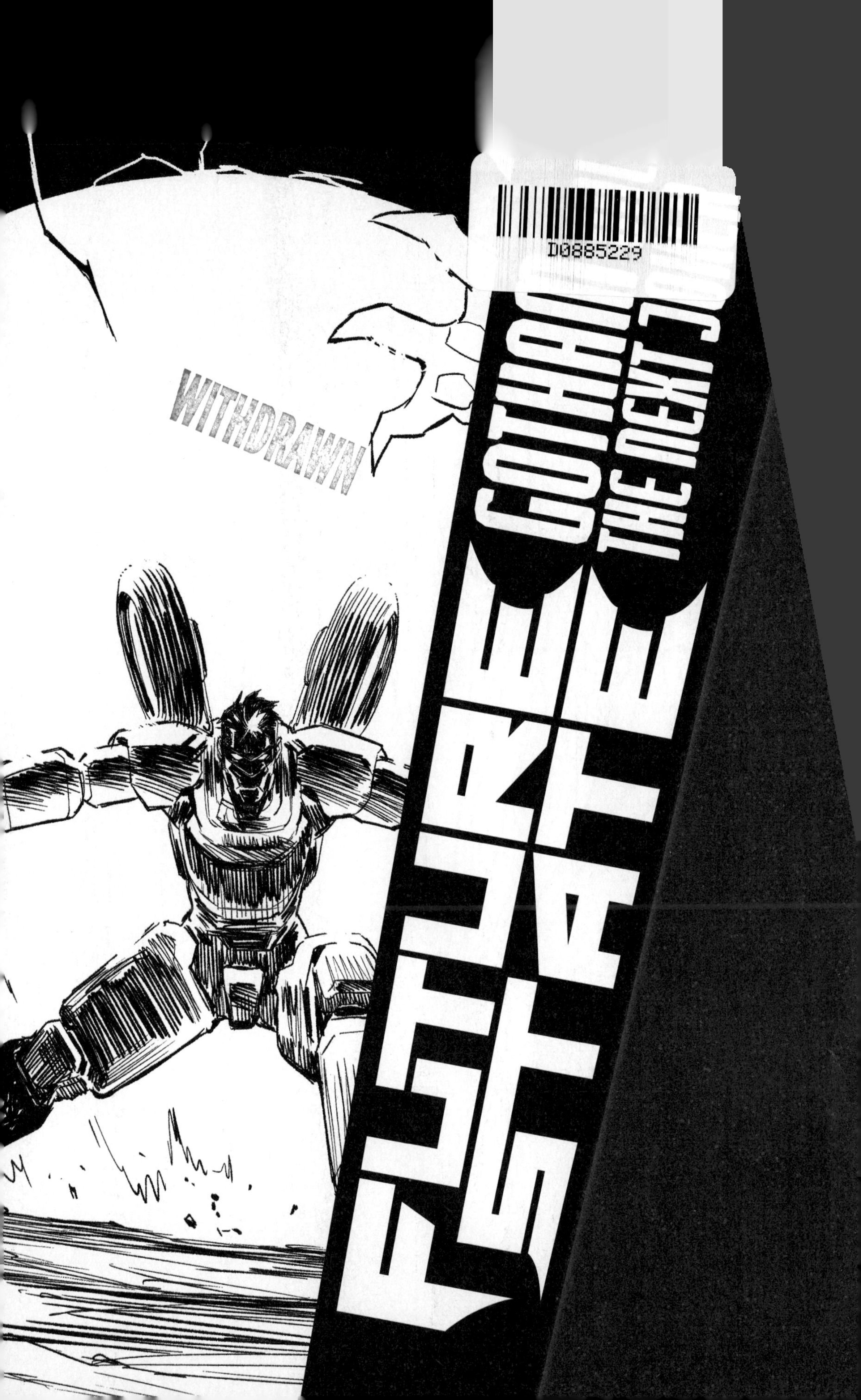
FUTURE STATE
GOTHAM
THE NEXT

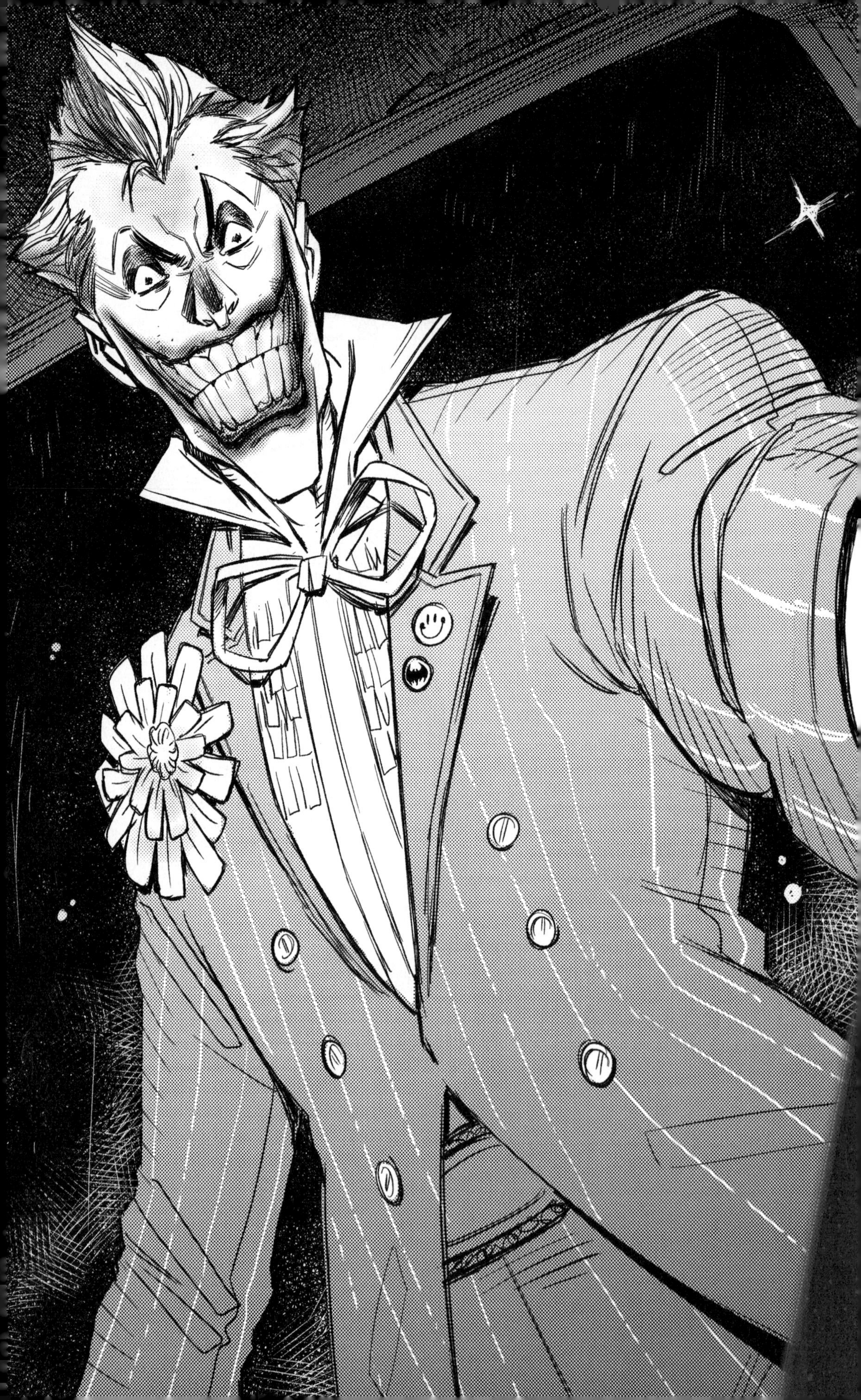

FUTURE STATE

GOTHAM VOL.2
THE NEXT JOKER

WRITER - DENNIS CULVER

ARTISTS - GIANNIS MILONOGIANNIS,
NIKOLA ČIŽMEŠIJA, AND GEOFFO

LETTERER - ALW'S TROY PETERI

COLLECTION COVER ARTIST -
SIMONE DI MEO

BEN ABERNATHY
Editor – Original Series & Collected Edition
STEVE COOK
Design Director – Books
SYDNEY LEE
Publication Design
ERIN VANOVER
Publication Production

MARIE JAVINS
Editor-in-Chief, DC Comics

ANNE DePIES
Senior VP – General Manager
JIM LEE
Publisher & Chief Creative Officer
DON FALLETTI
VP – Manufacturing Operations & Workflow Management
LAWRENCE GANEM
VP – Talent Services
ALISON GILL
Senior VP – Manufacturing & Operations
JEFFREY KAUFMAN
VP – Editorial Strategy & Programming
NICK J. NAPOLITANO
VP – Manufacturing Administration & Design
NANCY SPEARS
VP – Revenue

FUTURE STATE: GOTHAM VOL. 2: THE NEXT JOKER

DC Comics, 2900 West Alameda Ave., Burbank, CA 91505
Printed by LSC Communications, Owensville, MO, USA. 8/19/22.
First Printing.
ISBN: 978-1-77951-680-0

Library of Congress Cataloging-in-Publication Data is available.

PEFC Certified
This product is from sustainably managed forests and controlled sources
www.pefc.org
PEFC/29-31-337

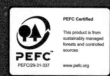

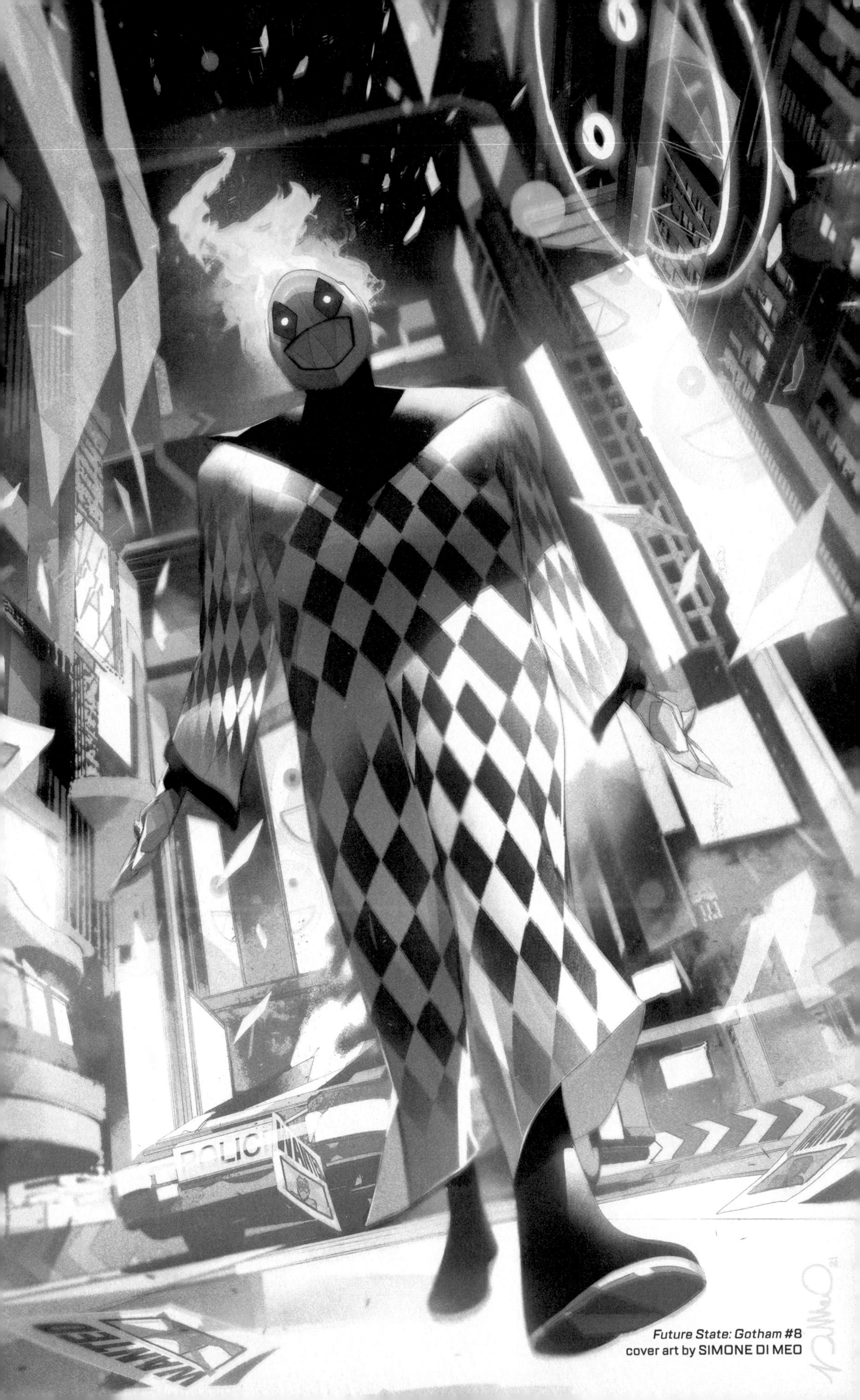

Future State: Gotham #8
cover art by SIMONE DI MEO

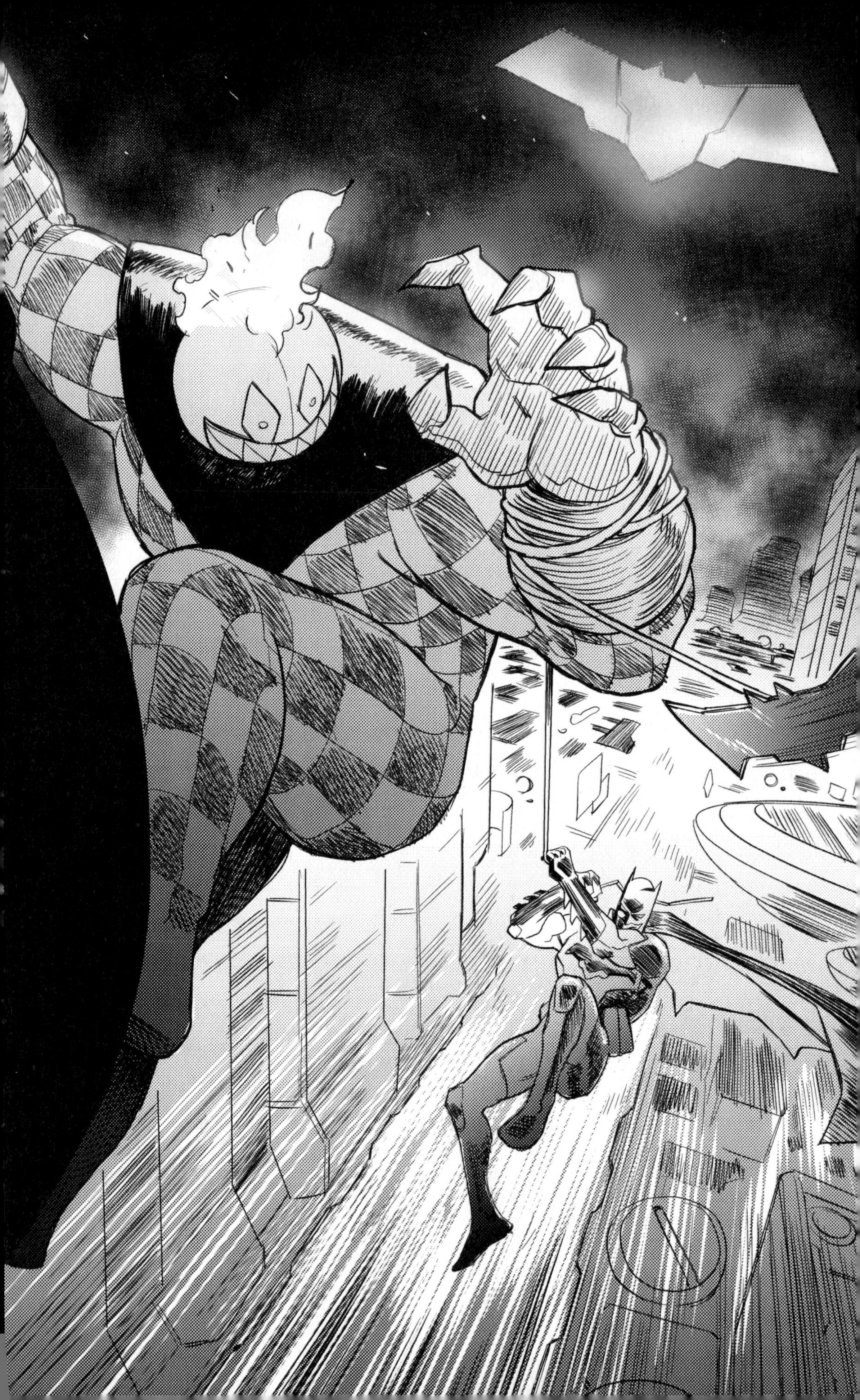

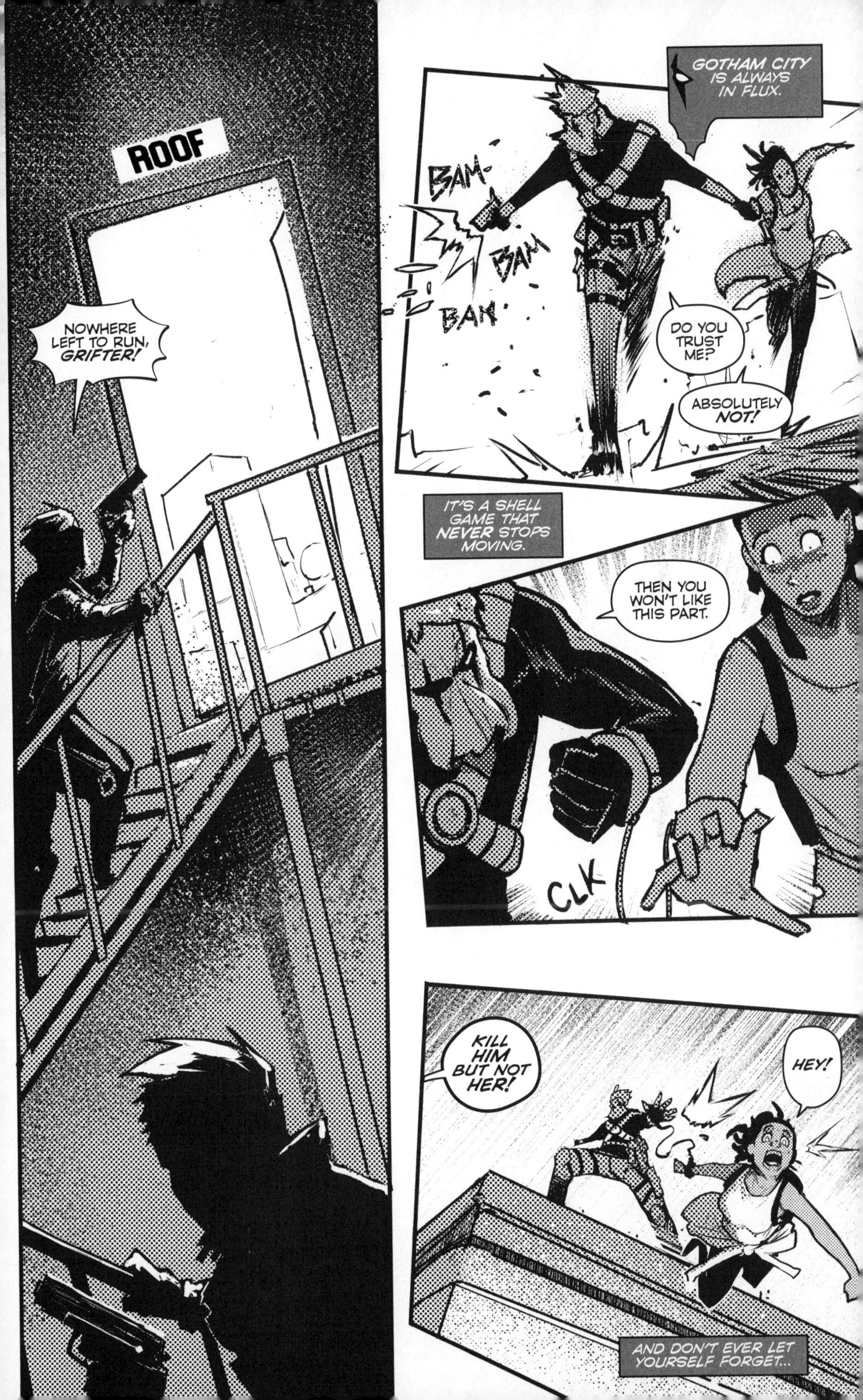
ROOF
NOWHERE LEFT TO RUN, GRIFTER!
GOTHAM CITY IS ALWAYS IN FLUX.
BAM
BAM
BAM
DO YOU TRUST ME?
ABSOLUTELY NOT!
IT'S A SHELL GAME THAT NEVER STOPS MOVING.
THEN YOU WON'T LIKE THIS PART.
CLK
KILL HIM BUT NOT HER!
HEY!
AND DON'T EVER LET YOURSELF FORGET...

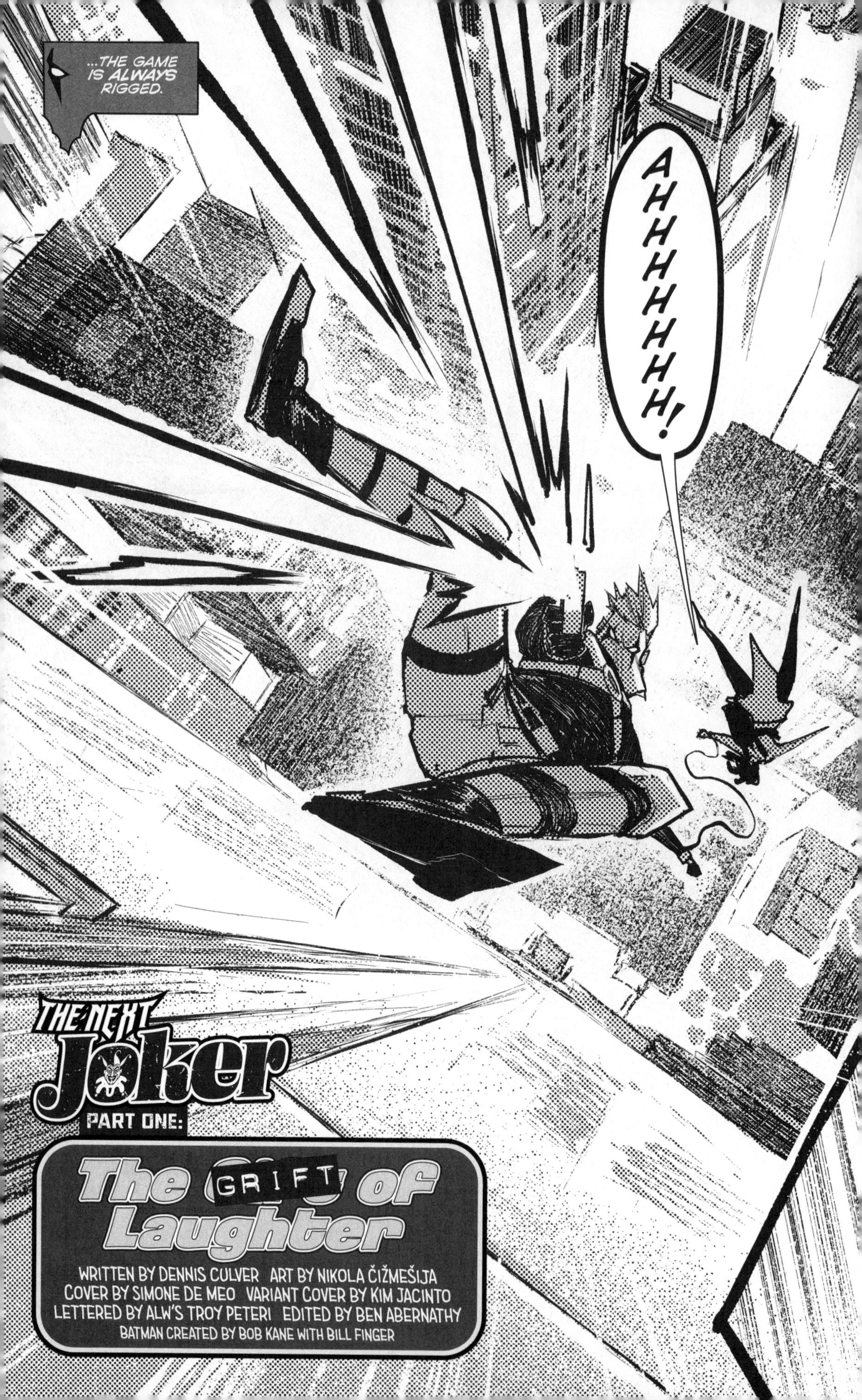
...THE GAME IS ALWAYS RIGGED.
AHHHHHHHH!
THE NEXT Joker
PART ONE:
The GRIFT of Laughter
WRITTEN BY DENNIS CULVER ART BY NIKOLA ČIŽMEŠIJA
COVER BY SIMONE DE MEO VARIANT COVER BY KIM JACINTO
LETTERED BY ALW'S TROY PETERI EDITED BY BEN ABERNATHY
BATMAN CREATED BY BOB KANE WITH BILL FINGER

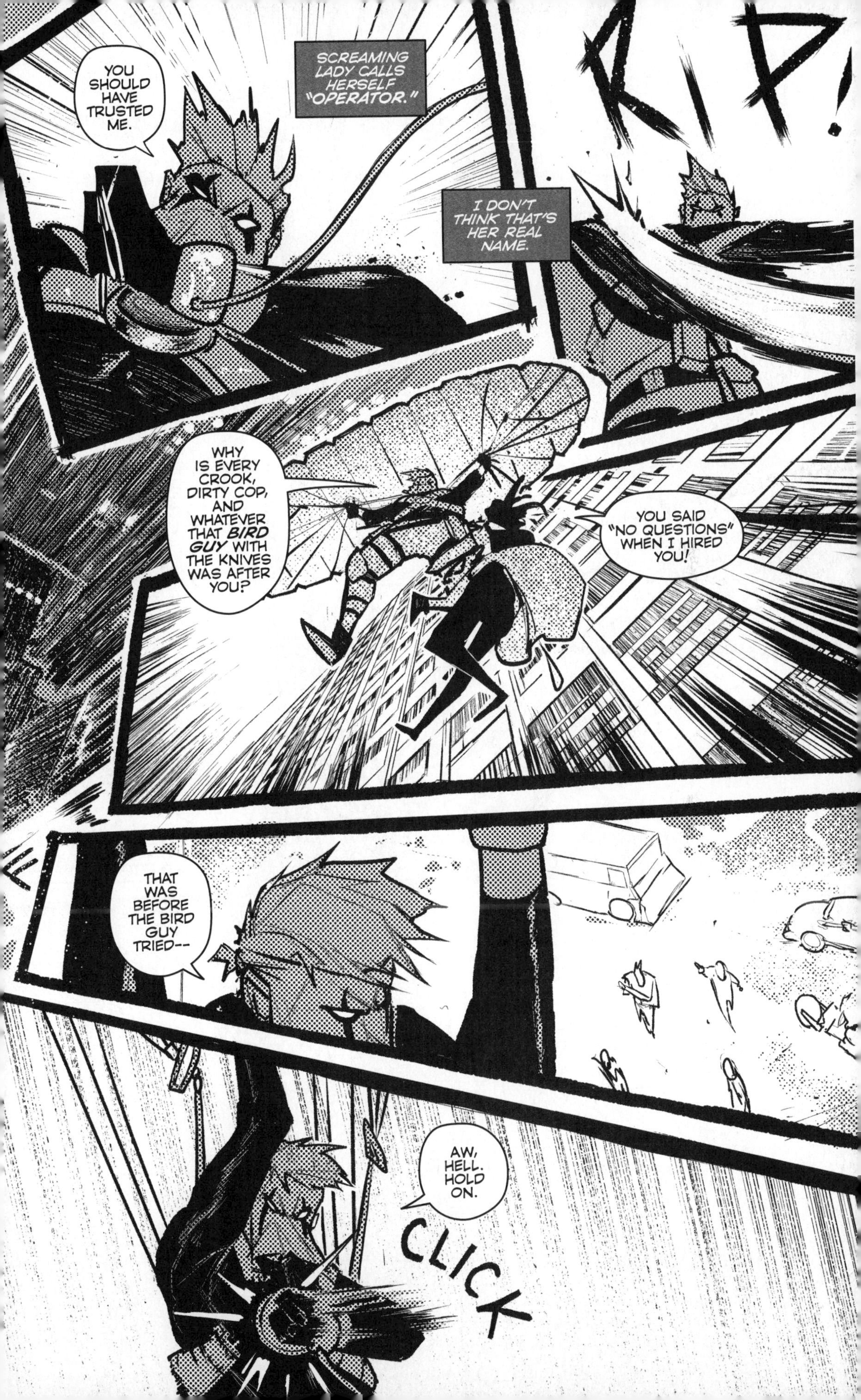
SCREAMING LADY CALLS HERSELF "OPERATOR."
YOU SHOULD HAVE TRUSTED ME.
RIP!
I DON'T THINK THAT'S HER REAL NAME.
WHY IS EVERY CROOK, DIRTY COP, AND WHATEVER THAT BIRD GUY WITH THE KNIVES WAS AFTER YOU?
YOU SAID "NO QUESTIONS" WHEN I HIRED YOU!
THAT WAS BEFORE THE BIRD GUY TRIED--
AW, HELL. HOLD ON.
CLICK

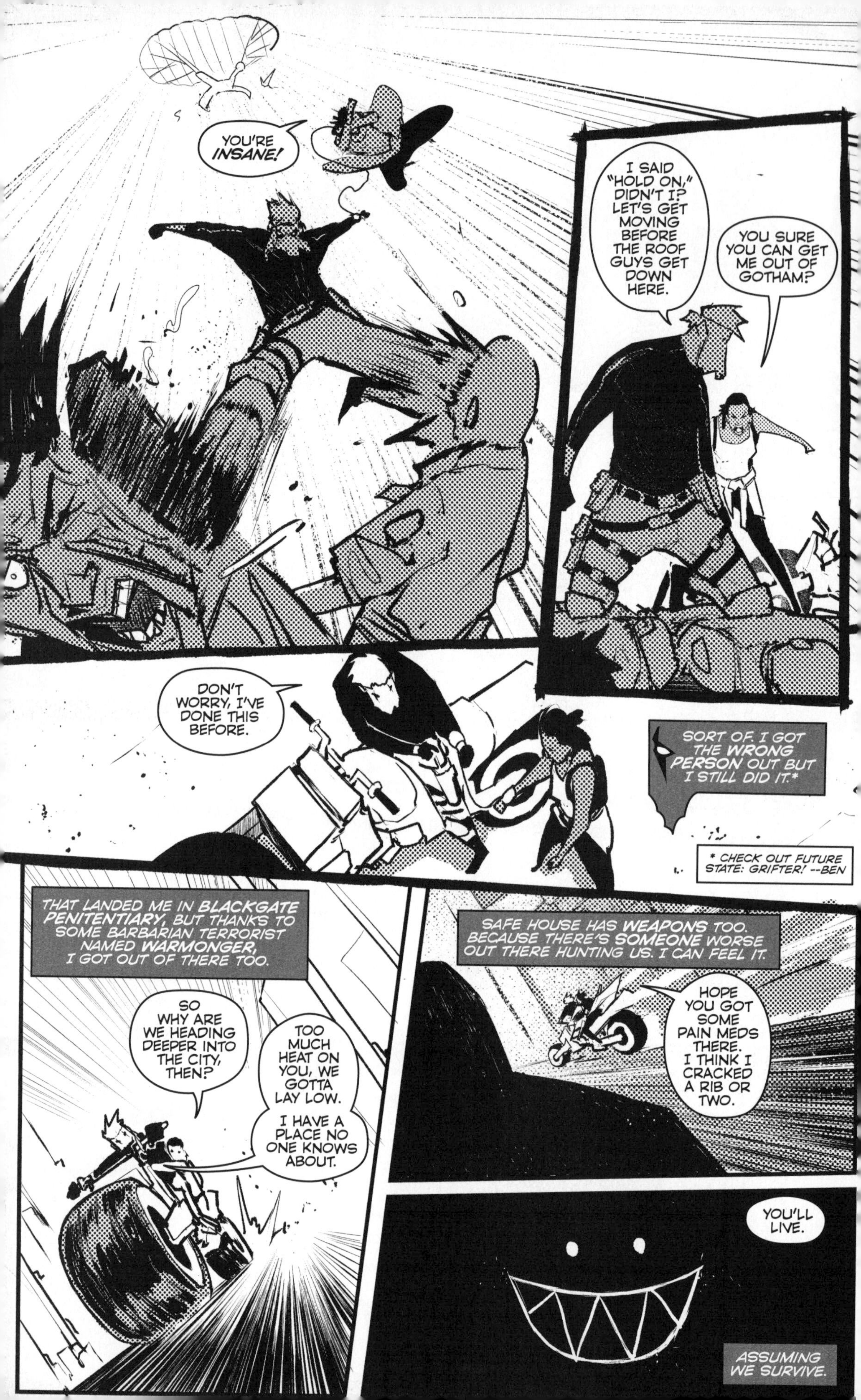
YOU'RE INSANE!
I SAID "HOLD ON," DIDN'T I? LET'S GET MOVING BEFORE THE ROOF GUYS GET DOWN HERE.
YOU SURE YOU CAN GET ME OUT OF GOTHAM?
DON'T WORRY, I'VE DONE THIS BEFORE.
SORT OF. I GOT THE WRONG PERSON OUT BUT I STILL DID IT.*
* CHECK OUT FUTURE STATE: GRIFTER! --BEN
THAT LANDED ME IN BLACKGATE PENITENTIARY, BUT THANKS TO SOME BARBARIAN TERRORIST NAMED WARMONGER, I GOT OUT OF THERE TOO.
SO WHY ARE WE HEADING DEEPER INTO THE CITY, THEN?
TOO MUCH HEAT ON YOU, WE GOTTA LAY LOW.
I HAVE A PLACE NO ONE KNOWS ABOUT.
SAFE HOUSE HAS WEAPONS TOO. BECAUSE THERE'S SOMEONE WORSE OUT THERE HUNTING US. I CAN FEEL IT.
HOPE YOU GOT SOME PAIN MEDS THERE. I THINK I CRACKED A RIB OR TWO.
YOU'LL LIVE.
ASSUMING WE SURVIVE.

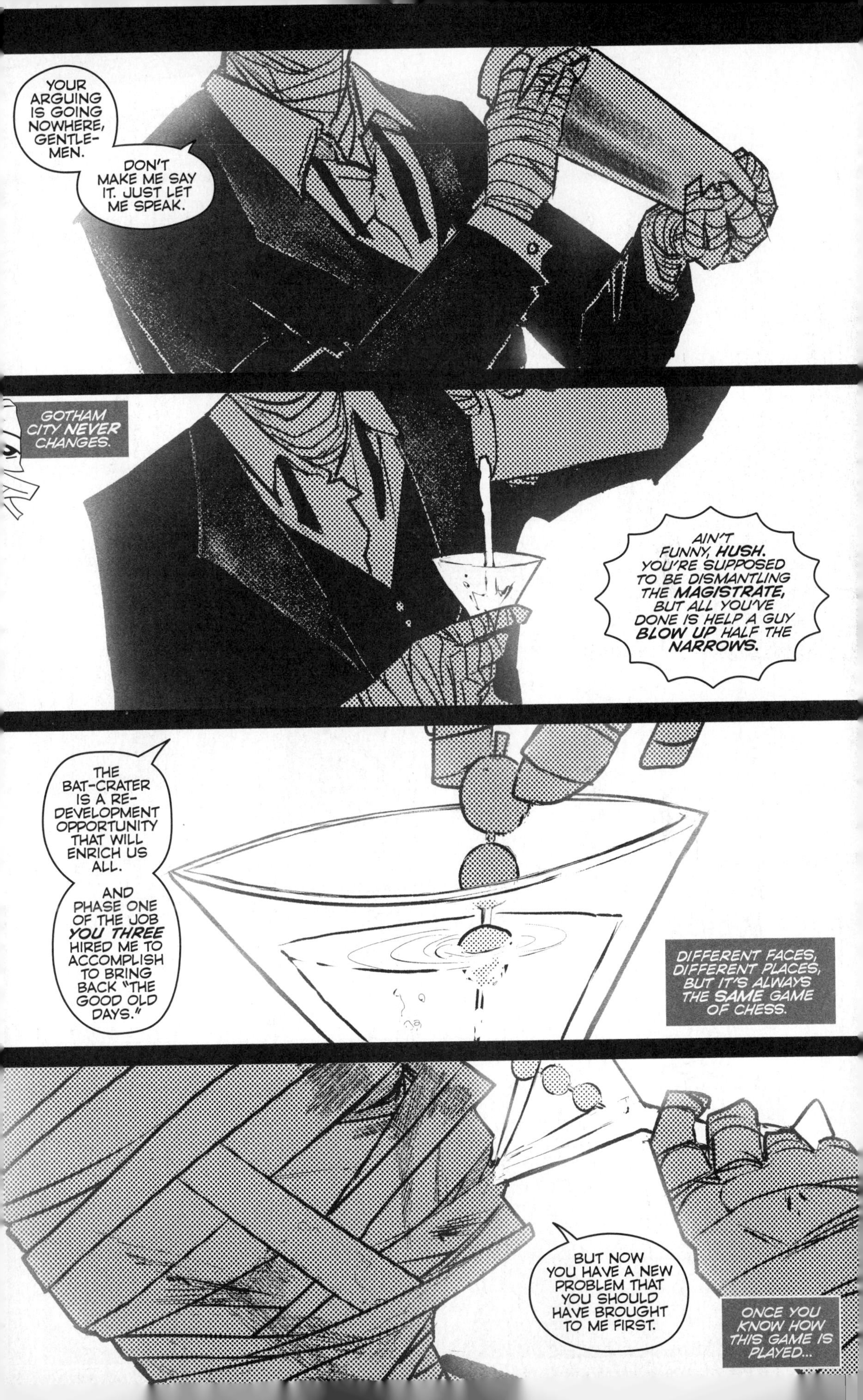
YOUR ARGUING IS GOING NOWHERE, GENTLE-MEN.
DON'T MAKE ME SAY IT. JUST LET ME SPEAK.
GOTHAM CITY NEVER CHANGES.
AIN'T FUNNY, HUSH. YOU'RE SUPPOSED TO BE DISMANTLING THE MAGISTRATE, BUT ALL YOU'VE DONE IS HELP A GUY BLOW UP HALF THE NARROWS.
THE BAT-CRATER IS A RE-DEVELOPMENT OPPORTUNITY THAT WILL ENRICH US ALL.
AND PHASE ONE OF THE JOB YOU THREE HIRED ME TO ACCOMPLISH TO BRING BACK "THE GOOD OLD DAYS."
DIFFERENT FACES, DIFFERENT PLACES, BUT IT'S ALWAYS THE SAME GAME OF CHESS.
BUT NOW YOU HAVE A NEW PROBLEM THAT YOU SHOULD HAVE BROUGHT TO ME FIRST.
ONCE YOU KNOW HOW THIS GAME IS PLAYED...

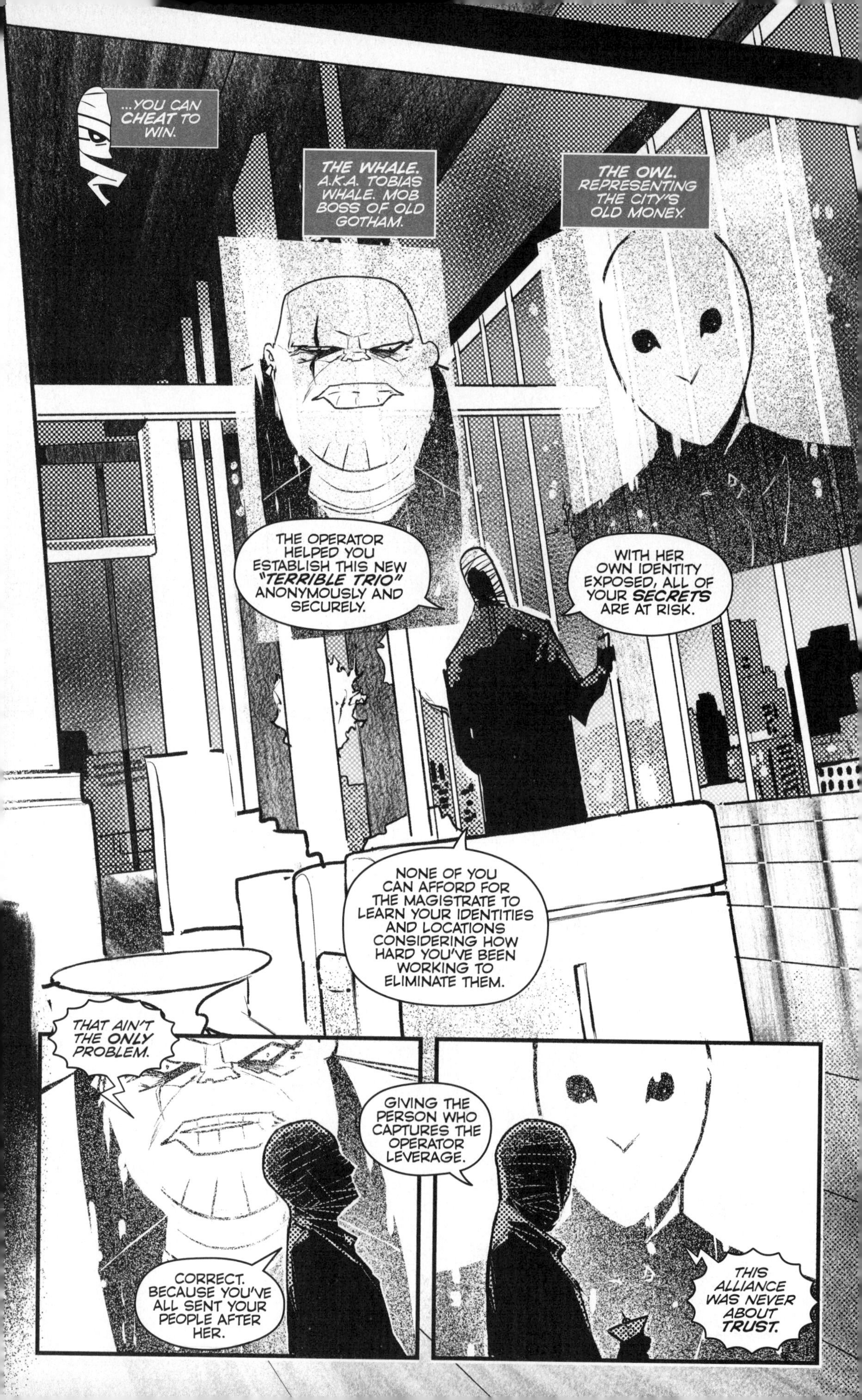
...YOU CAN CHEAT TO WIN.
THE WHALE. A.K.A. TOBIAS WHALE. MOB BOSS OF OLD GOTHAM.
THE OWL. REPRESENTING THE CITY'S OLD MONEY.
THE OPERATOR HELPED YOU ESTABLISH THIS NEW "TERRIBLE TRIO" ANONYMOUSLY AND SECURELY.
WITH HER OWN IDENTITY EXPOSED, ALL OF YOUR SECRETS ARE AT RISK.
NONE OF YOU CAN AFFORD FOR THE MAGISTRATE TO LEARN YOUR IDENTITIES AND LOCATIONS CONSIDERING HOW HARD YOU'VE BEEN WORKING TO ELIMINATE THEM.
THAT AIN'T THE ONLY PROBLEM.
GIVING THE PERSON WHO CAPTURES THE OPERATOR LEVERAGE.
CORRECT. BECAUSE YOU'VE ALL SENT YOUR PEOPLE AFTER HER.
THIS ALLIANCE WAS NEVER ABOUT TRUST.

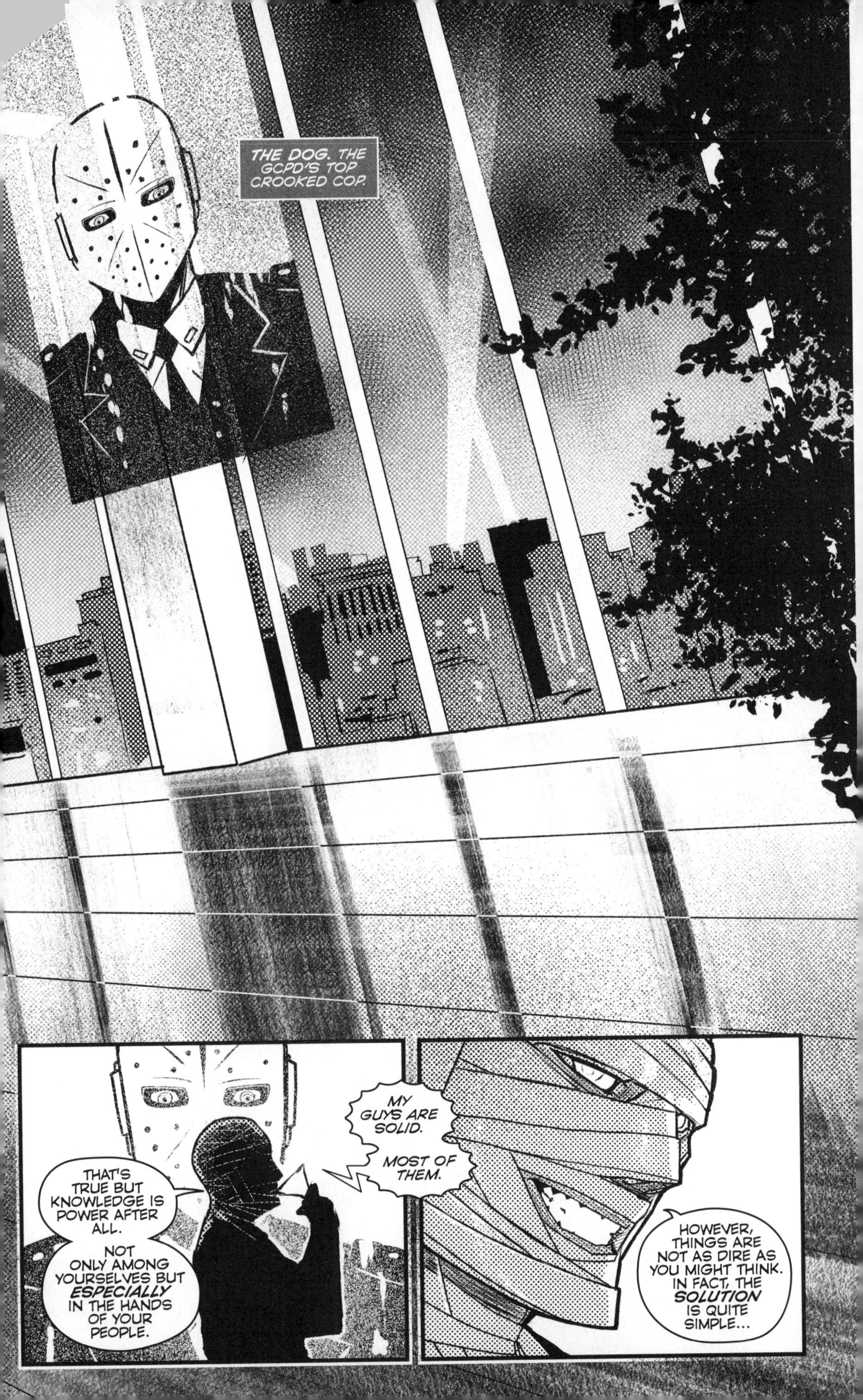
THE DOG. THE GCPD'S TOP CROOKED COP.
MY GUYS ARE SOLID.
MOST OF THEM.
THAT'S TRUE BUT KNOWLEDGE IS POWER AFTER ALL.
NOT ONLY AMONG YOURSELVES BUT ESPECIALLY IN THE HANDS OF YOUR PEOPLE.
HOWEVER, THINGS ARE NOT AS DIRE AS YOU MIGHT THINK. IN FACT, THE SOLUTION IS QUITE SIMPLE...

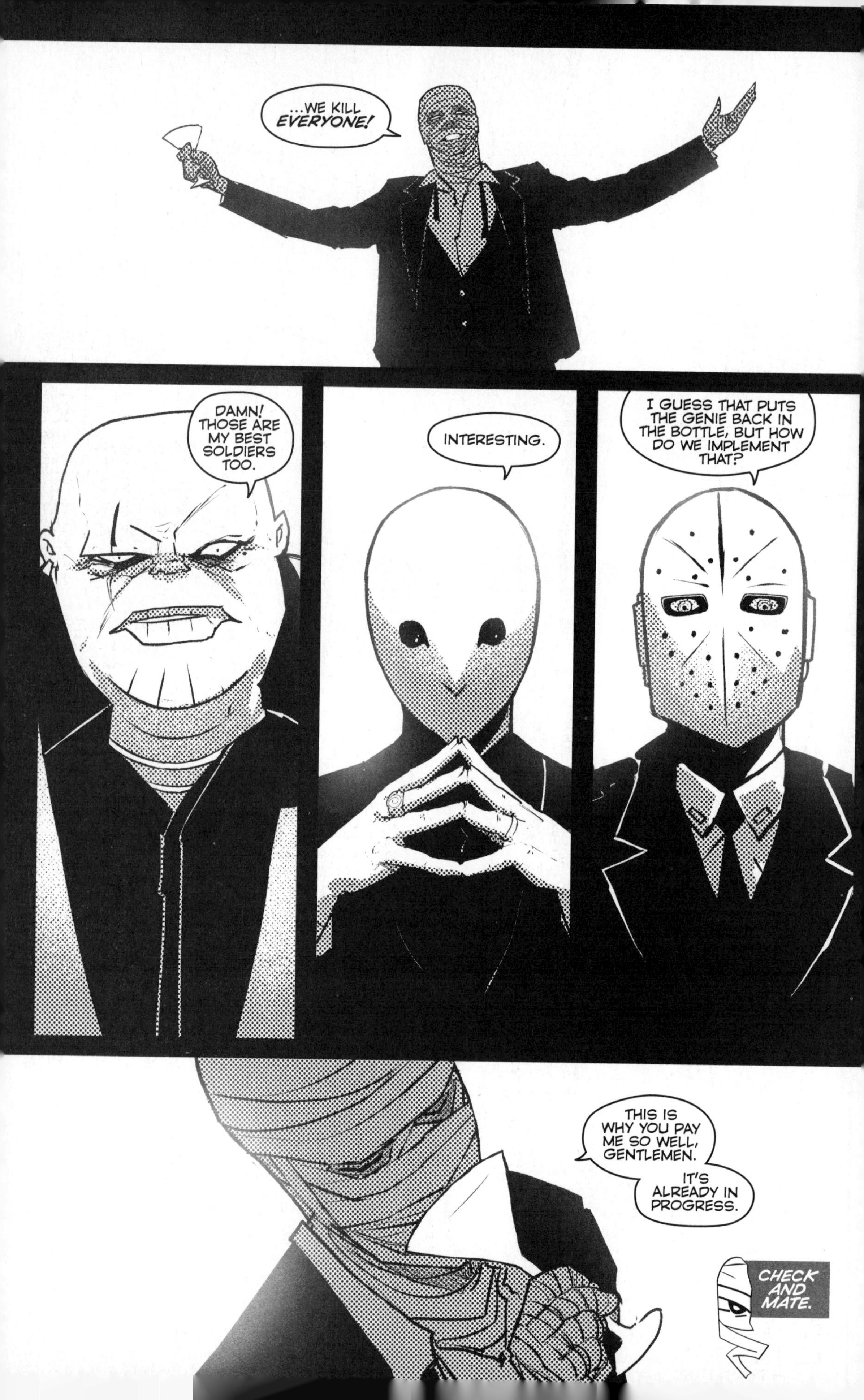
...WE KILL EVERYONE!
DAMN! THOSE ARE MY BEST SOLDIERS TOO.
INTERESTING.
I GUESS THAT PUTS THE GENIE BACK IN THE BOTTLE, BUT HOW DO WE IMPLEMENT THAT?
THIS IS WHY YOU PAY ME SO WELL, GENTLEMEN.
IT'S ALREADY IN PROGRESS.
CHECK AND MATE.

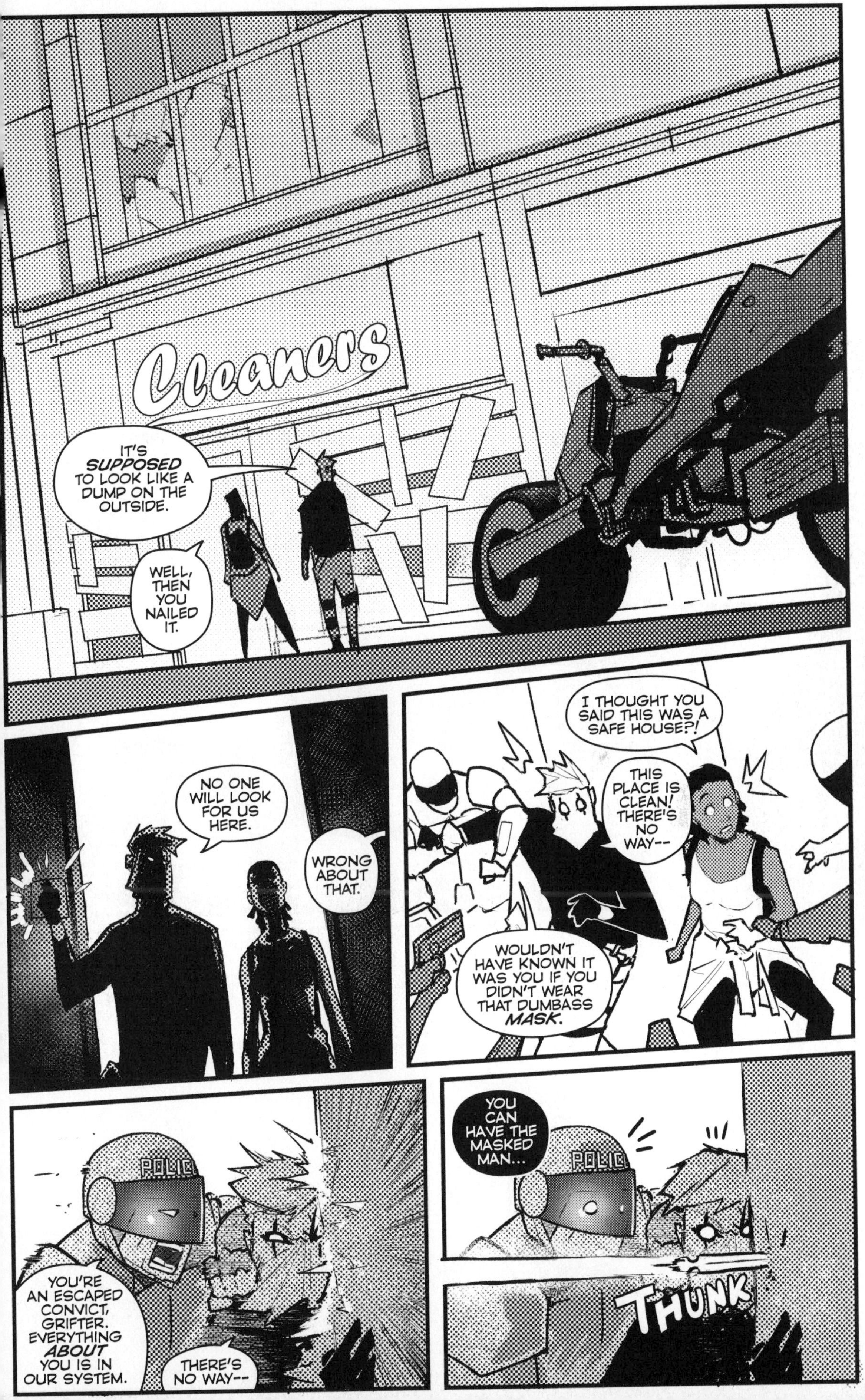
Cleaners
IT'S *SUPPOSED* TO LOOK LIKE A DUMP ON THE OUTSIDE.
WELL, THEN YOU NAILED IT.
NO ONE WILL LOOK FOR US HERE.
WRONG ABOUT THAT.
I THOUGHT YOU SAID THIS WAS A SAFE HOUSE?!
THIS PLACE IS CLEAN! THERE'S NO WAY--
WOULDN'T HAVE KNOWN IT WAS YOU IF YOU DIDN'T WEAR THAT DUMBASS *MASK*.
YOU'RE AN ESCAPED CONVICT, GRIFTER. EVERYTHING *ABOUT* YOU IS IN OUR SYSTEM.
THERE'S NO WAY--
YOU CAN HAVE THE MASKED MAN...
THUNK

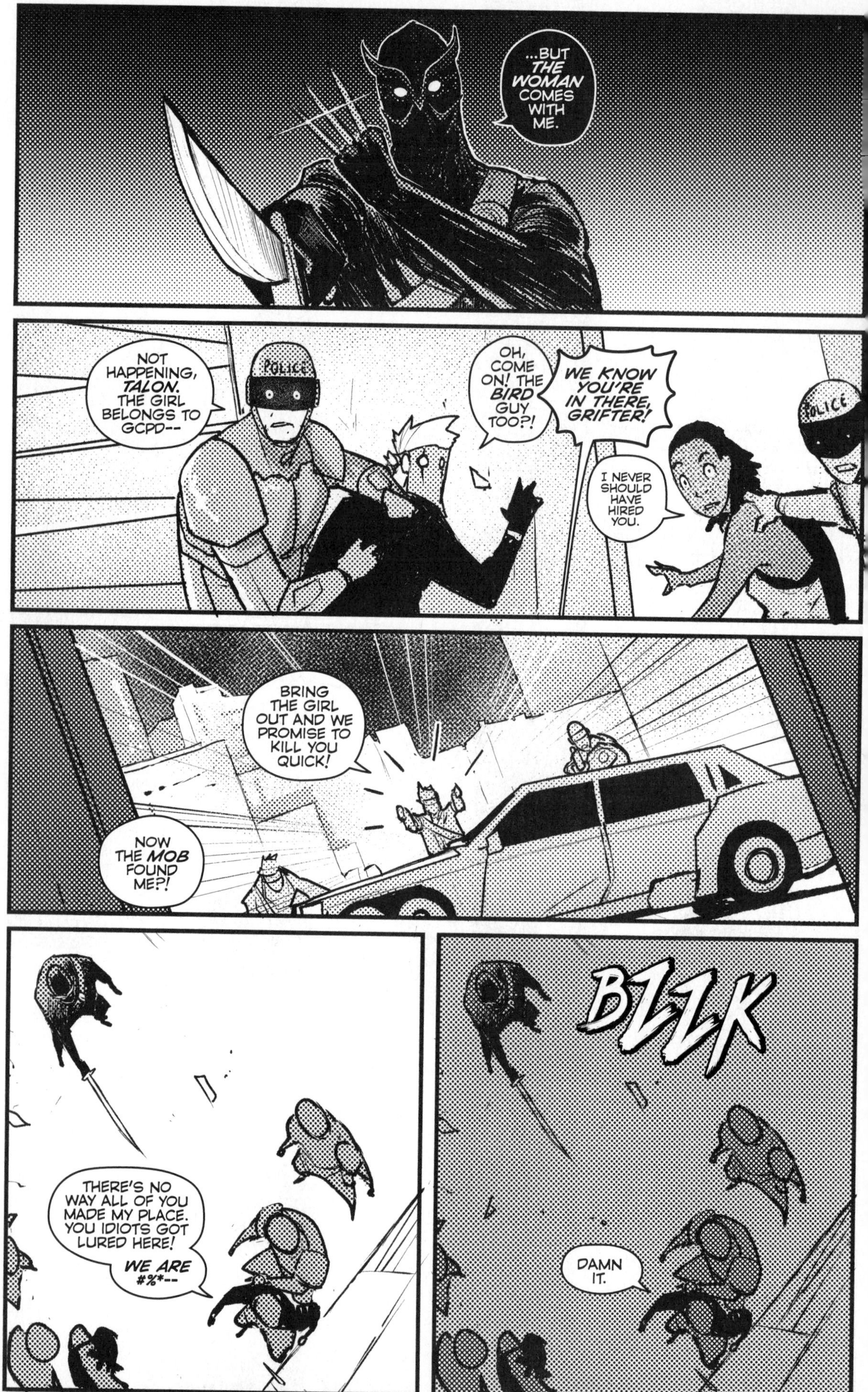
...BUT THE WOMAN COMES WITH ME.
NOT HAPPENING, TALON. THE GIRL BELONGS TO GCPD--
POLICE
OH, COME ON! THE BIRD GUY TOO?!
WE KNOW YOU'RE IN THERE, GRIFTER!
I NEVER SHOULD HAVE HIRED YOU.
POLICE
BRING THE GIRL OUT AND WE PROMISE TO KILL YOU QUICK!
NOW THE MOB FOUND ME?!
THERE'S NO WAY ALL OF YOU MADE MY PLACE. YOU IDIOTS GOT LURED HERE!
WE ARE #%*--
BZZK
DAMN IT.

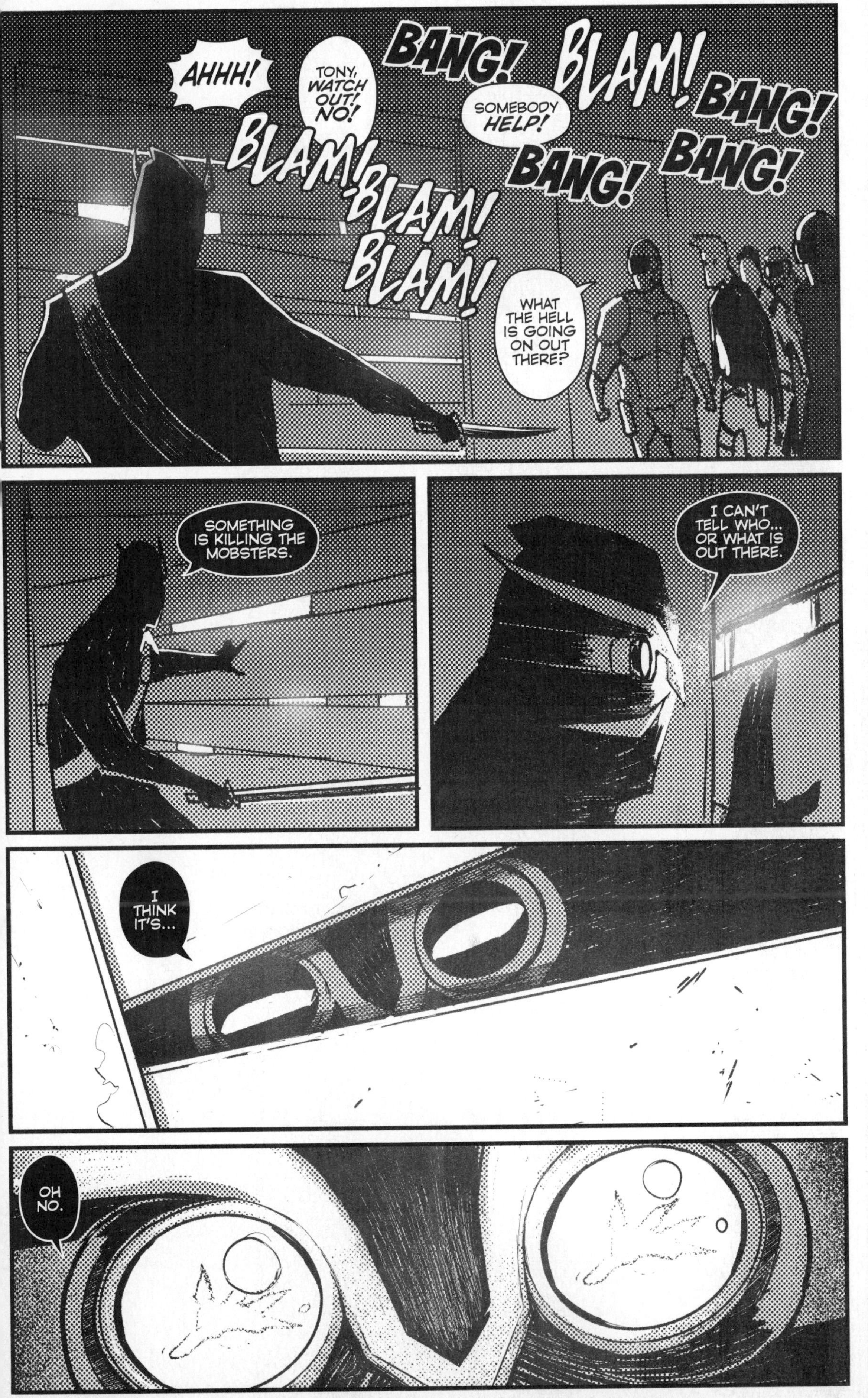
AHHH!
TONY, WATCH OUT! NO!
BANG!
BLAM!
BANG!
SOMEBODY HELP!
BANG!
BANG!
BLAM! -BLAM! BLAM!
WHAT THE HELL IS GOING ON OUT THERE?
SOMETHING IS KILLING THE MOBSTERS.
I CAN'T TELL WHO... OR WHAT IS OUT THERE.
I THINK IT'S...
OH NO.

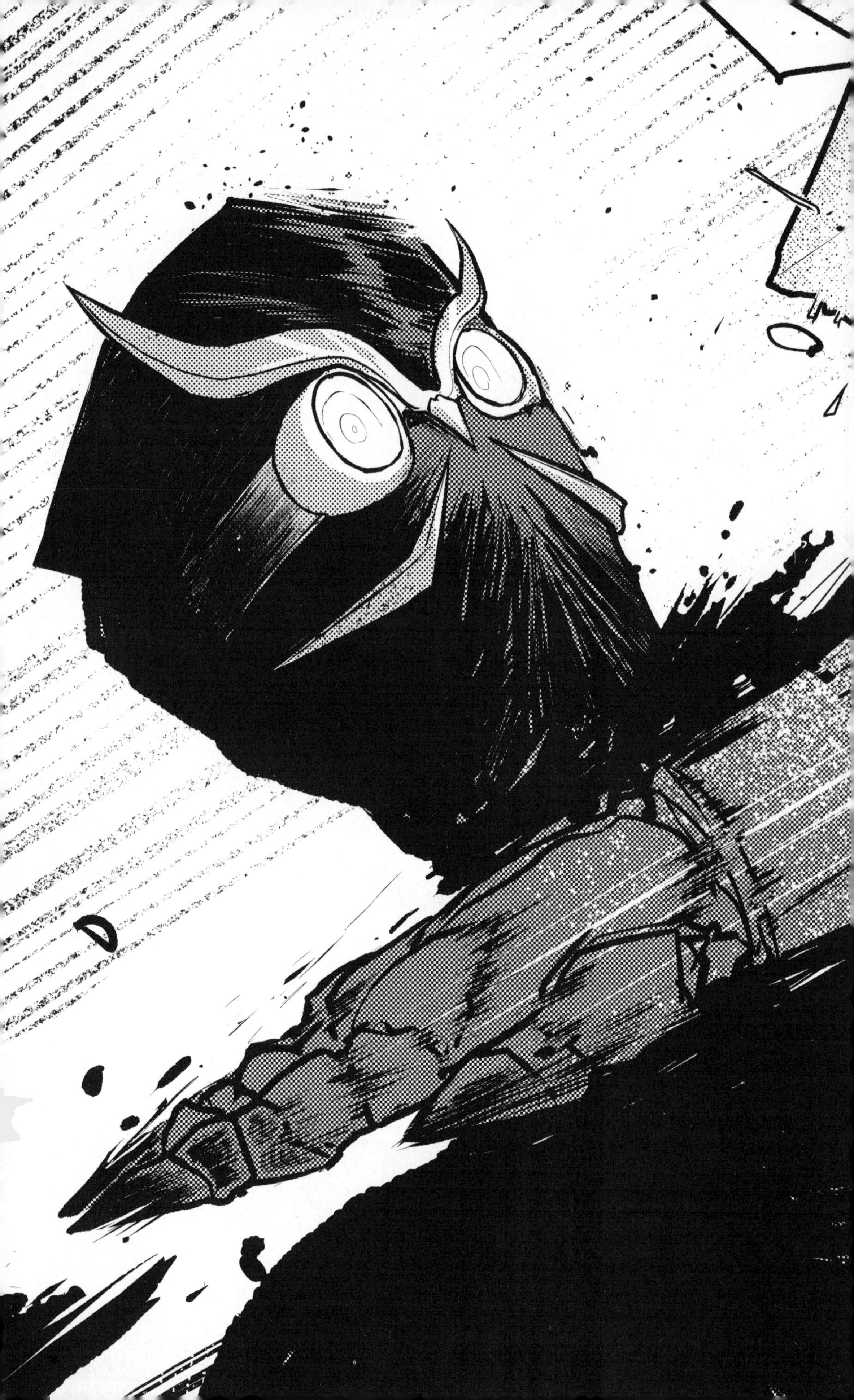

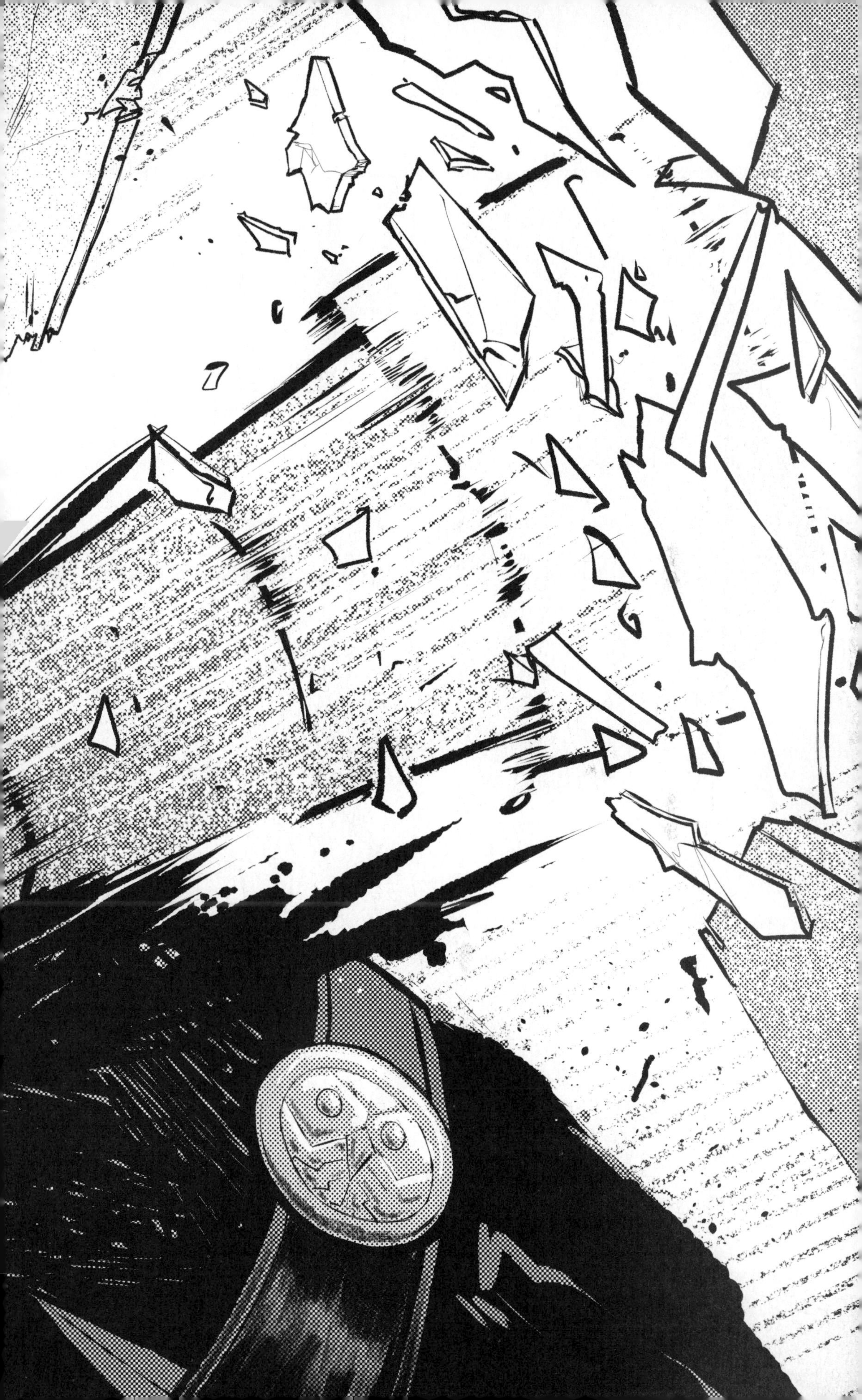

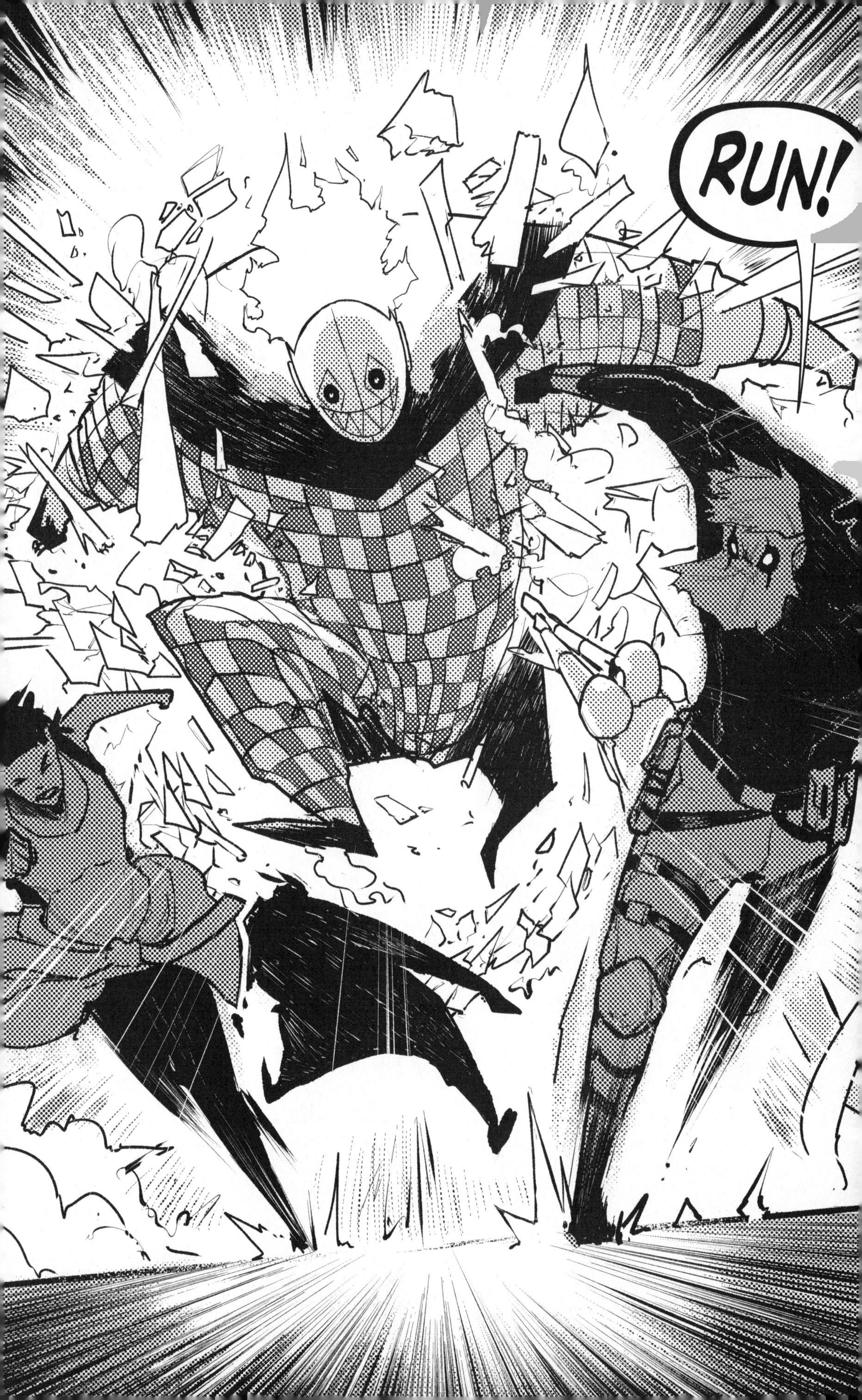
RUN!

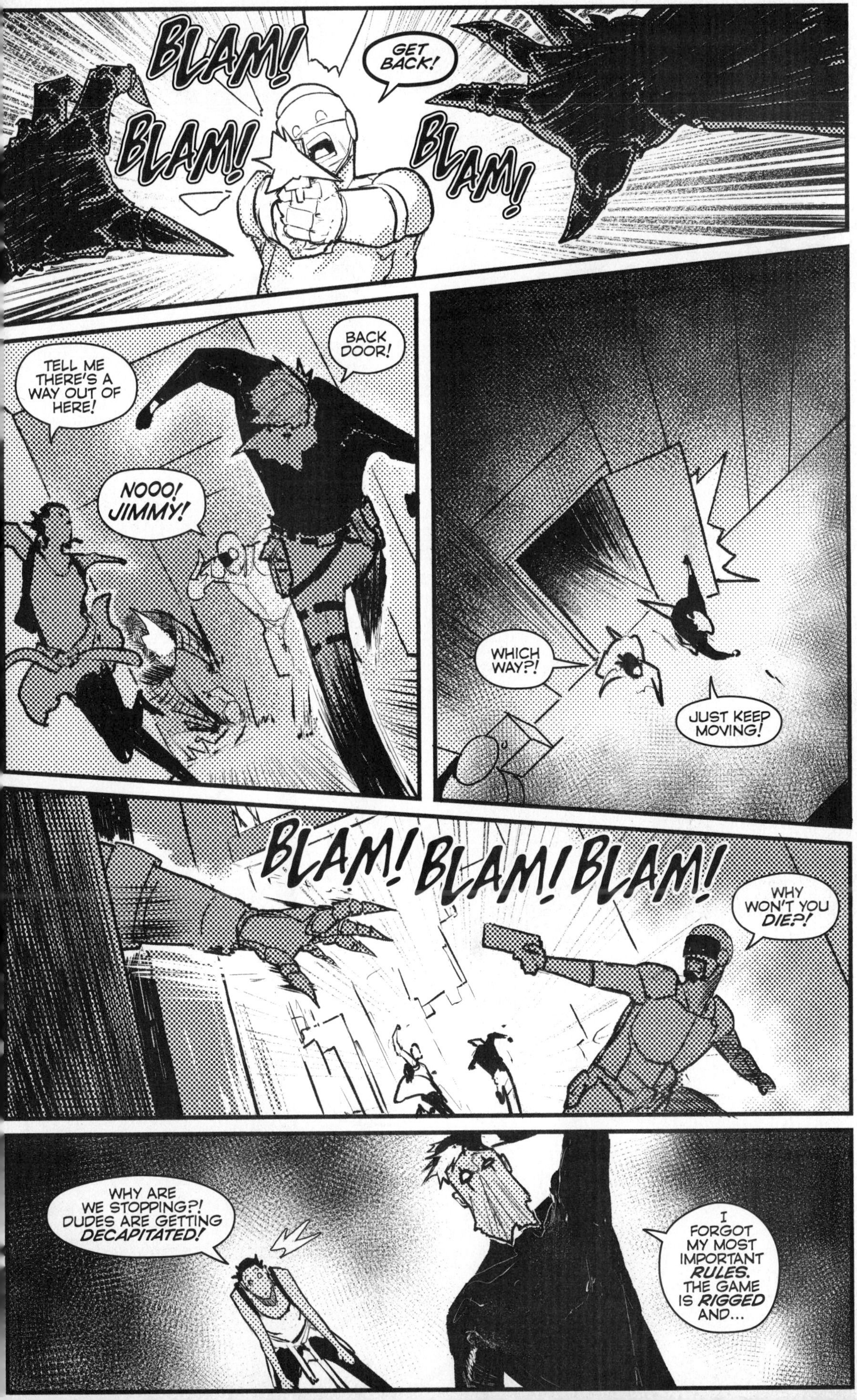
BLAM!
BLAM!
GET BACK!
BLAM!
TELL ME THERE'S A WAY OUT OF HERE!
BACK DOOR!
NOOO! JIMMY!
WHICH WAY?!
JUST KEEP MOVING!
BLAM! BLAM! BLAM!
WHY WON'T YOU DIE?!
WHY ARE WE STOPPING?! DUDES ARE GETTING DECAPITATED!
I FORGOT MY MOST IMPORTANT RULES. THE GAME IS RIGGED AND...

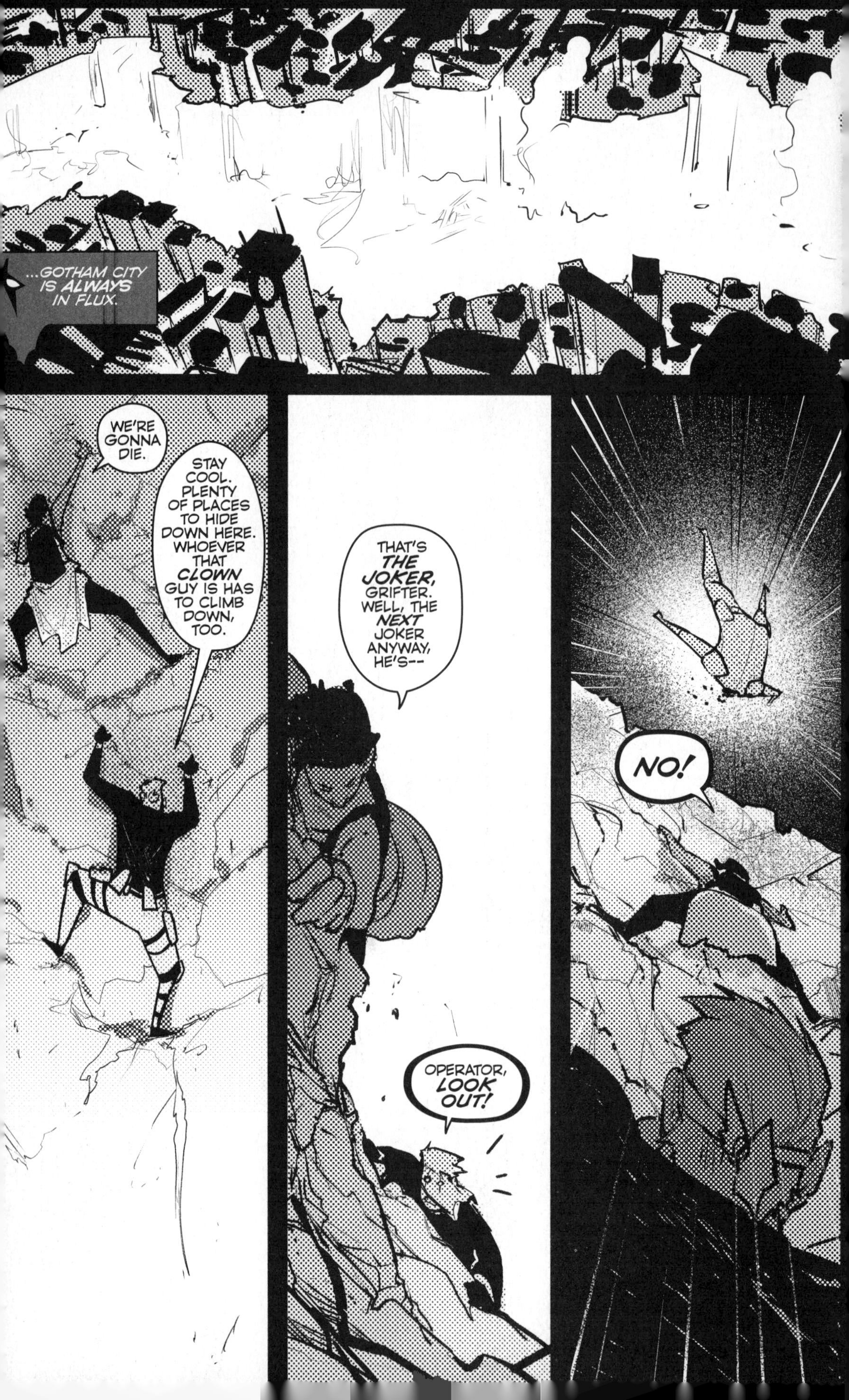
...GOTHAM CITY IS ALWAYS IN FLUX.
WE'RE GONNA DIE.
STAY COOL. PLENTY OF PLACES TO HIDE DOWN HERE. WHOEVER THAT CLOWN GUY IS HAS TO CLIMB DOWN, TOO.
THAT'S THE JOKER, GRIFTER. WELL, THE NEXT JOKER ANYWAY, HE'S--
OPERATOR, LOOK OUT!
NO!

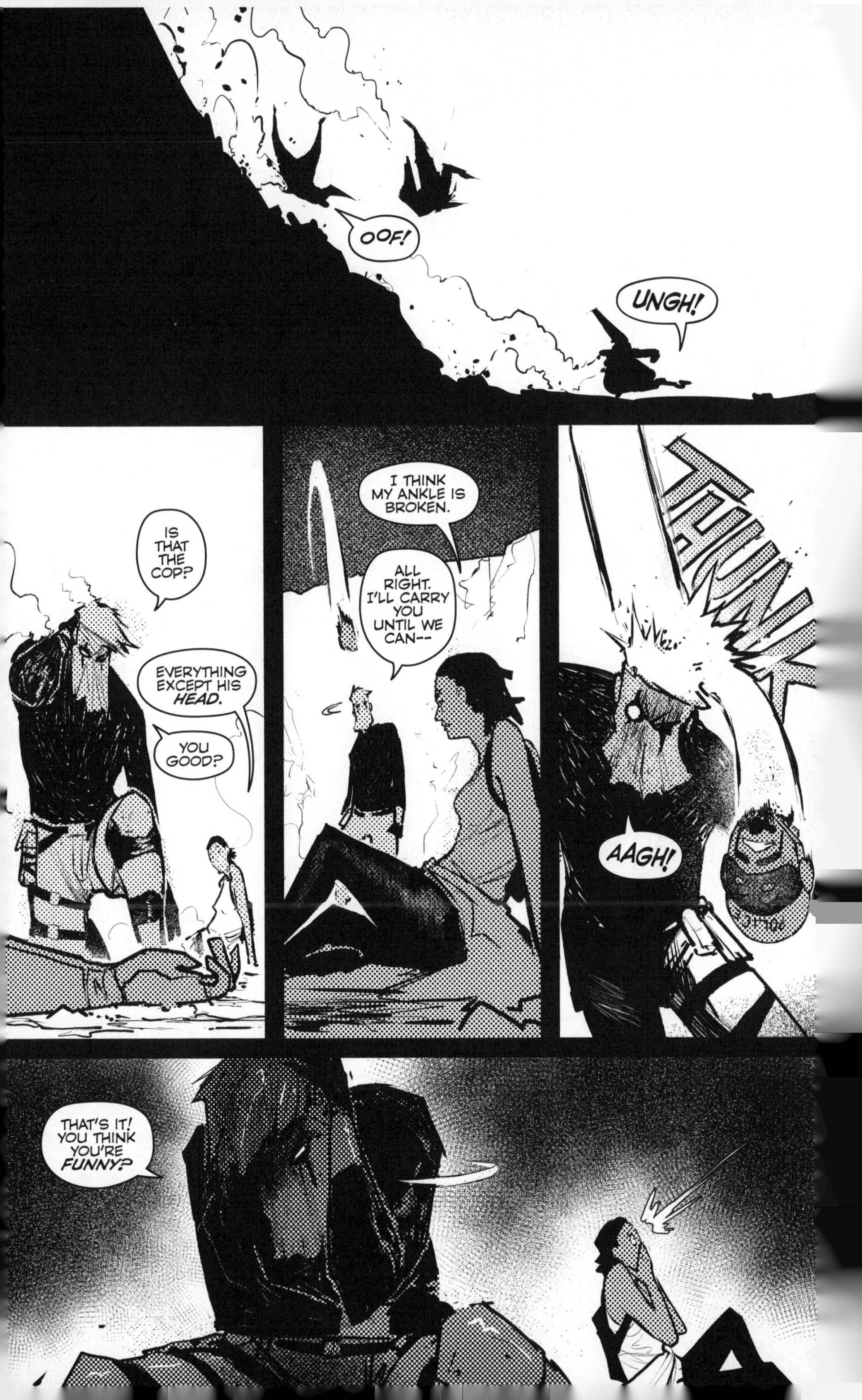
OOF!
UNGH!
IS THAT THE COP?
EVERYTHING EXCEPT HIS HEAD.
YOU GOOD?
I THINK MY ANKLE IS BROKEN.
ALL RIGHT. I'LL CARRY YOU UNTIL WE CAN--
AAGH!
THAT'S IT! YOU THINK YOU'RE FUNNY?

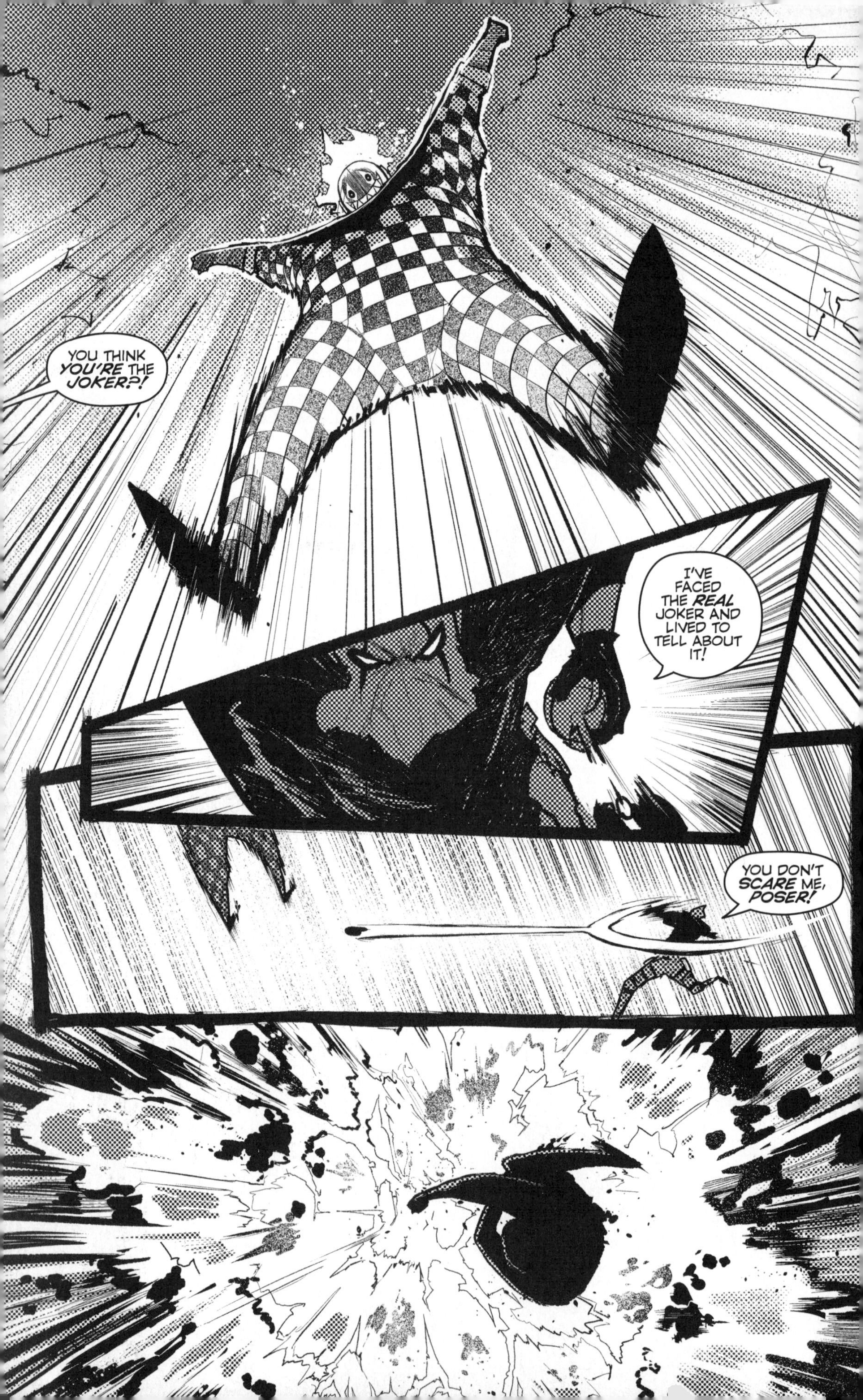
YOU THINK YOU'RE THE JOKER?!
I'VE FACED THE REAL JOKER AND LIVED TO TELL ABOUT IT!
YOU DON'T SCARE ME, POSER!

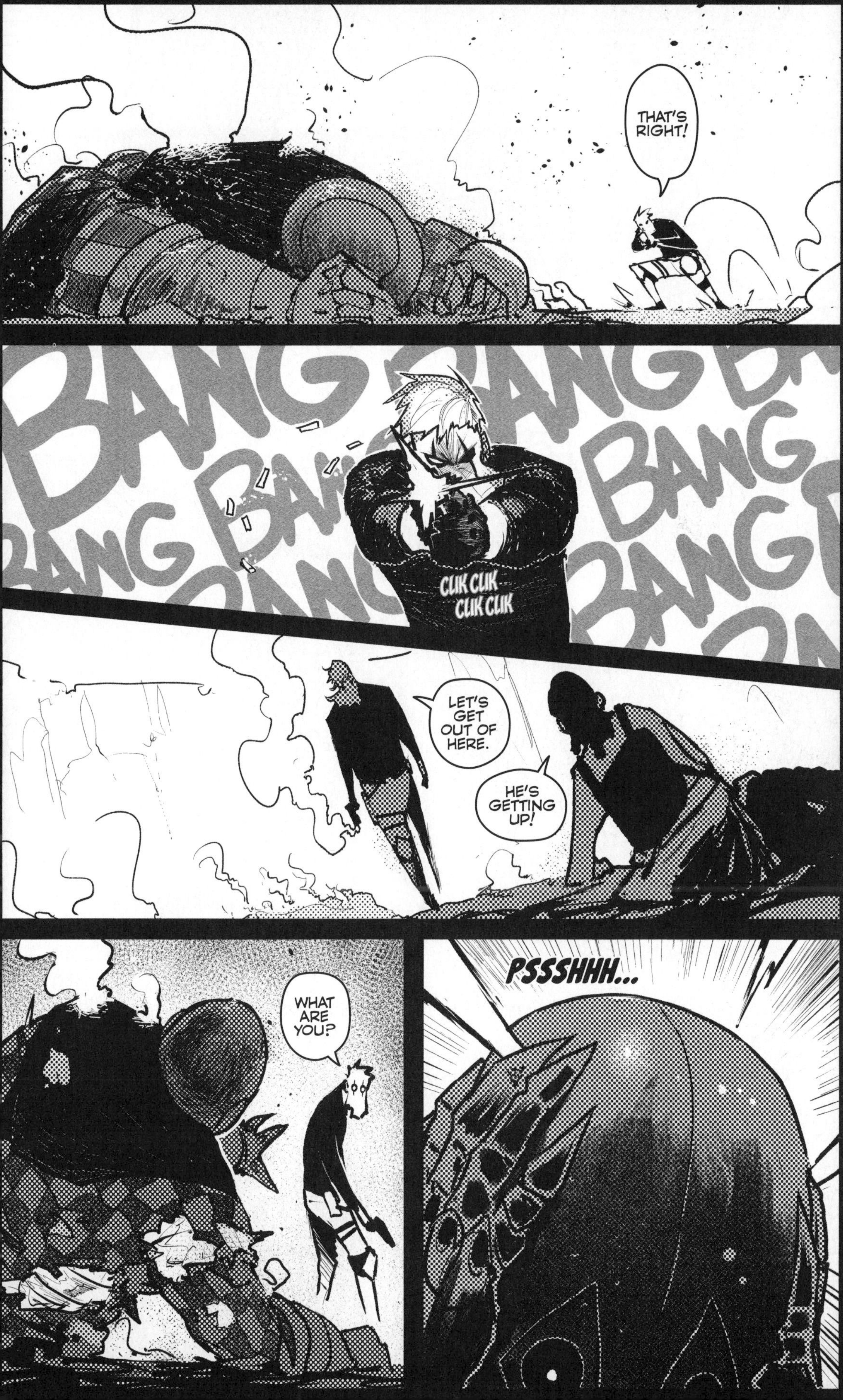
THAT'S RIGHT!
BANG BANG BANG BANG BANG BANG BANG
CLIK CLIK CLIK CLIK
LET'S GET OUT OF HERE.
HE'S GETTING UP!
WHAT ARE YOU?
PSSSHHH...

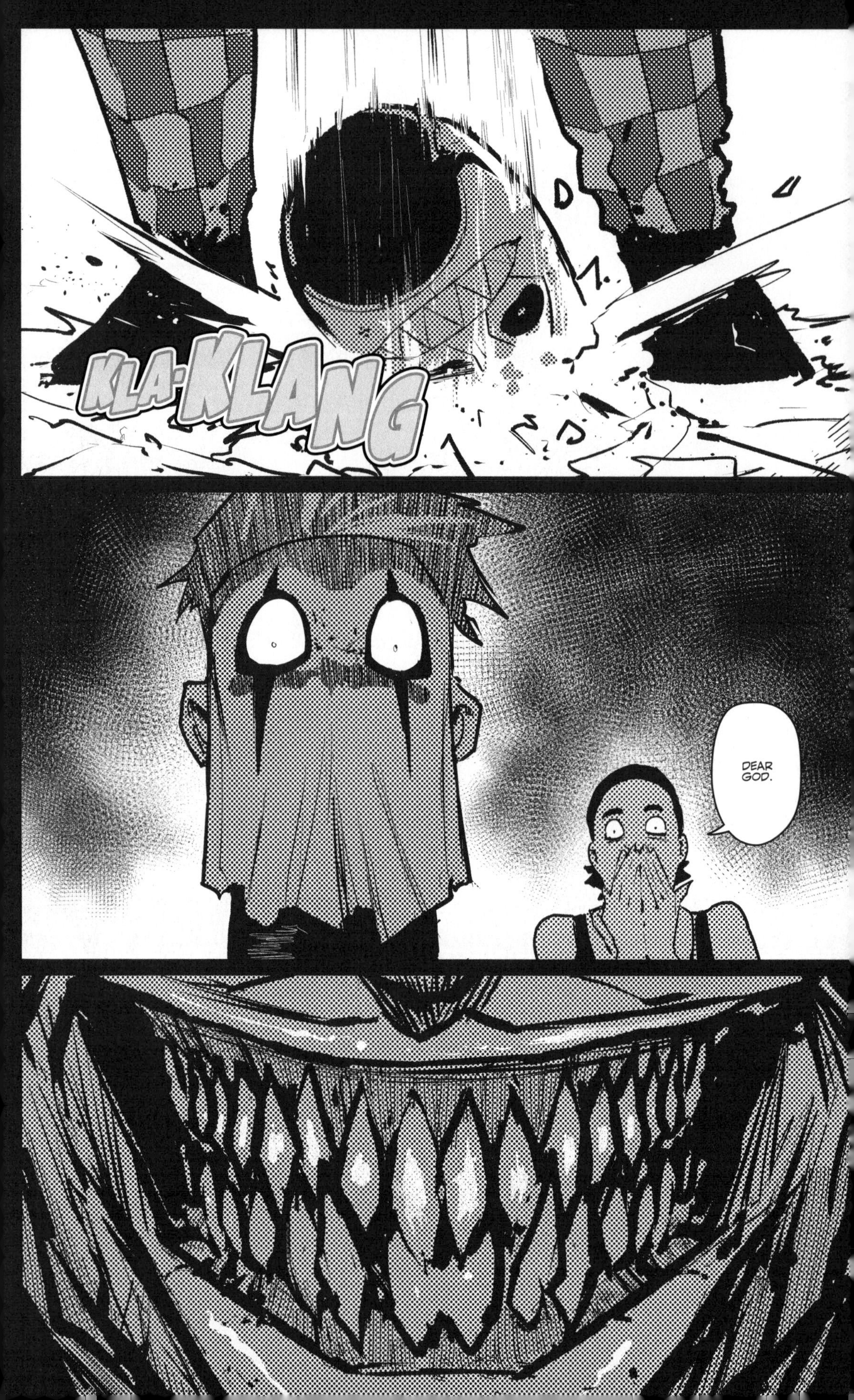
KLA-KLANG
DEAR GOD.

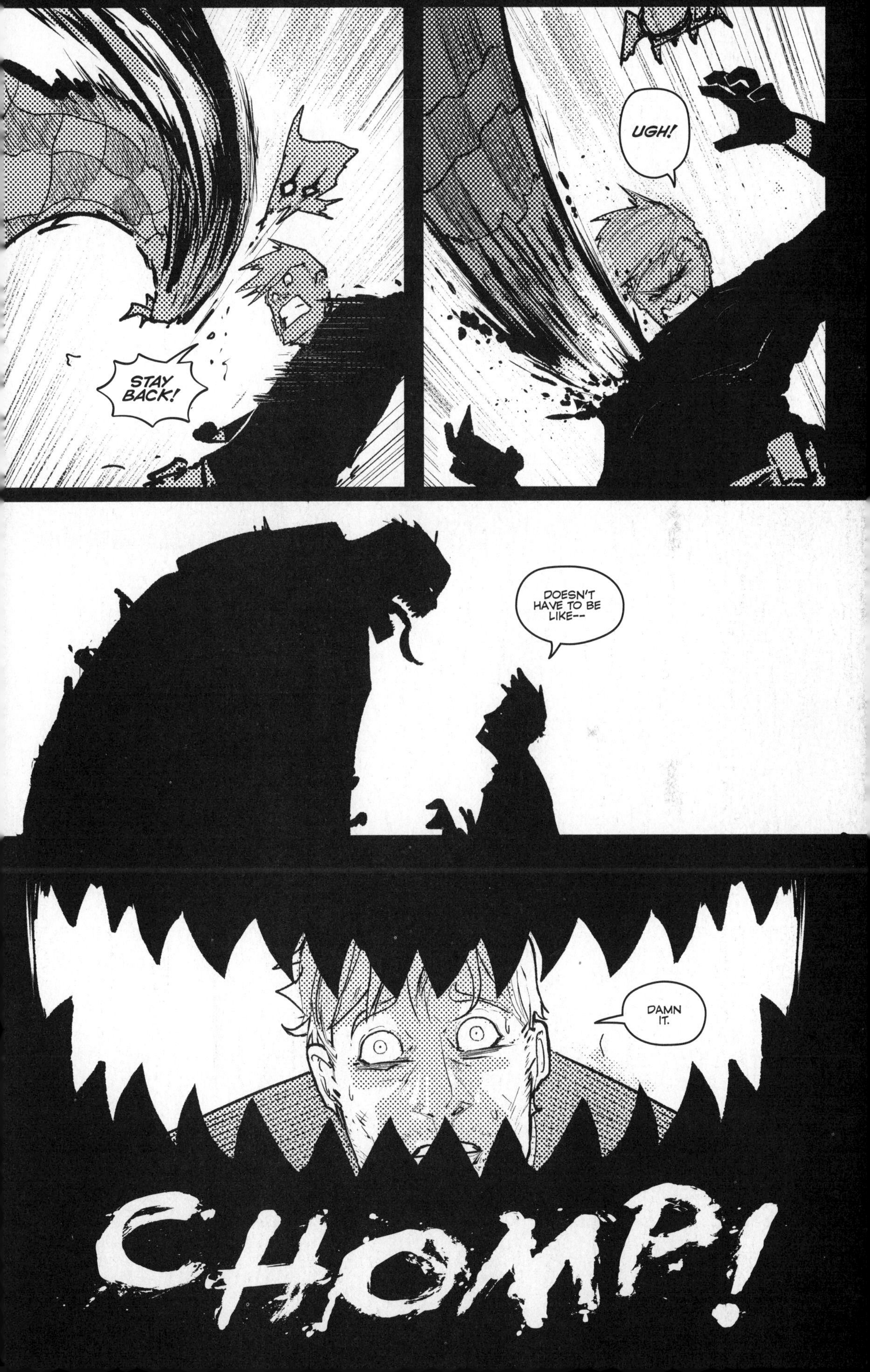
STAY BACK!
UGH!
DOESN'T HAVE TO BE LIKE--
DAMN IT.
CHOMP!

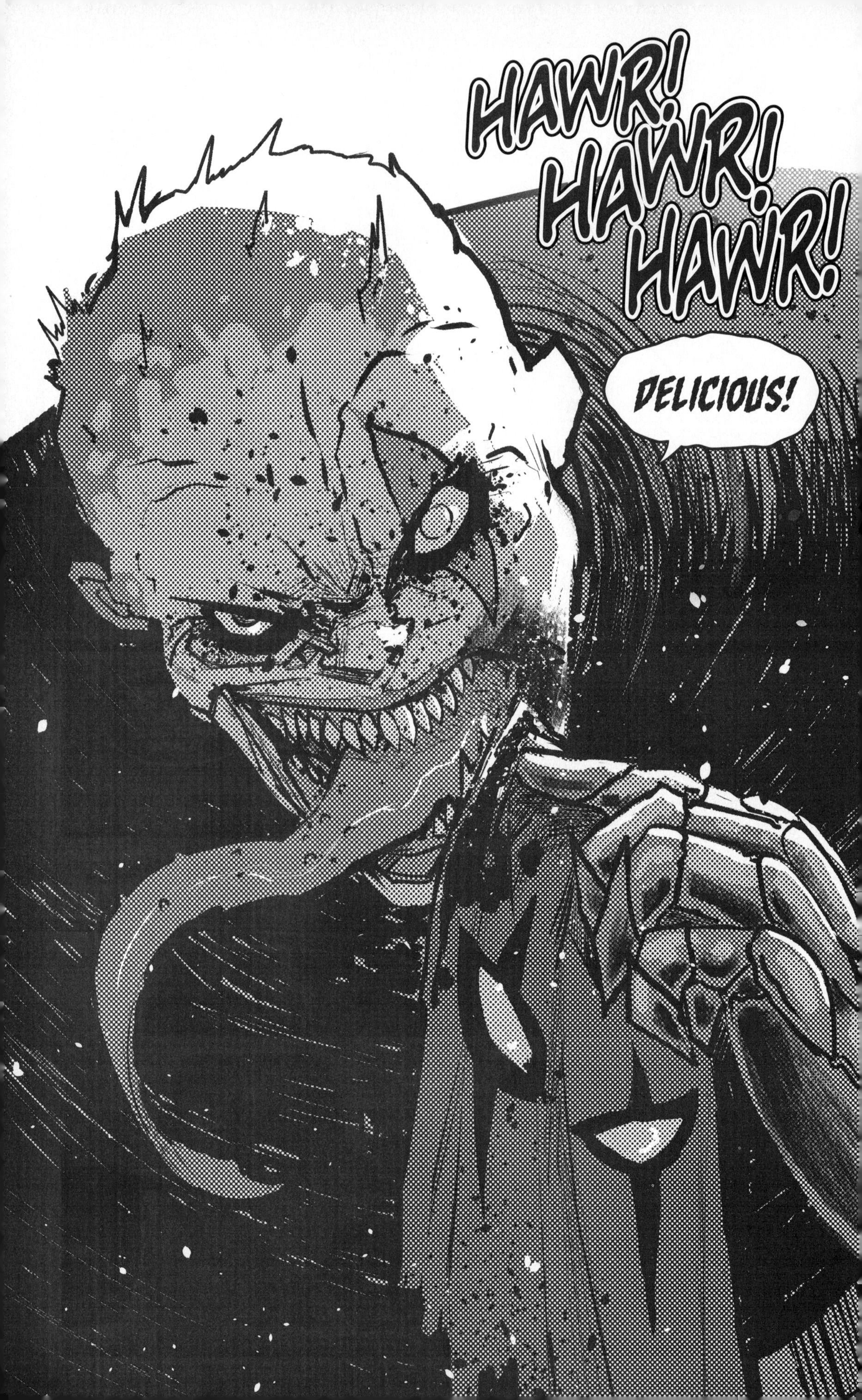
HAWR! HAWR! HAWR!
DELICIOUS!

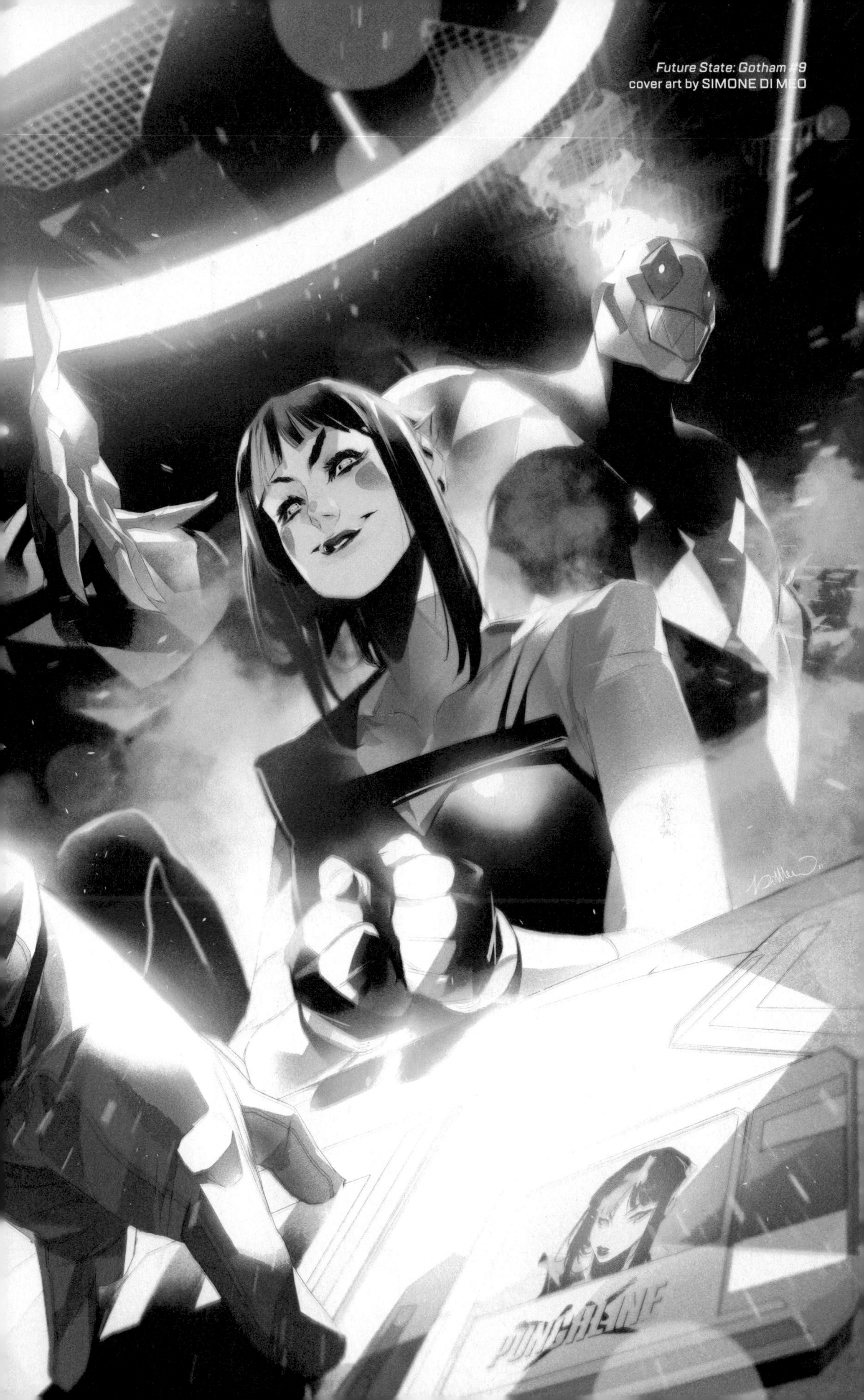
PUNCHLINE

Future State: Gotham #9
cover art by SIMONE DI MEO

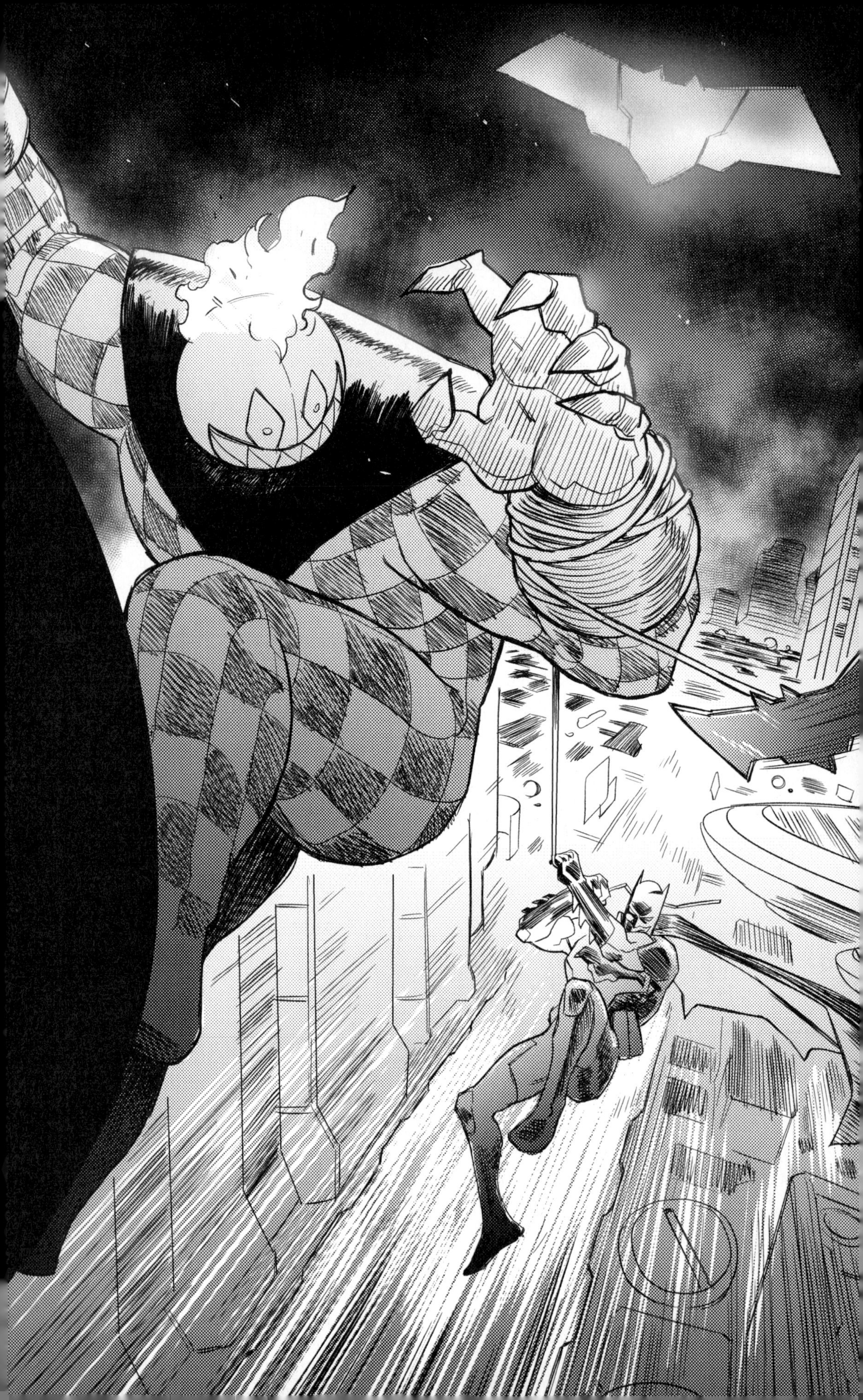

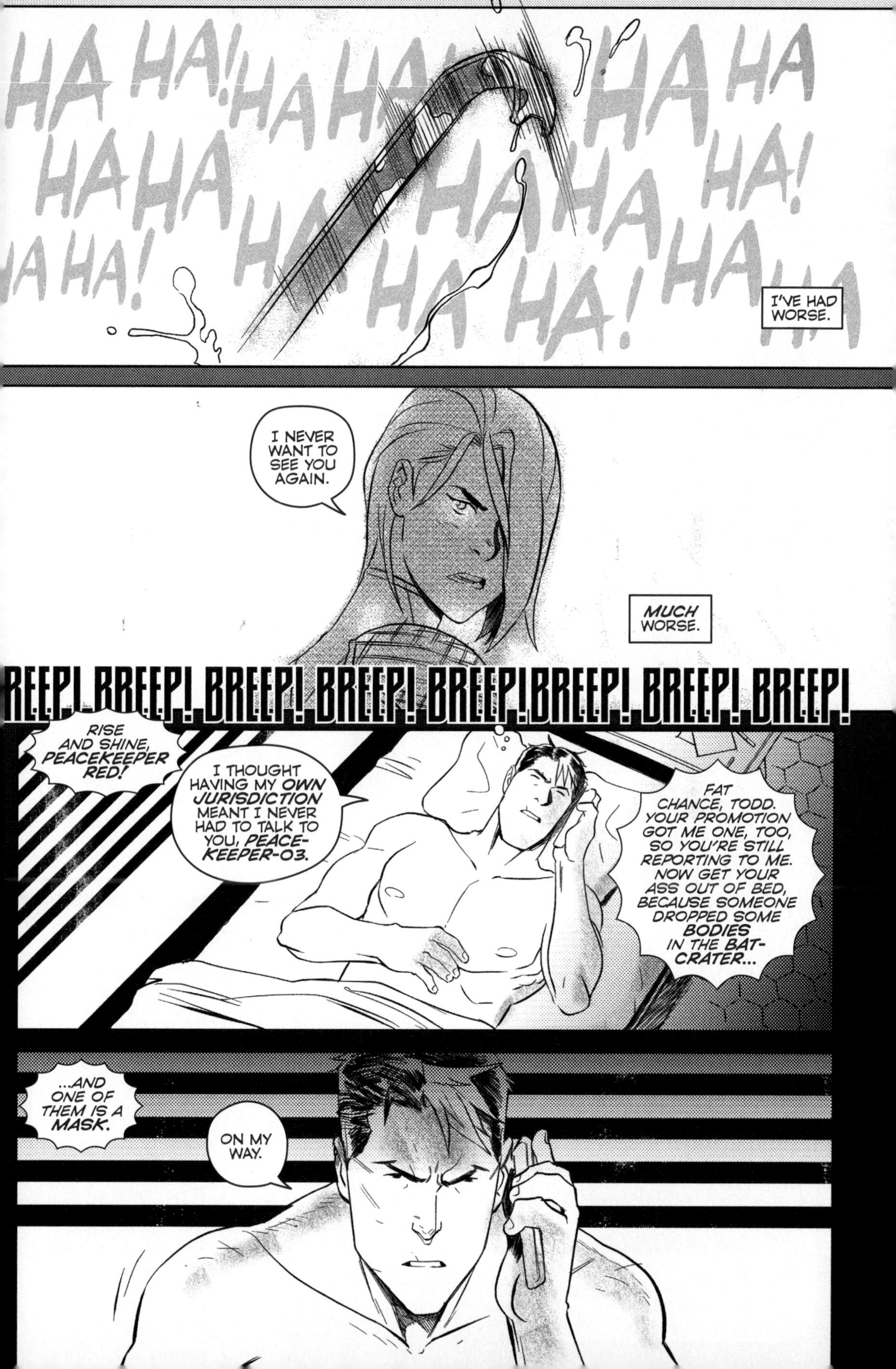
HA HA! HA HA HA HA HA HA HA HA HA HA HA HA! HA HA! HA HA HA HA! HA HA
I'VE HAD WORSE.
I NEVER WANT TO SEE YOU AGAIN.
MUCH WORSE.
BREEP! BREEP! BREEP! BREEP! BREEP! BREEP! BREEP! BREEP!
RISE AND SHINE, PEACEKEEPER RED!
I THOUGHT HAVING MY OWN JURISDICTION MEANT I NEVER HAD TO TALK TO YOU, PEACE-KEEPER-03.
FAT CHANCE, TODD. YOUR PROMOTION GOT ME ONE, TOO, SO YOU'RE STILL REPORTING TO ME. NOW GET YOUR ASS OUT OF BED, BECAUSE SOMEONE DROPPED SOME BODIES IN THE BAT-CRATER...
...AND ONE OF THEM IS A MASK.
ON MY WAY.

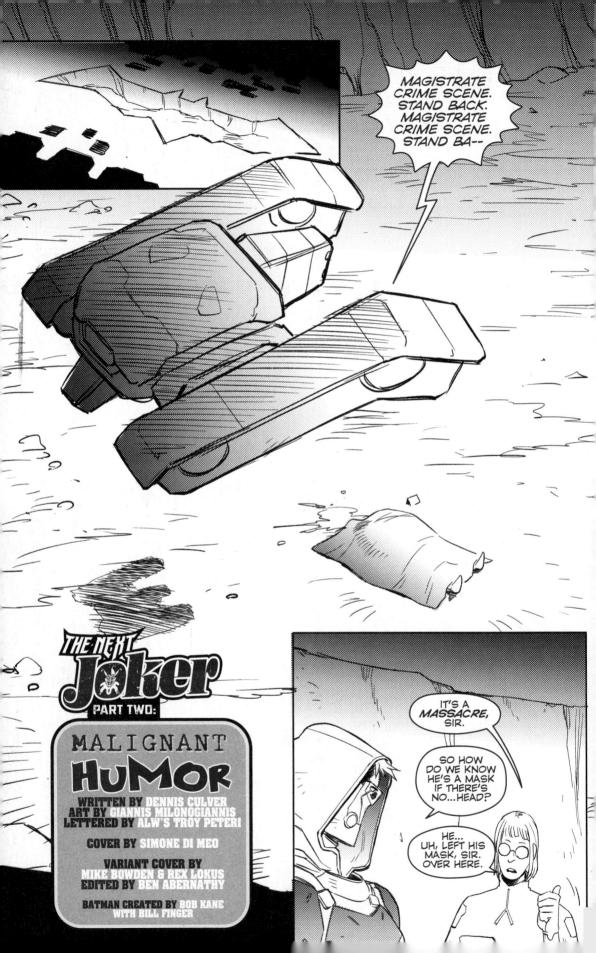

MAGISTRATE CRIME SCENE. STAND BACK. MAGISTRATE CRIME SCENE. STAND BA--

THE NEXT Joker
PART TWO:
MALIGNANT HuMor

WRITTEN BY DENNIS CULVER
ART BY GIANNIS MILONOGIANNIS
LETTERED BY ALW'S TROY PETERI

COVER BY SIMONE DI MEO

VARIANT COVER BY
MIKE BOWDEN & REX LOKUS
EDITED BY BEN ABERNATHY

BATMAN CREATED BY BOB KANE
WITH BILL FINGER

IT'S A MASSACRE, SIR.

SO HOW DO WE KNOW HE'S A MASK IF THERE'S NO...HEAD?

HE... UH, LEFT HIS MASK, SIR. OVER HERE.

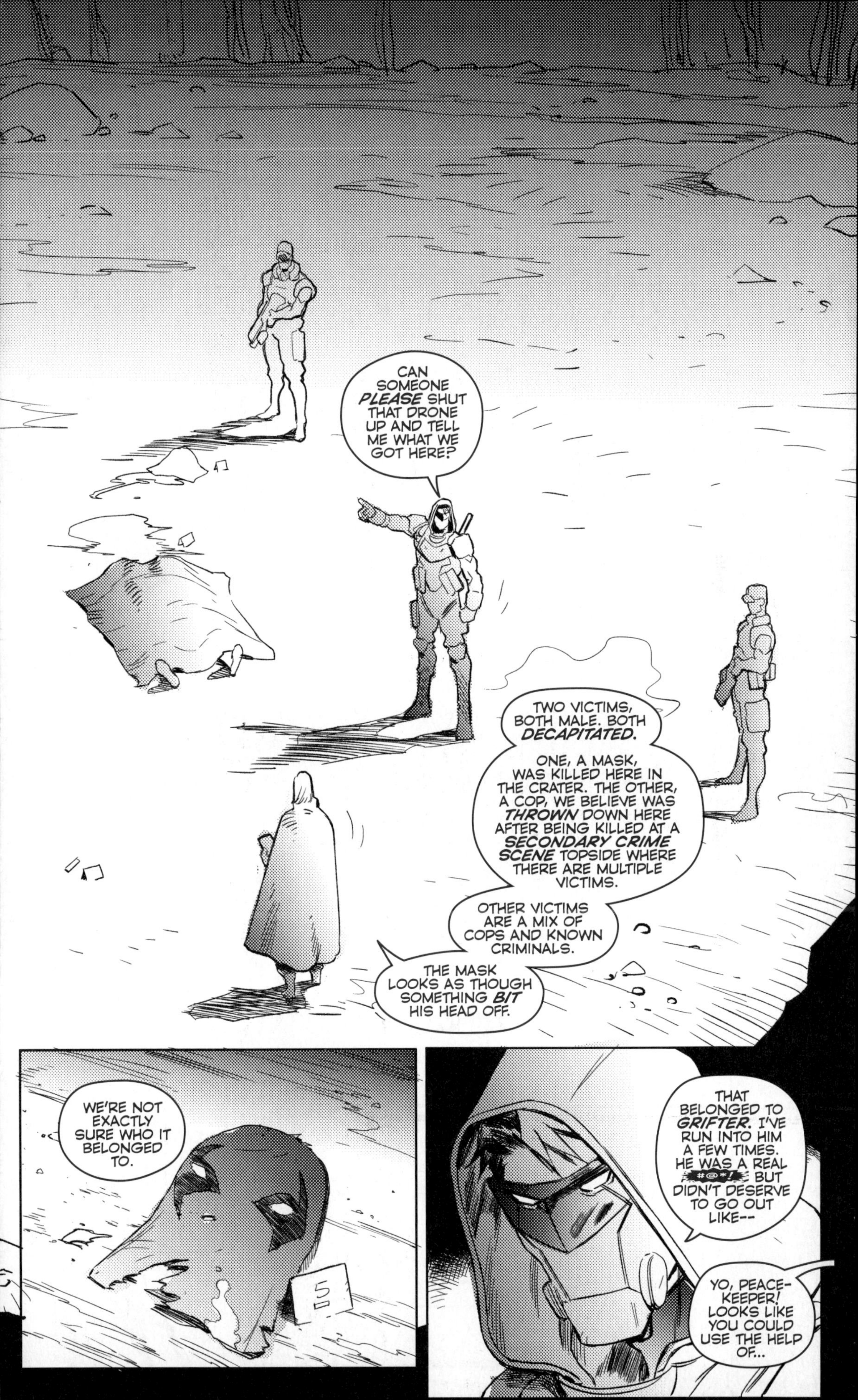

CAN SOMEONE PLEASE SHUT THAT DRONE UP AND TELL ME WHAT WE GOT HERE?
TWO VICTIMS, BOTH MALE. BOTH DECAPITATED.
ONE, A MASK, WAS KILLED HERE IN THE CRATER. THE OTHER, A COP, WE BELIEVE WAS THROWN DOWN HERE AFTER BEING KILLED AT A SECONDARY CRIME SCENE TOPSIDE WHERE THERE ARE MULTIPLE VICTIMS.
OTHER VICTIMS ARE A MIX OF COPS AND KNOWN CRIMINALS.
THE MASK LOOKS AS THOUGH SOMETHING BIT HIS HEAD OFF.
WE'RE NOT EXACTLY SURE WHO IT BELONGED TO.
5
THAT BELONGED TO GRIFTER. I'VE RUN INTO HIM A FEW TIMES. HE WAS A REAL #@*! BUT DIDN'T DESERVE TO GO OUT LIKE--
YO, PEACE-KEEPER! LOOKS LIKE YOU COULD USE THE HELP OF...

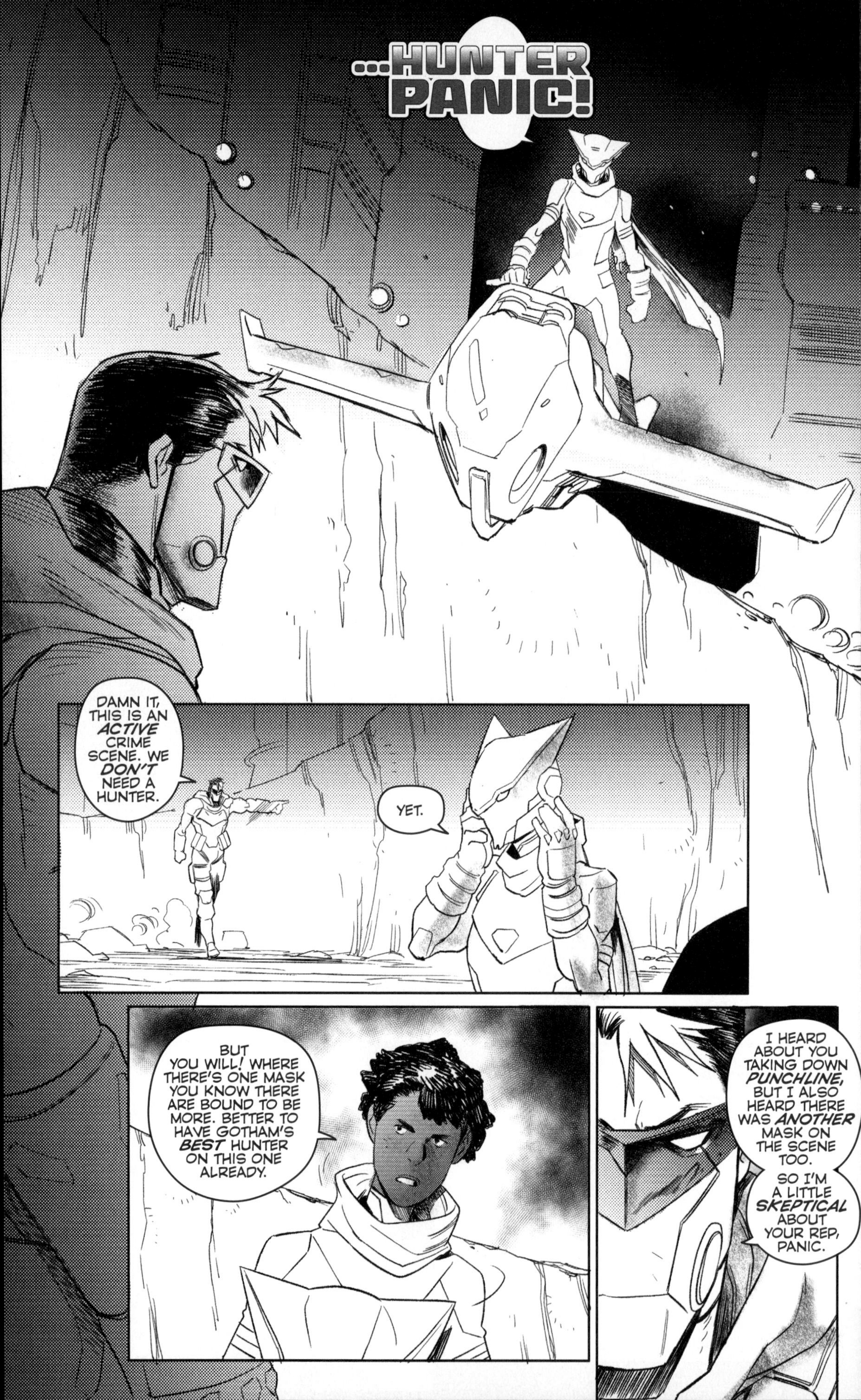
...HUNTER PANIC!
DAMN IT, THIS IS AN ACTIVE CRIME SCENE. WE DON'T NEED A HUNTER.
YET.
BUT YOU WILL! WHERE THERE'S ONE MASK YOU KNOW THERE ARE BOUND TO BE MORE. BETTER TO HAVE GOTHAM'S BEST HUNTER ON THIS ONE ALREADY.
I HEARD ABOUT YOU TAKING DOWN PUNCHLINE, BUT I ALSO HEARD THERE WAS ANOTHER MASK ON THE SCENE TOO.
SO I'M A LITTLE SKEPTICAL ABOUT YOUR REP, PANIC.

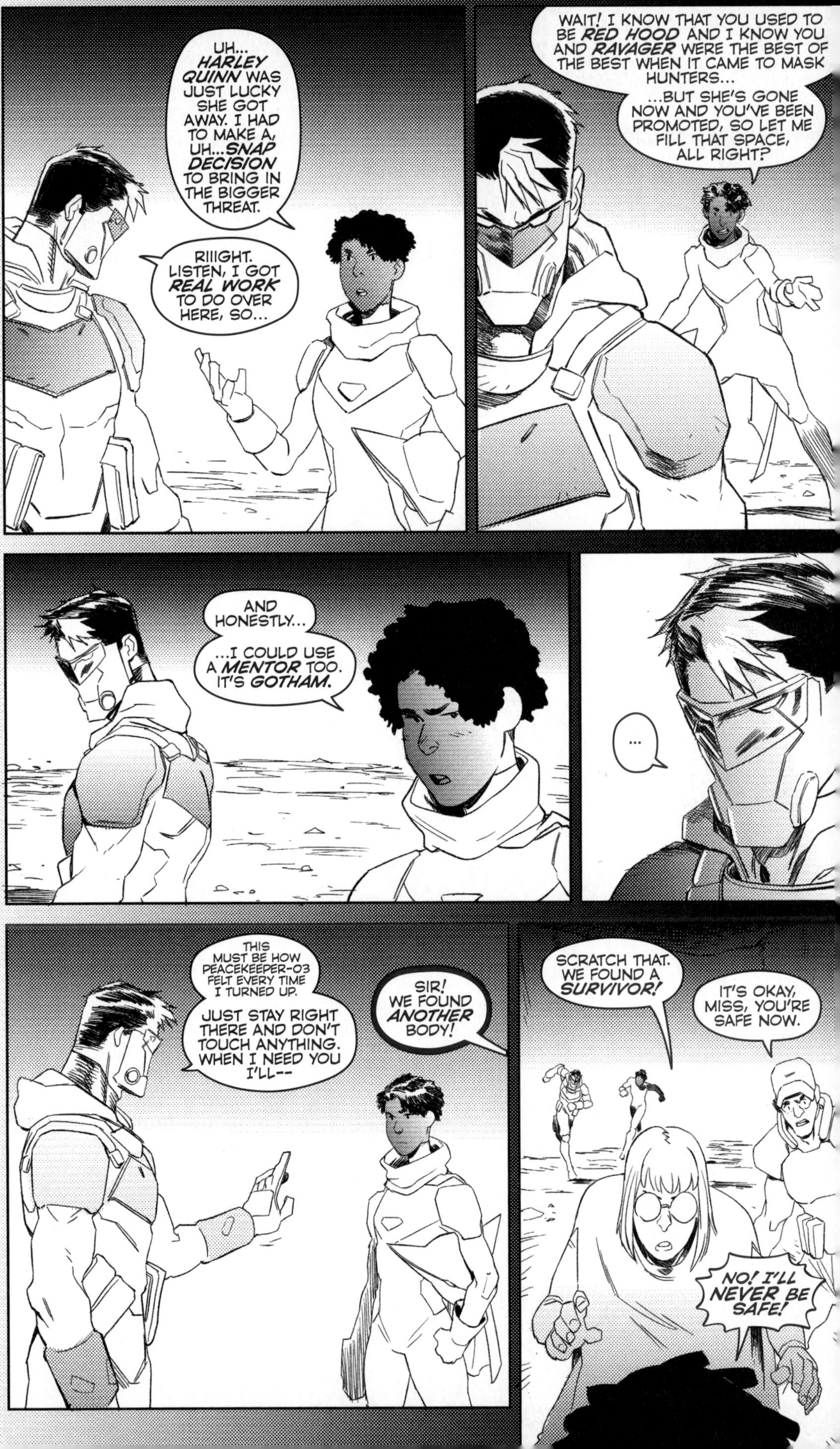
UH... HARLEY QUINN WAS JUST LUCKY SHE GOT AWAY. I HAD TO MAKE A, UH...SNAP DECISION TO BRING IN THE BIGGER THREAT.
RIIIGHT. LISTEN, I GOT REAL WORK TO DO OVER HERE, SO...
WAIT! I KNOW THAT YOU USED TO BE RED HOOD AND I KNOW YOU AND RAVAGER WERE THE BEST OF THE BEST WHEN IT CAME TO MASK HUNTERS...
...BUT SHE'S GONE NOW AND YOU'VE BEEN PROMOTED, SO LET ME FILL THAT SPACE, ALL RIGHT?
AND HONESTLY...
...I COULD USE A MENTOR TOO. IT'S GOTHAM.
...
THIS MUST BE HOW PEACEKEEPER-03 FELT EVERY TIME I TURNED UP.
JUST STAY RIGHT THERE AND DON'T TOUCH ANYTHING. WHEN I NEED YOU I'LL--
SIR! WE FOUND ANOTHER BODY!
SCRATCH THAT. WE FOUND A SURVIVOR!
IT'S OKAY, MISS, YOU'RE SAFE NOW.
NO! I'LL NEVER BE SAFE!

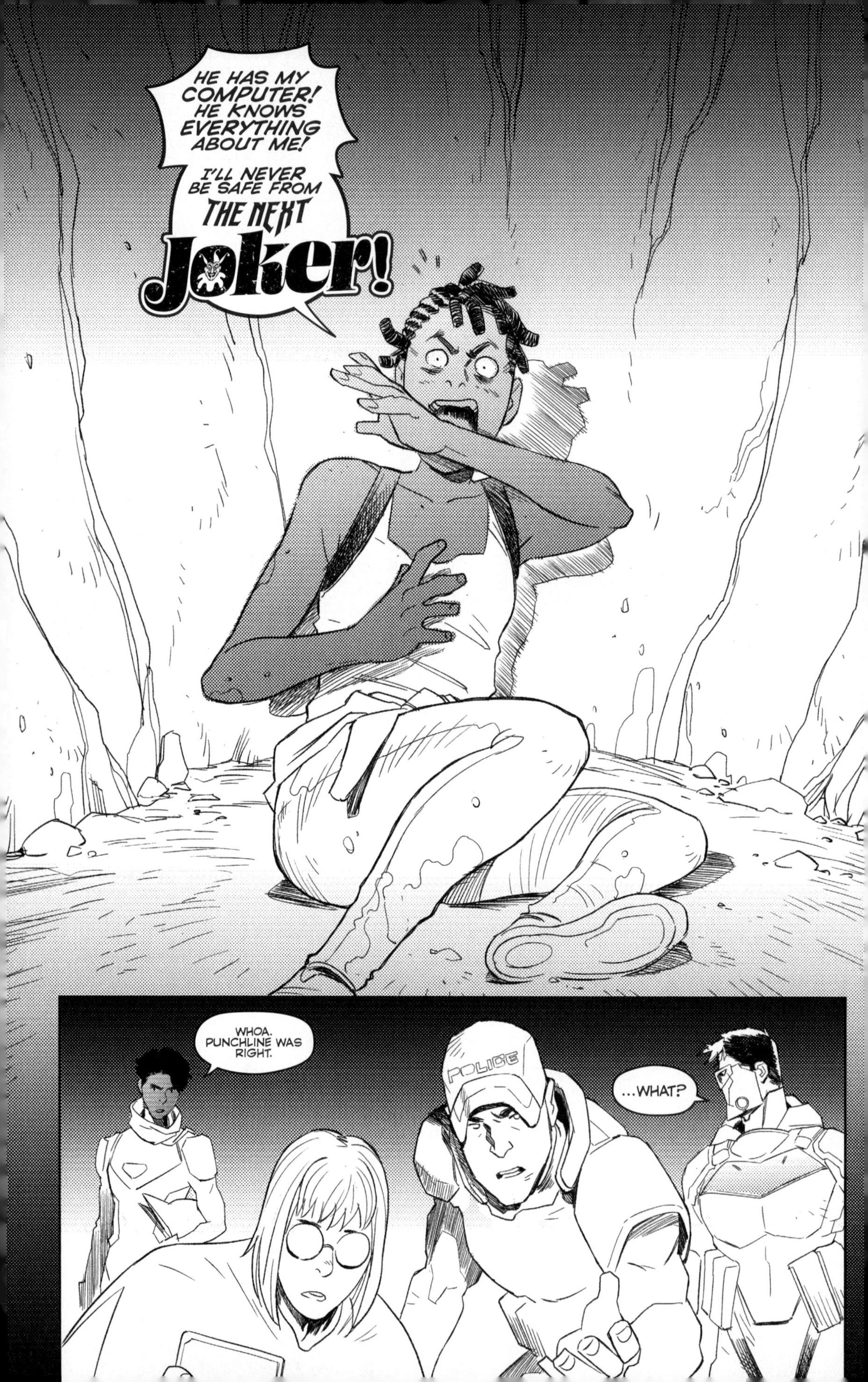
HE HAS MY COMPUTER! HE KNOWS EVERYTHING ABOUT ME!
I'LL NEVER BE SAFE FROM THE NEXT JOKER!
WHOA. PUNCHLINE WAS RIGHT.
POLICE
...WHAT?

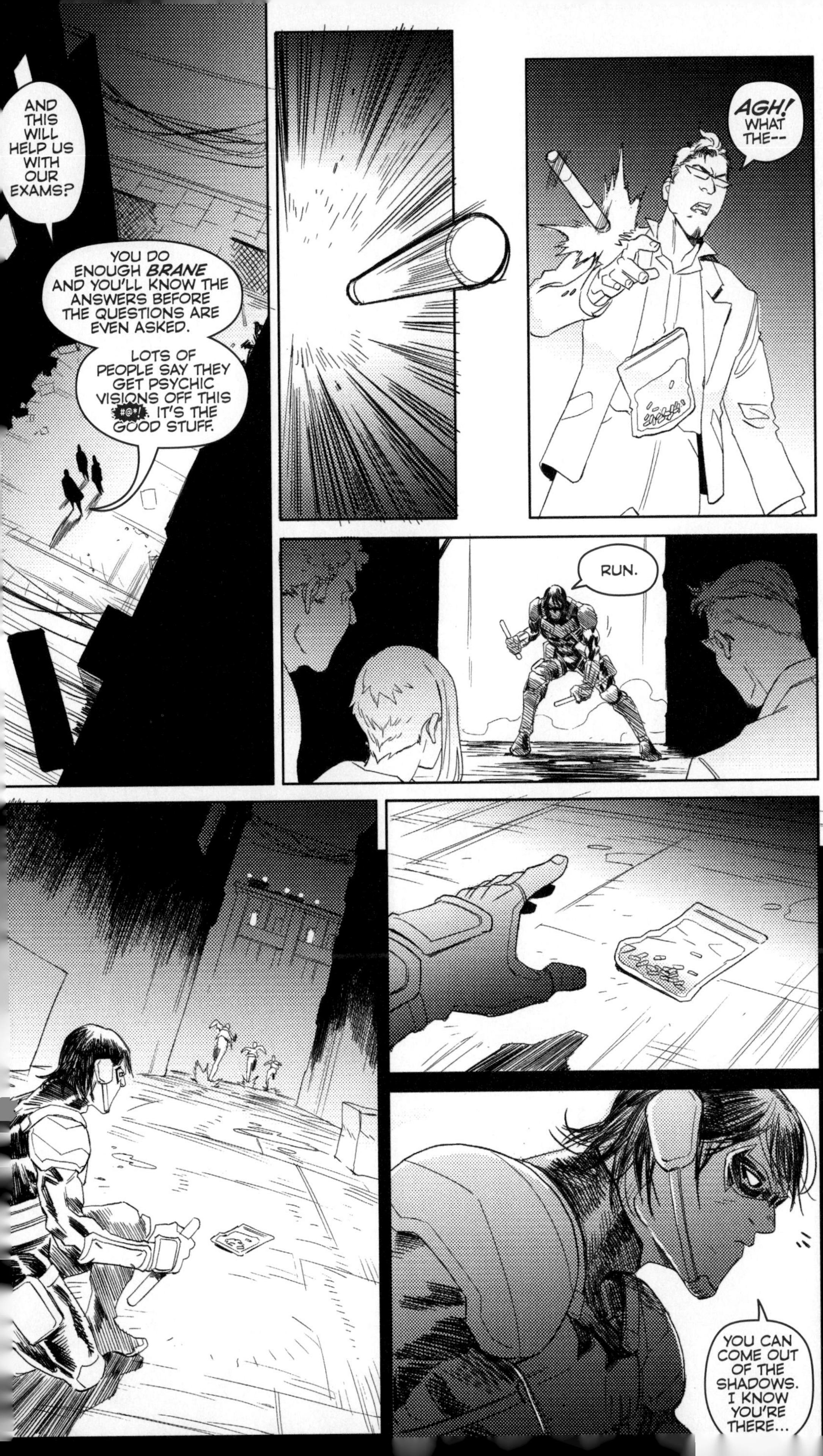
AND THIS WILL HELP US WITH OUR EXAMS?
YOU DO ENOUGH BRANE AND YOU'LL KNOW THE ANSWERS BEFORE THE QUESTIONS ARE EVEN ASKED.
LOTS OF PEOPLE SAY THEY GET PSYCHIC VISIONS OFF THIS #@*!. IT'S THE GOOD STUFF.
AGH! WHAT THE--
RUN.
YOU CAN COME OUT OF THE SHADOWS. I KNOW YOU'RE THERE...

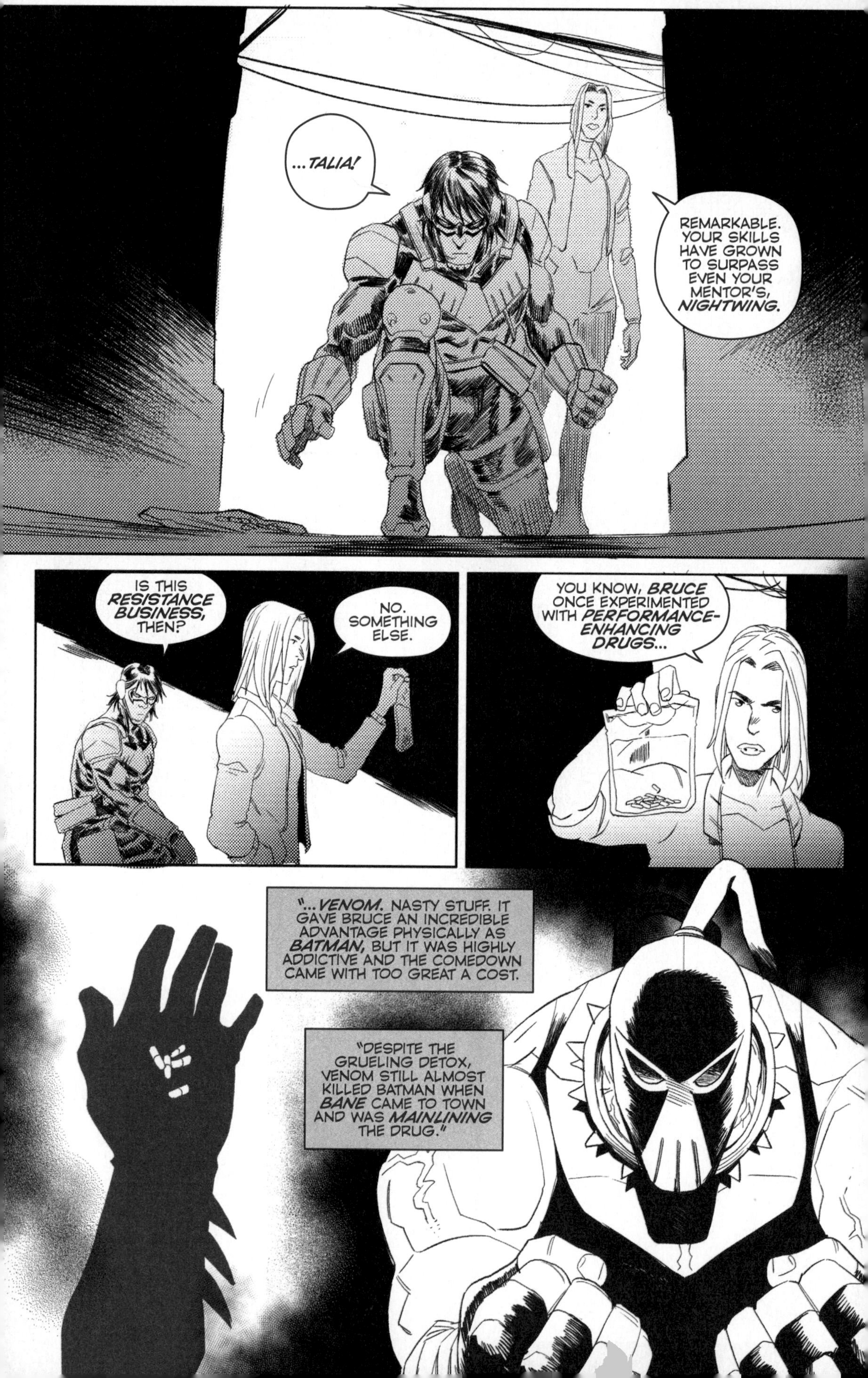
...TALIA!
REMARKABLE. YOUR SKILLS HAVE GROWN TO SURPASS EVEN YOUR MENTOR'S, NIGHTWING.
IS THIS RESISTANCE BUSINESS, THEN?
NO. SOMETHING ELSE.
YOU KNOW, BRUCE ONCE EXPERIMENTED WITH PERFORMANCE-ENHANCING DRUGS...
"...VENOM. NASTY STUFF. IT GAVE BRUCE AN INCREDIBLE ADVANTAGE PHYSICALLY AS BATMAN, BUT IT WAS HIGHLY ADDICTIVE AND THE COMEDOWN CAME WITH TOO GREAT A COST.
"DESPITE THE GRUELING DETOX, VENOM STILL ALMOST KILLED BATMAN WHEN BANE CAME TO TOWN AND WAS MAINLINING THE DRUG."

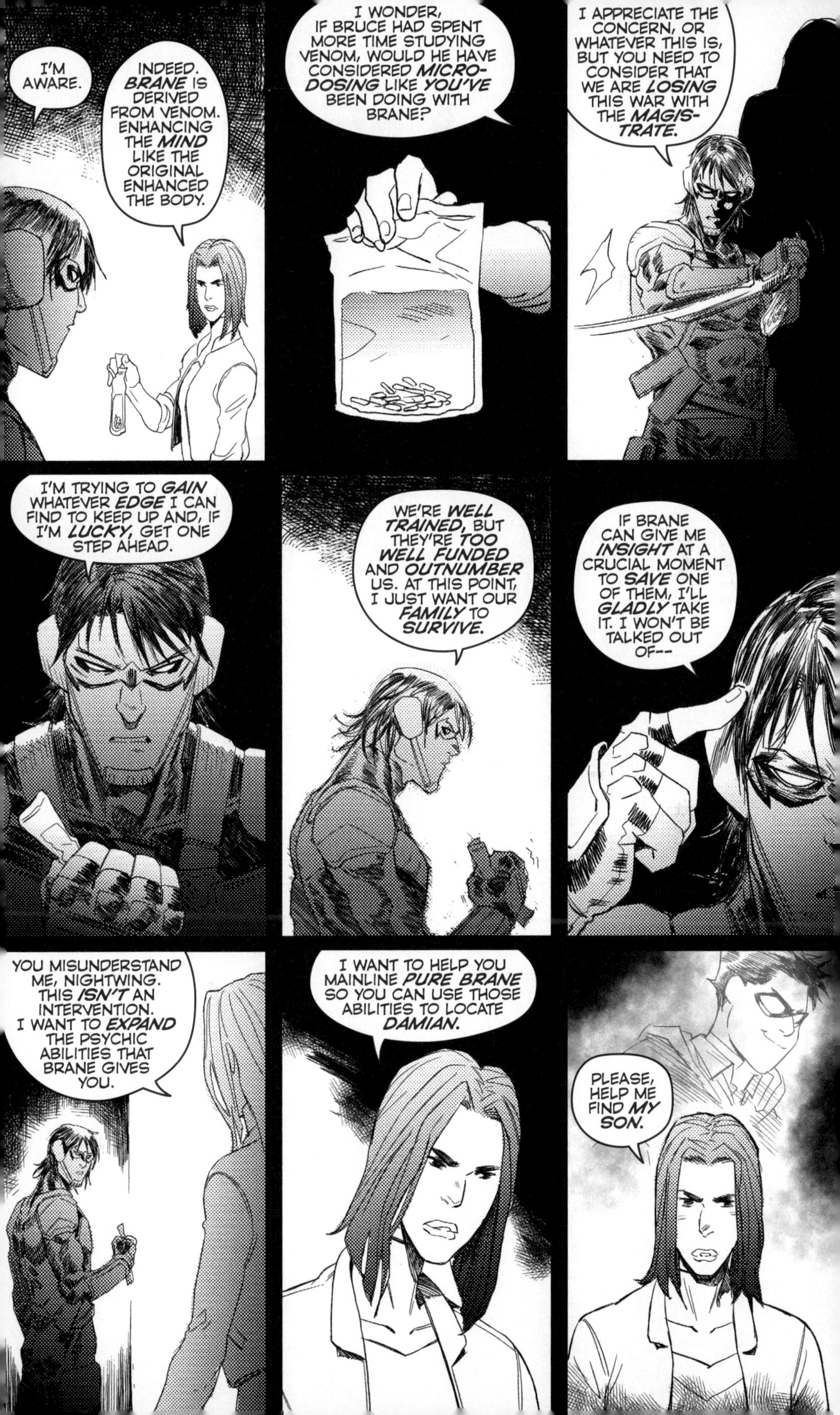
I'M AWARE.
INDEED. BRANE IS DERIVED FROM VENOM. ENHANCING THE MIND LIKE THE ORIGINAL ENHANCED THE BODY.
I WONDER, IF BRUCE HAD SPENT MORE TIME STUDYING VENOM, WOULD HE HAVE CONSIDERED MICRO-DOSING LIKE YOU'VE BEEN DOING WITH BRANE?
I APPRECIATE THE CONCERN, OR WHATEVER THIS IS, BUT YOU NEED TO CONSIDER THAT WE ARE LOSING THIS WAR WITH THE MAGIS-TRATE.
I'M TRYING TO GAIN WHATEVER EDGE I CAN FIND TO KEEP UP AND, IF I'M LUCKY, GET ONE STEP AHEAD.
WE'RE WELL TRAINED, BUT THEY'RE TOO WELL FUNDED AND OUTNUMBER US. AT THIS POINT, I JUST WANT OUR FAMILY TO SURVIVE.
IF BRANE CAN GIVE ME INSIGHT AT A CRUCIAL MOMENT TO SAVE ONE OF THEM, I'LL GLADLY TAKE IT. I WON'T BE TALKED OUT OF--
YOU MISUNDERSTAND ME, NIGHTWING. THIS ISN'T AN INTERVENTION. I WANT TO EXPAND THE PSYCHIC ABILITIES THAT BRANE GIVES YOU.
I WANT TO HELP YOU MAINLINE PURE BRANE SO YOU CAN USE THOSE ABILITIES TO LOCATE DAMIAN.
PLEASE, HELP ME FIND MY SON.

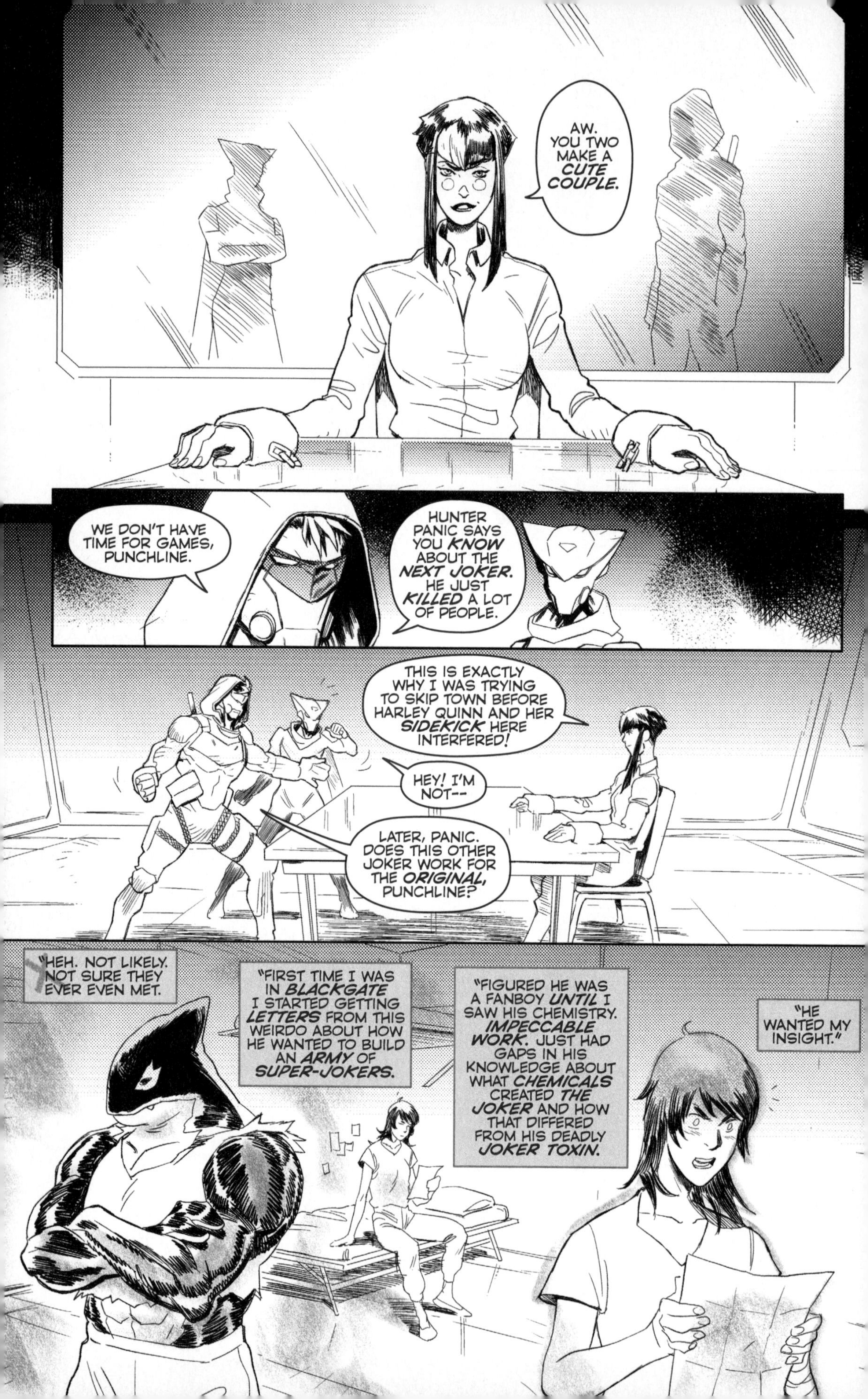
AW. YOU TWO MAKE A CUTE COUPLE.
WE DON'T HAVE TIME FOR GAMES, PUNCHLINE.
HUNTER PANIC SAYS YOU KNOW ABOUT THE NEXT JOKER. HE JUST KILLED A LOT OF PEOPLE.
THIS IS EXACTLY WHY I WAS TRYING TO SKIP TOWN BEFORE HARLEY QUINN AND HER SIDEKICK HERE INTERFERED!
HEY! I'M NOT--
LATER, PANIC. DOES THIS OTHER JOKER WORK FOR THE ORIGINAL, PUNCHLINE?
"HEH. NOT LIKELY. NOT SURE THEY EVER EVEN MET.
"FIRST TIME I WAS IN BLACKGATE I STARTED GETTING LETTERS FROM THIS WEIRDO ABOUT HOW HE WANTED TO BUILD AN ARMY OF SUPER-JOKERS.
"FIGURED HE WAS A FANBOY UNTIL I SAW HIS CHEMISTRY. IMPECCABLE WORK. JUST HAD GAPS IN HIS KNOWLEDGE ABOUT WHAT CHEMICALS CREATED THE JOKER AND HOW THAT DIFFERED FROM HIS DEADLY JOKER TOXIN.
"HE WANTED MY INSIGHT."

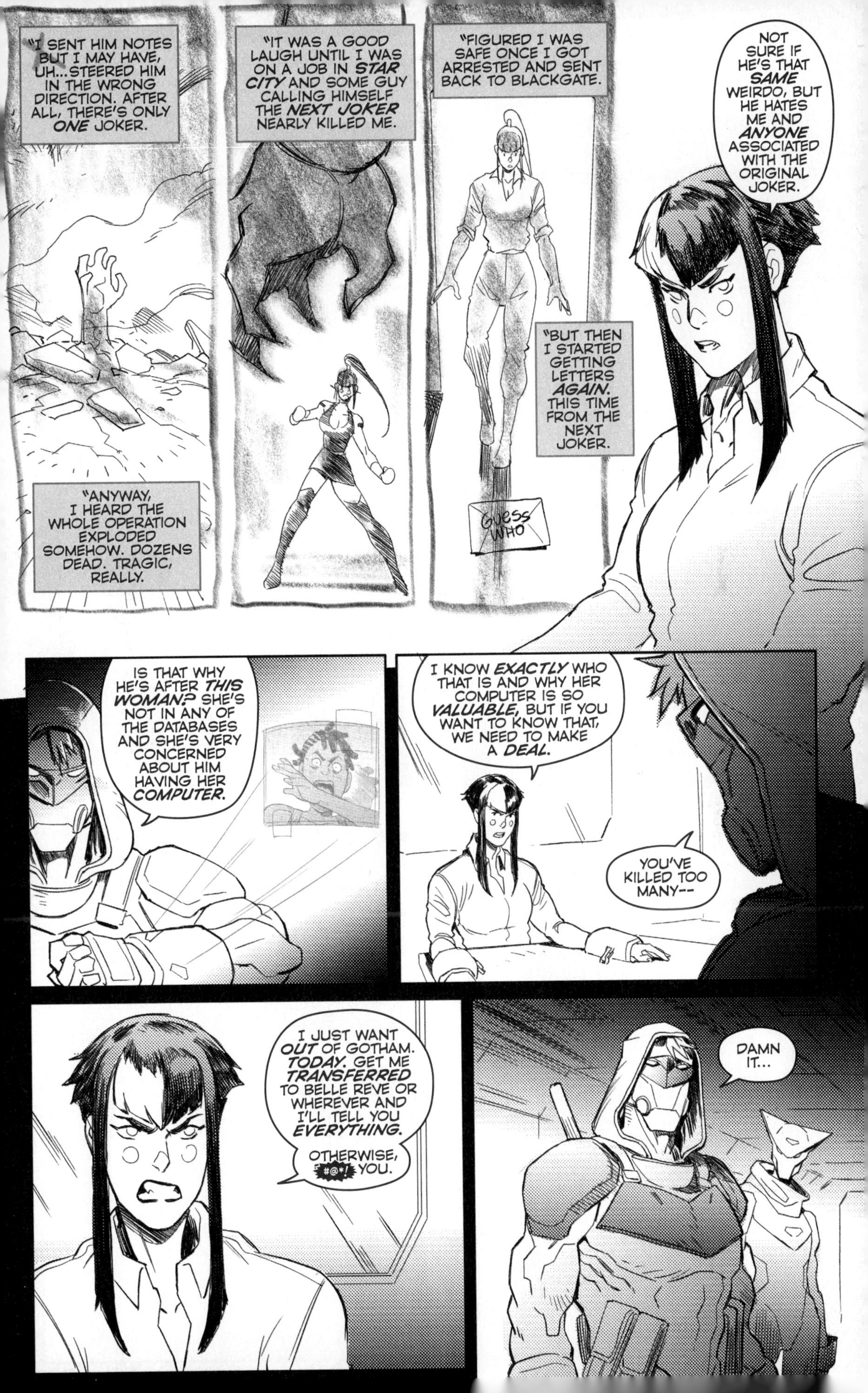
"I SENT HIM NOTES BUT I MAY HAVE, UH...STEERED HIM IN THE WRONG DIRECTION. AFTER ALL, THERE'S ONLY ONE JOKER.
"ANYWAY, I HEARD THE WHOLE OPERATION EXPLODED SOMEHOW. DOZENS DEAD. TRAGIC, REALLY.
"IT WAS A GOOD LAUGH UNTIL I WAS ON A JOB IN STAR CITY AND SOME GUY CALLING HIMSELF THE NEXT JOKER NEARLY KILLED ME.
"FIGURED I WAS SAFE ONCE I GOT ARRESTED AND SENT BACK TO BLACKGATE.
"BUT THEN I STARTED GETTING LETTERS AGAIN. THIS TIME FROM THE NEXT JOKER.
GUESS WHO
NOT SURE IF HE'S THAT SAME WEIRDO, BUT HE HATES ME AND ANYONE ASSOCIATED WITH THE ORIGINAL JOKER.
IS THAT WHY HE'S AFTER THIS WOMAN? SHE'S NOT IN ANY OF THE DATABASES AND SHE'S VERY CONCERNED ABOUT HIM HAVING HER COMPUTER.
I KNOW EXACTLY WHO THAT IS AND WHY HER COMPUTER IS SO VALUABLE, BUT IF YOU WANT TO KNOW THAT, WE NEED TO MAKE A DEAL.
YOU'VE KILLED TOO MANY--
I JUST WANT OUT OF GOTHAM. TODAY. GET ME TRANSFERRED TO BELLE REVE OR WHEREVER AND I'LL TELL YOU EVERYTHING.
OTHERWISE, #@*! YOU.
DAMN IT...

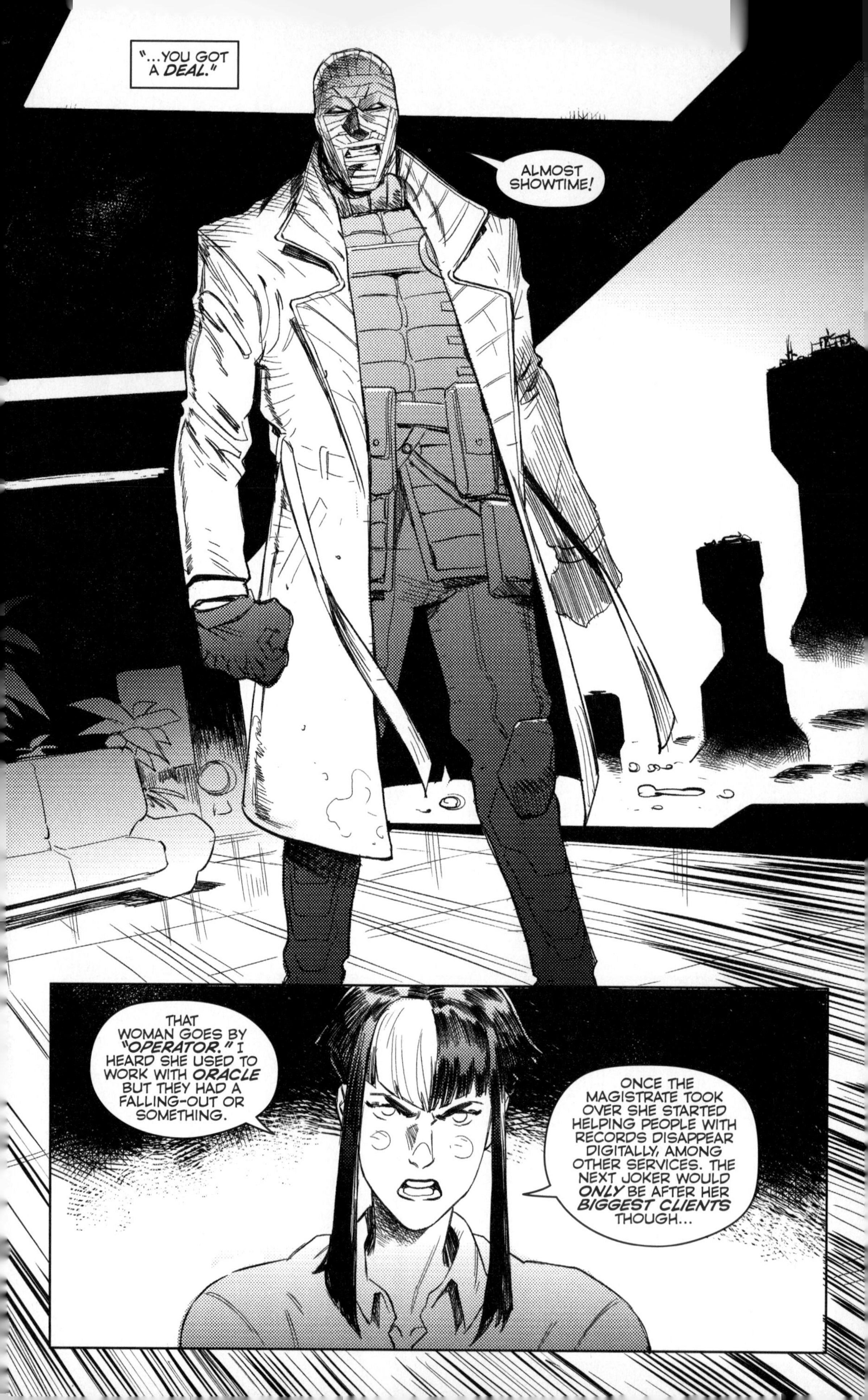
"...YOU GOT A DEAL."
ALMOST SHOWTIME!
THAT WOMAN GOES BY "OPERATOR." I HEARD SHE USED TO WORK WITH ORACLE BUT THEY HAD A FALLING-OUT OR SOMETHING.
ONCE THE MAGISTRATE TOOK OVER SHE STARTED HELPING PEOPLE WITH RECORDS DISAPPEAR DIGITALLY, AMONG OTHER SERVICES. THE NEXT JOKER WOULD ONLY BE AFTER HER BIGGEST CLIENTS THOUGH...

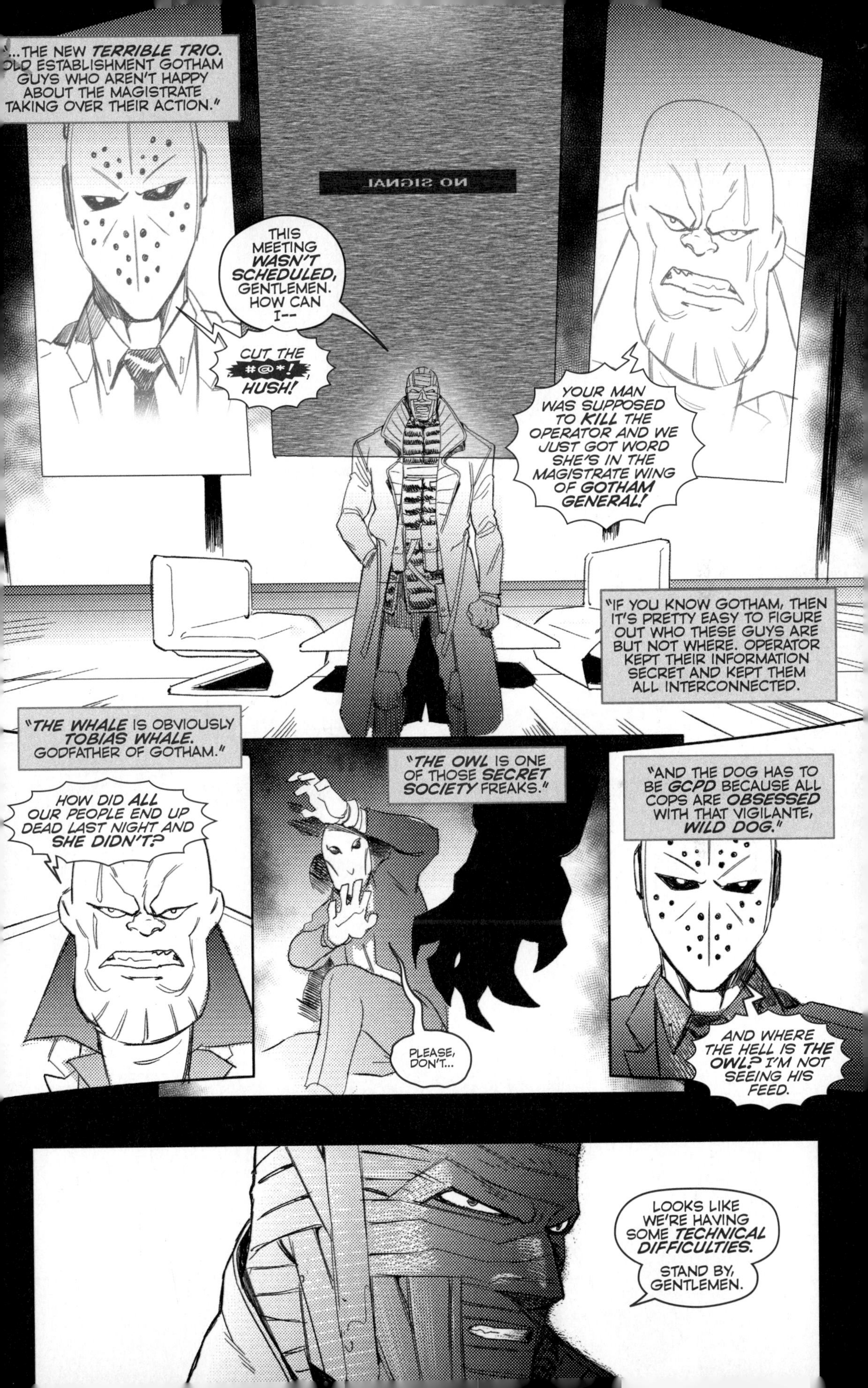
"...THE NEW TERRIBLE TRIO. OLD ESTABLISHMENT GOTHAM GUYS WHO AREN'T HAPPY ABOUT THE MAGISTRATE TAKING OVER THEIR ACTION."
NO SIGNAL
THIS MEETING WASN'T SCHEDULED, GENTLEMEN. HOW CAN I--
CUT THE #@*!, HUSH!
YOUR MAN WAS SUPPOSED TO KILL THE OPERATOR AND WE JUST GOT WORD SHE'S IN THE MAGISTRATE WING OF GOTHAM GENERAL!
"IF YOU KNOW GOTHAM, THEN IT'S PRETTY EASY TO FIGURE OUT WHO THESE GUYS ARE BUT NOT WHERE. OPERATOR KEPT THEIR INFORMATION SECRET AND KEPT THEM ALL INTERCONNECTED.
"THE WHALE IS OBVIOUSLY TOBIAS WHALE. GODFATHER OF GOTHAM."
HOW DID ALL OUR PEOPLE END UP DEAD LAST NIGHT AND SHE DIDN'T?
"THE OWL IS ONE OF THOSE SECRET SOCIETY FREAKS."
PLEASE, DON'T...
"AND THE DOG HAS TO BE GCPD BECAUSE ALL COPS ARE OBSESSED WITH THAT VIGILANTE, WILD DOG."
AND WHERE THE HELL IS THE OWL? I'M NOT SEEING HIS FEED.
LOOKS LIKE WE'RE HAVING SOME TECHNICAL DIFFICULTIES.
STAND BY, GENTLEMEN.

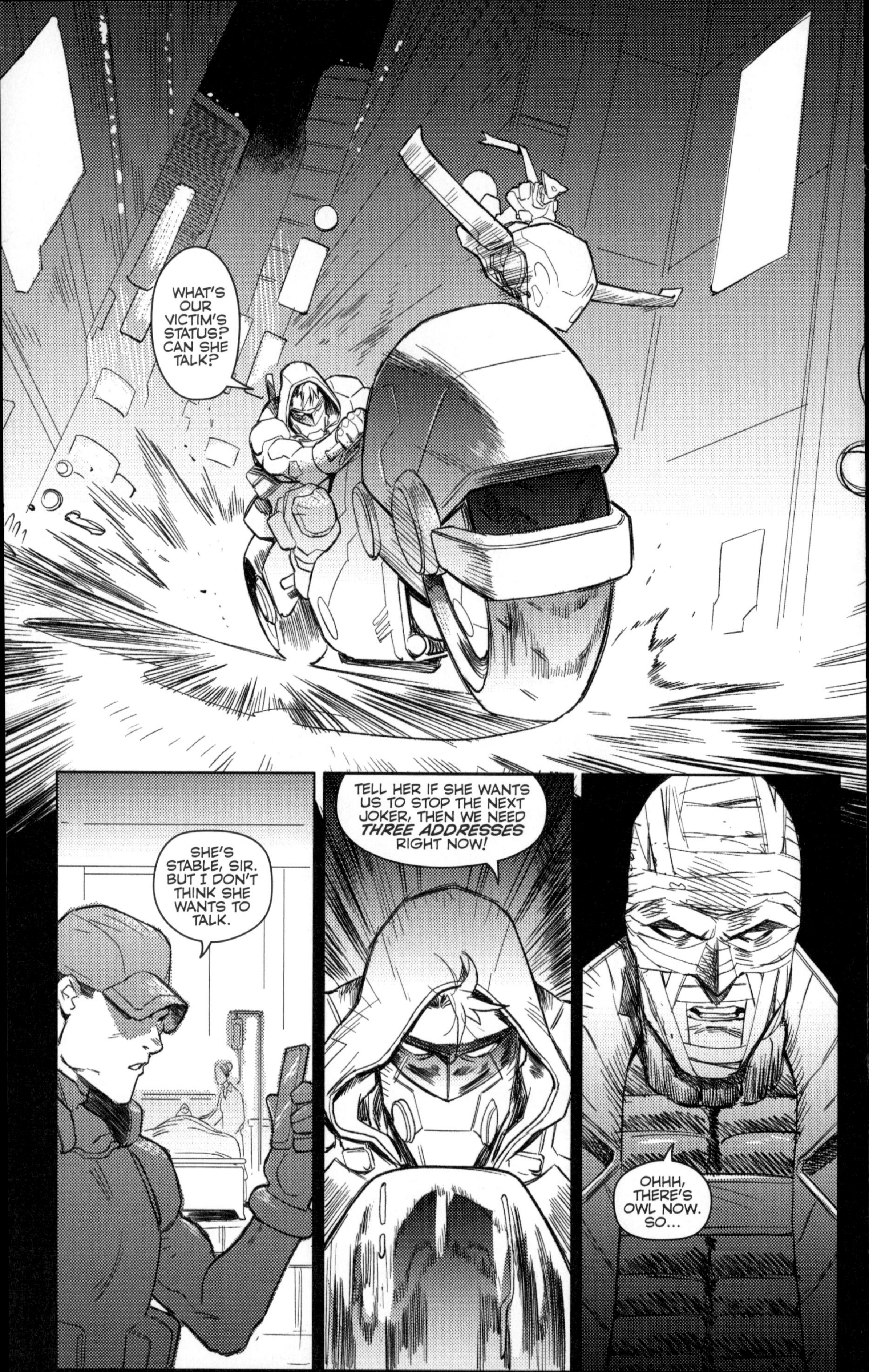
WHAT'S OUR VICTIM'S STATUS? CAN SHE TALK?
SHE'S STABLE, SIR. BUT I DON'T THINK SHE WANTS TO TALK.
TELL HER IF SHE WANTS US TO STOP THE NEXT JOKER, THEN WE NEED THREE ADDRESSES RIGHT NOW!
OHHH, THERE'S OWL NOW. SO...

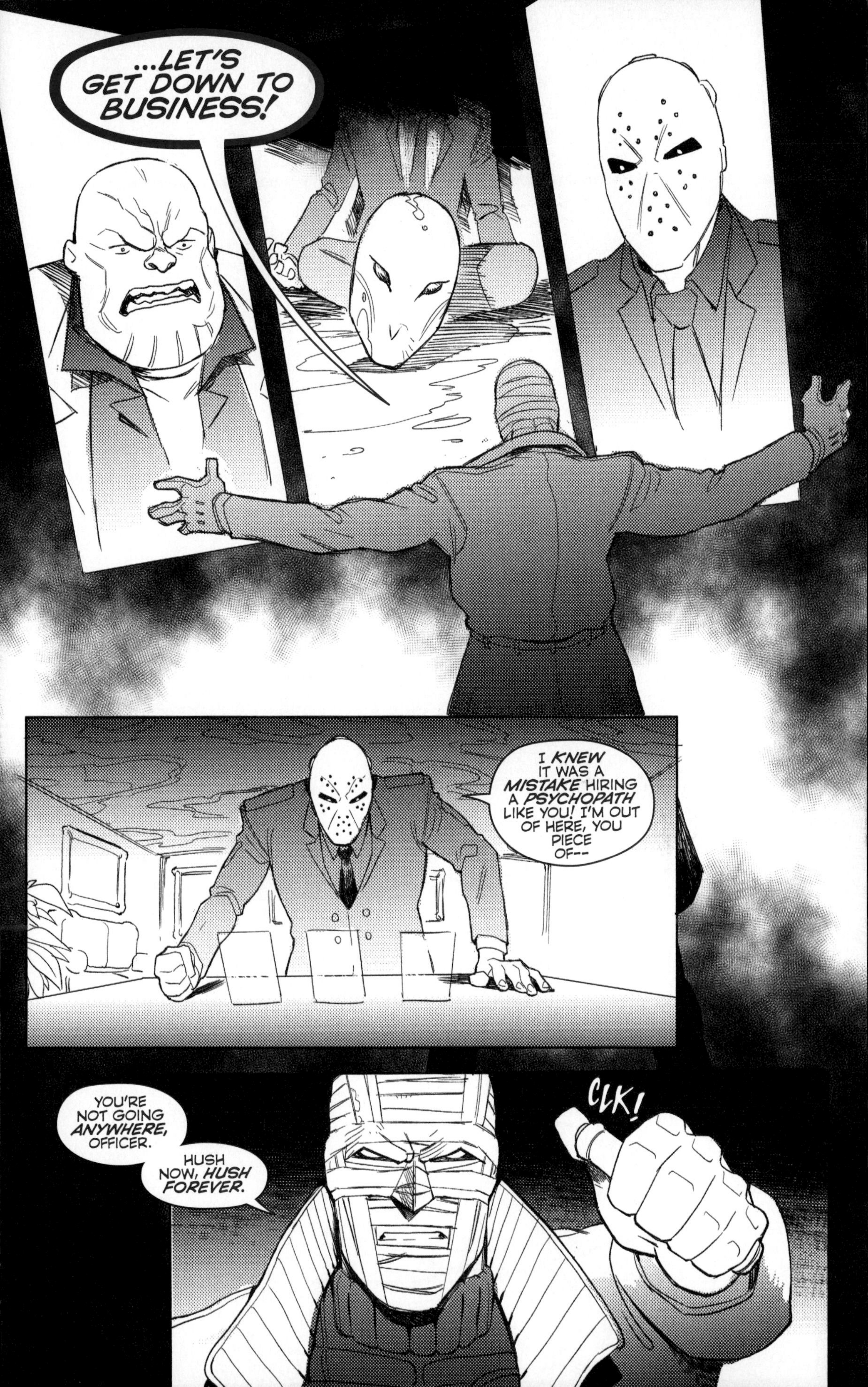
...LET'S GET DOWN TO BUSINESS!
I KNEW IT WAS A MISTAKE HIRING A PSYCHOPATH LIKE YOU! I'M OUT OF HERE, YOU PIECE OF--
YOU'RE NOT GOING ANYWHERE, OFFICER.
HUSH NOW, HUSH FOREVER.
CLK!

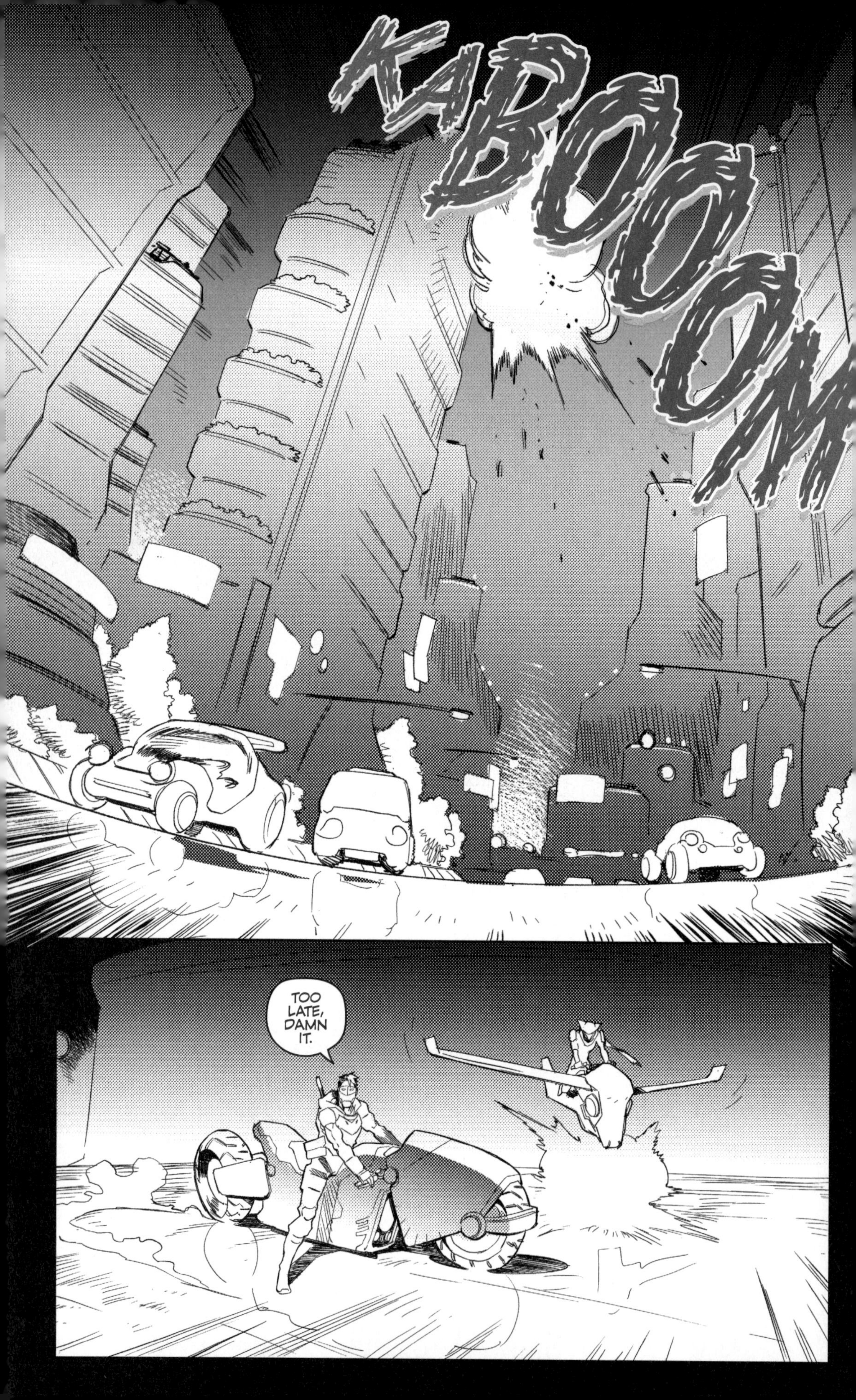
KABOOOOM
TOO LATE, DAMN IT.

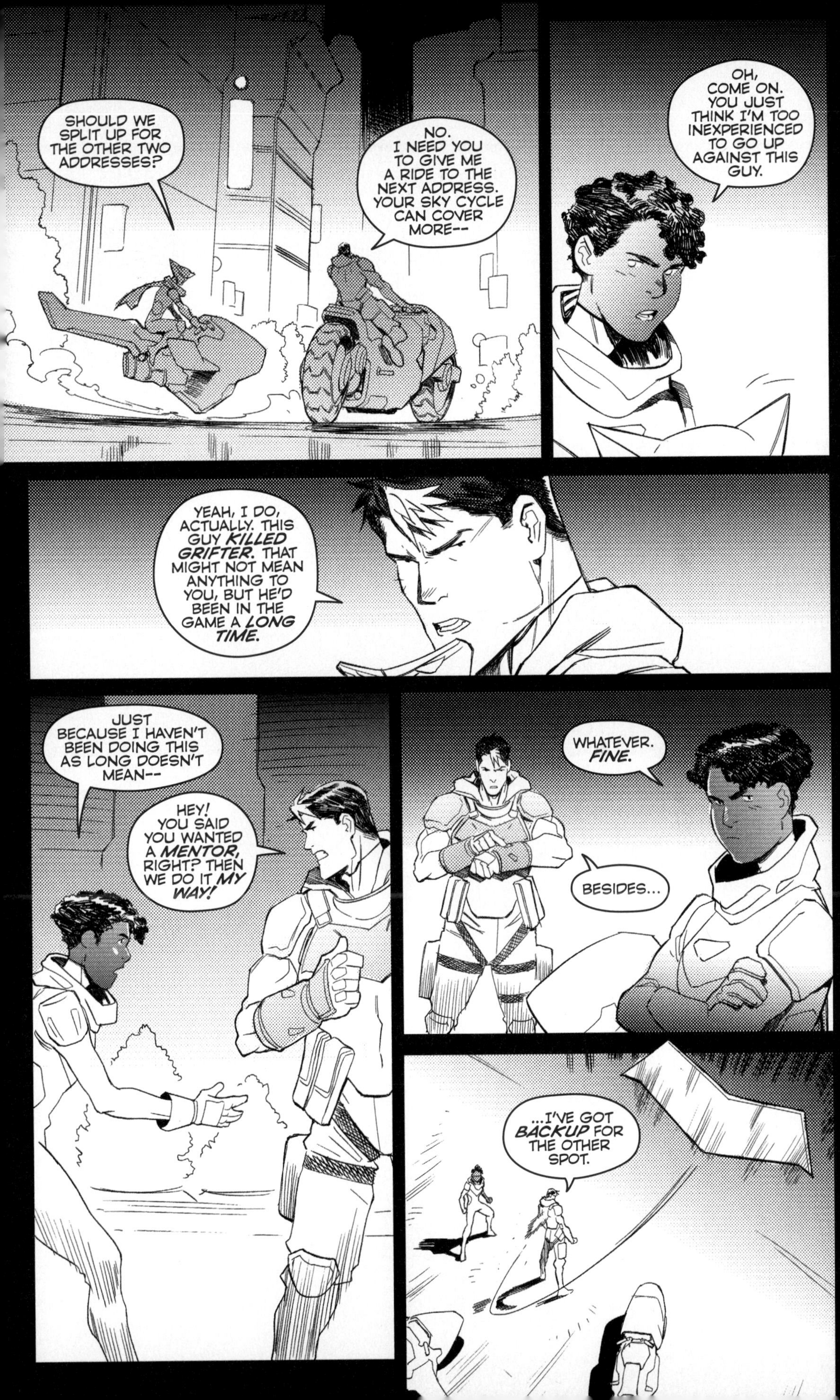
SHOULD WE SPLIT UP FOR THE OTHER TWO ADDRESSES?
NO. I NEED YOU TO GIVE ME A RIDE TO THE NEXT ADDRESS. YOUR SKY CYCLE CAN COVER MORE--
OH, COME ON. YOU JUST THINK I'M TOO INEXPERIENCED TO GO UP AGAINST THIS GUY.
YEAH, I DO, ACTUALLY. THIS GUY *KILLED GRIFTER*. THAT MIGHT NOT MEAN ANYTHING TO YOU, BUT HE'D BEEN IN THE GAME A *LONG TIME*.
JUST BECAUSE I HAVEN'T BEEN DOING THIS AS LONG DOESN'T MEAN--
HEY! YOU SAID YOU WANTED A *MENTOR*, RIGHT? THEN WE DO IT *MY WAY!*
WHATEVER. *FINE*.
BESIDES...
...I'VE GOT *BACKUP* FOR THE OTHER SPOT.

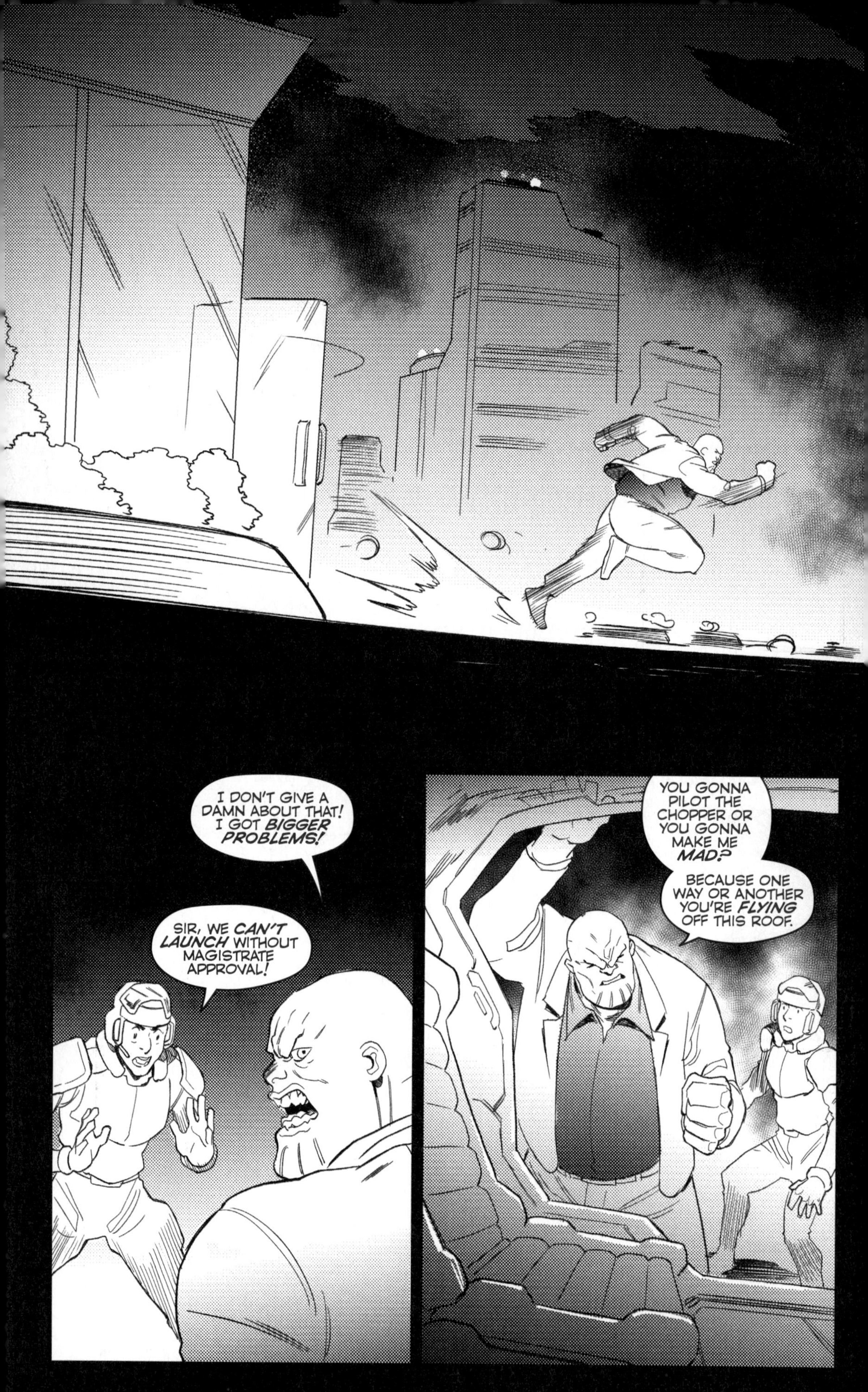
I DON'T GIVE A DAMN ABOUT THAT! I GOT *BIGGER PROBLEMS!*
SIR, WE *CAN'T LAUNCH* WITHOUT MAGISTRATE APPROVAL!
YOU GONNA PILOT THE CHOPPER OR YOU GONNA MAKE ME *MAD?*
BECAUSE ONE WAY OR ANOTHER YOU'RE *FLYING* OFF THIS ROOF.

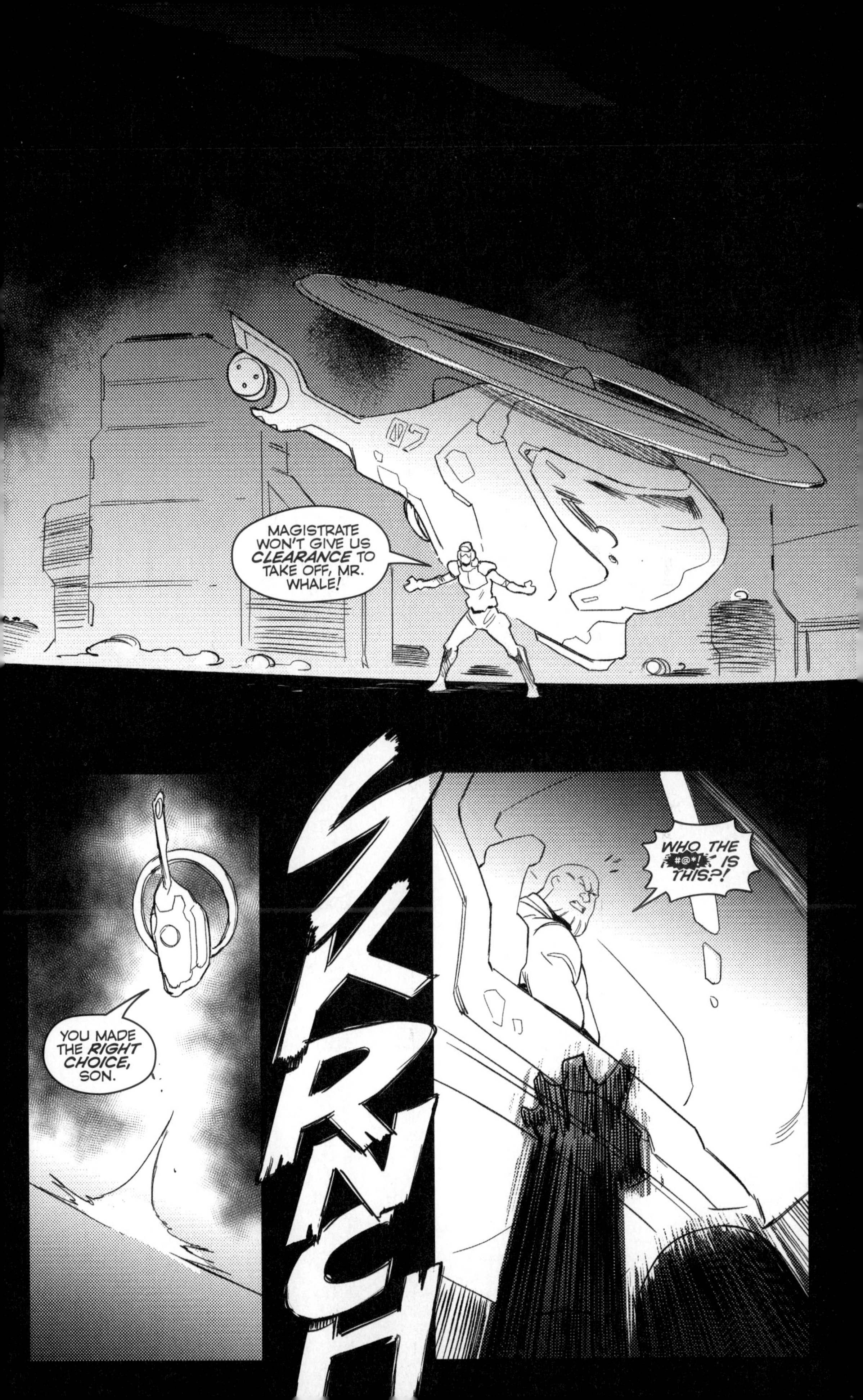
MAGISTRATE WON'T GIVE US CLEARANCE TO TAKE OFF, MR. WHALE!
YOU MADE THE RIGHT CHOICE, SON.
SKRNCH
WHO THE #@*! IS THIS?!

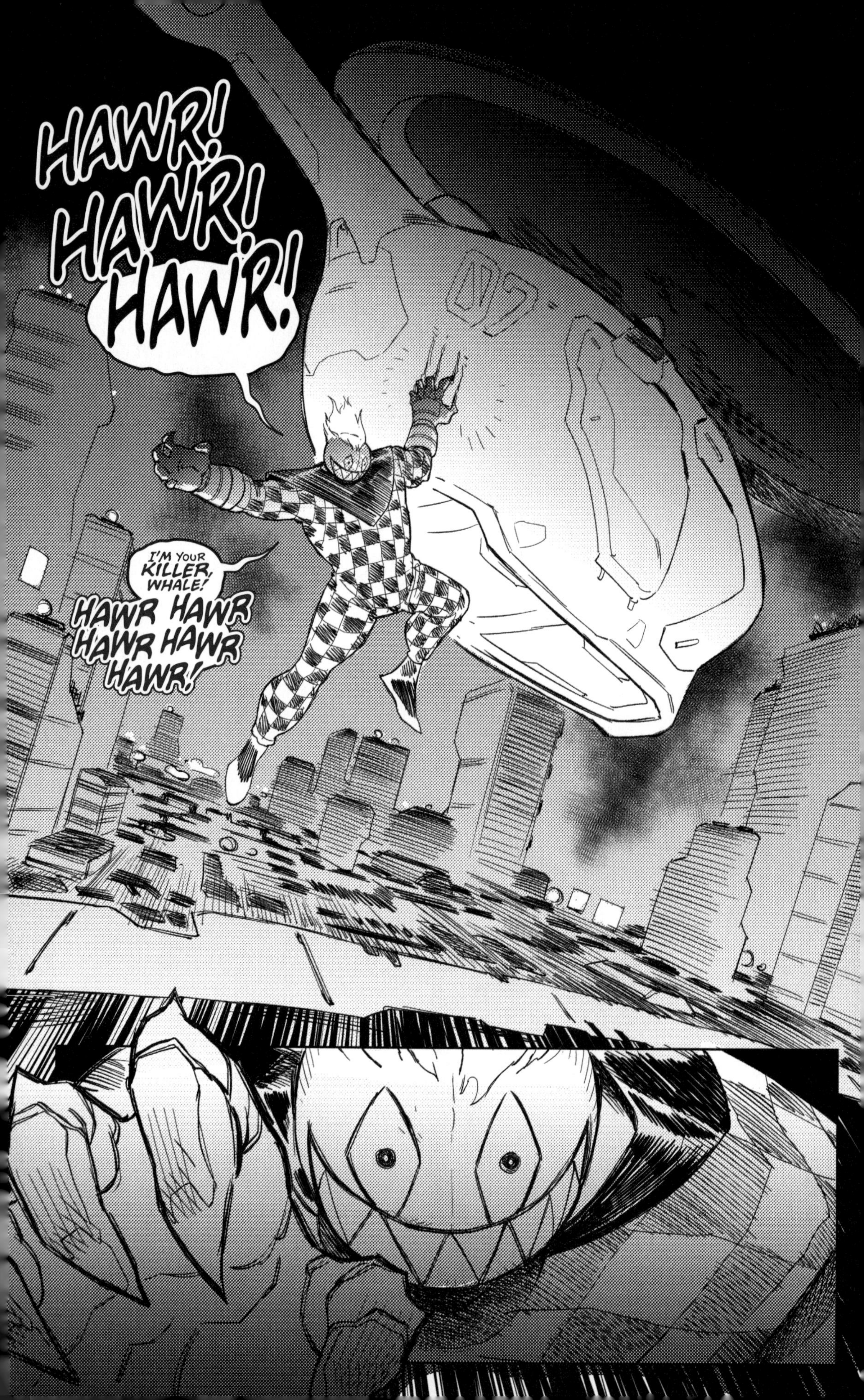
HAWR! HAWR! HAWR!
I'M YOUR KILLER, WHALE!
HAWR HAWR HAWR HAWR HAWR!

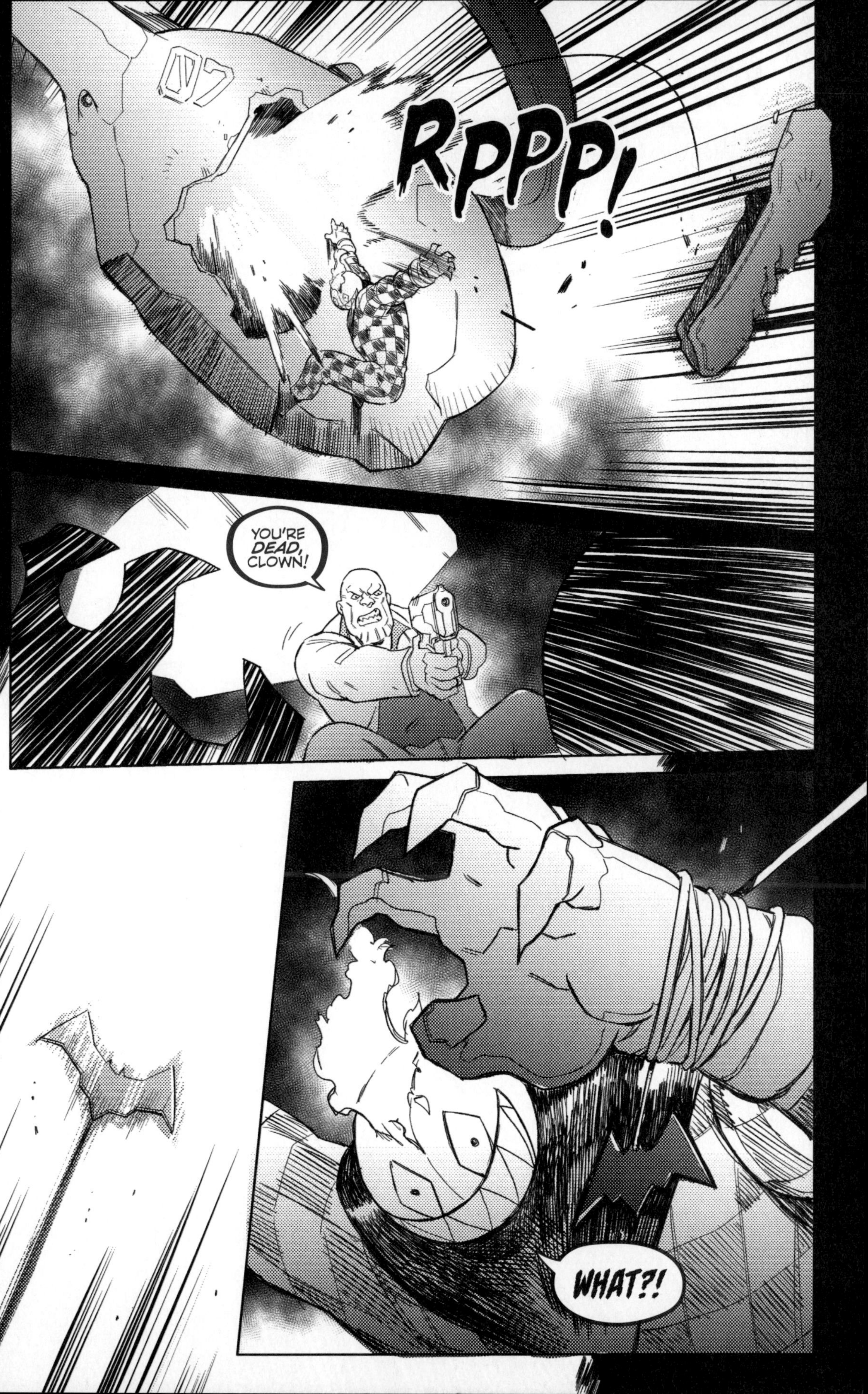
RPPP!
YOU'RE DEAD, CLOWN!
WHAT?!

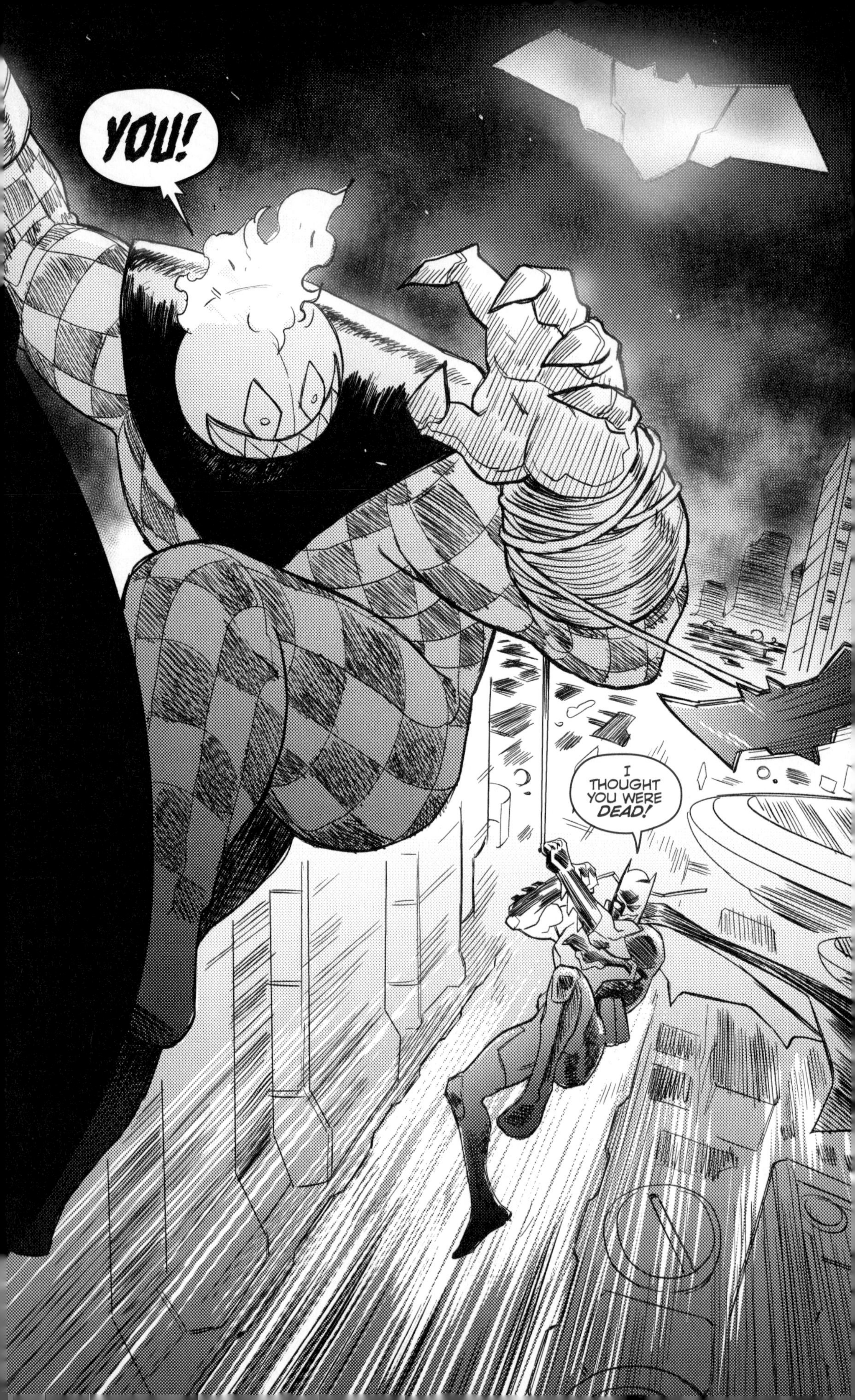
YOU!
I THOUGHT YOU WERE DEAD!

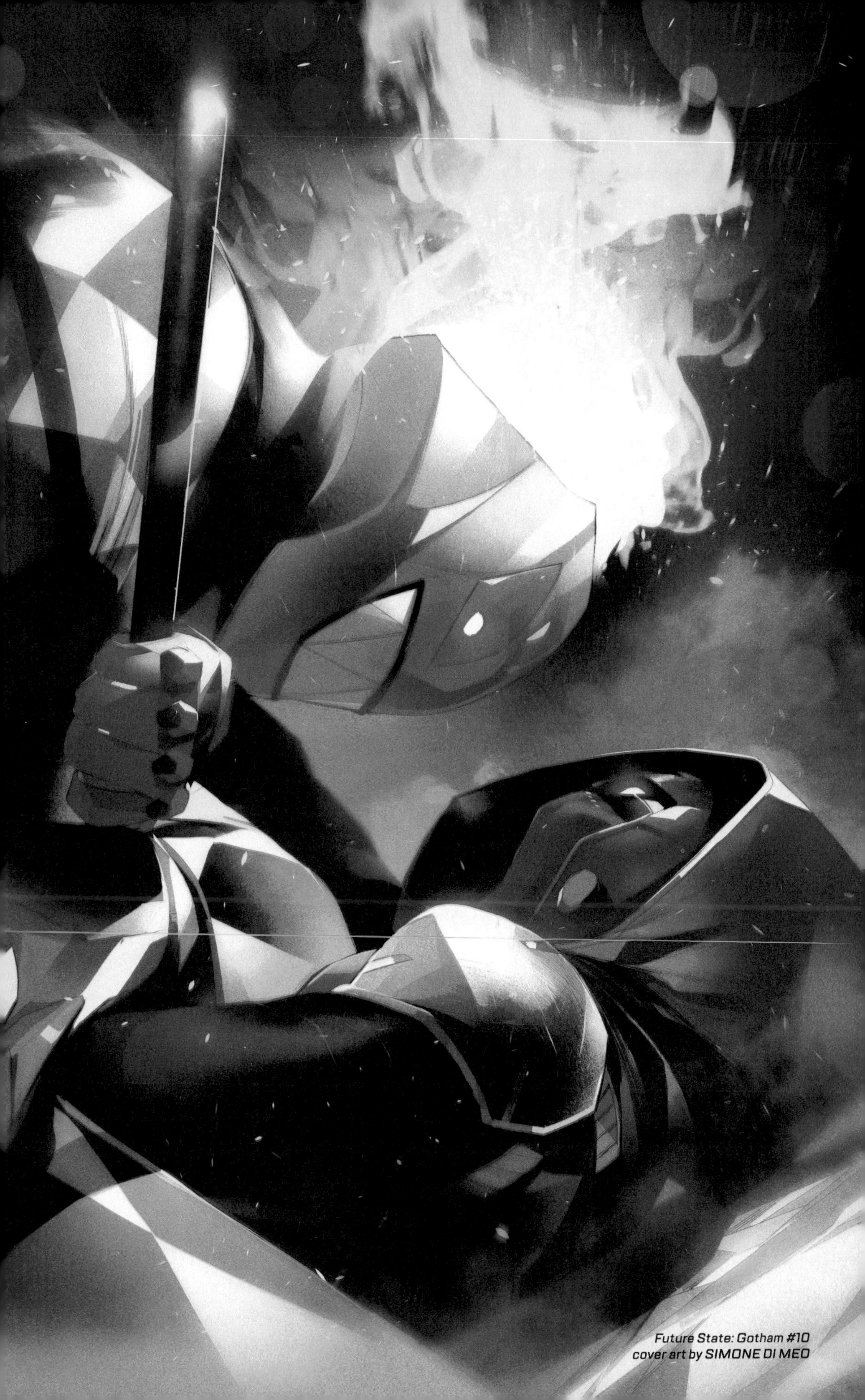

Future State: Gotham #10
cover art by SIMONE DI MEO

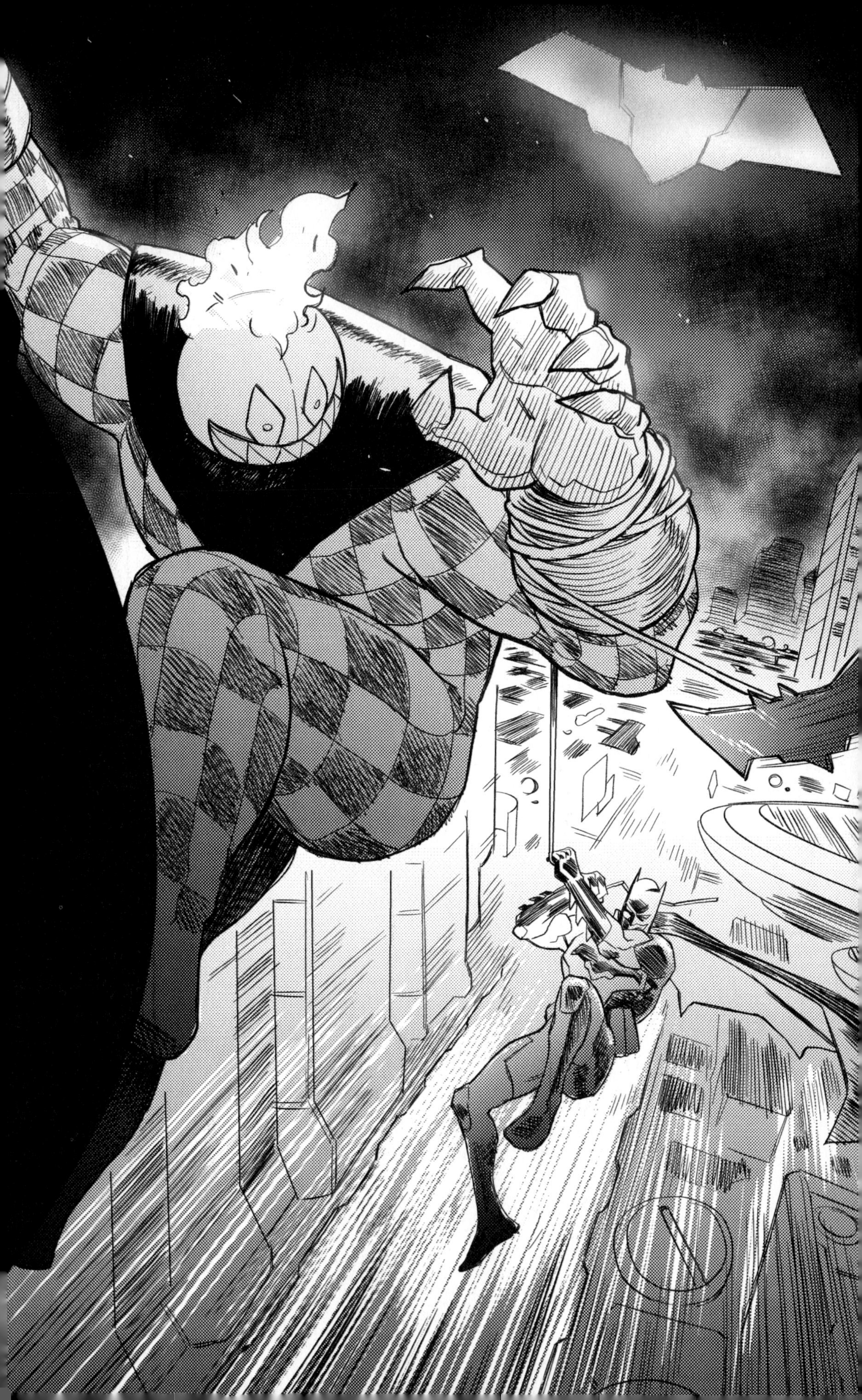

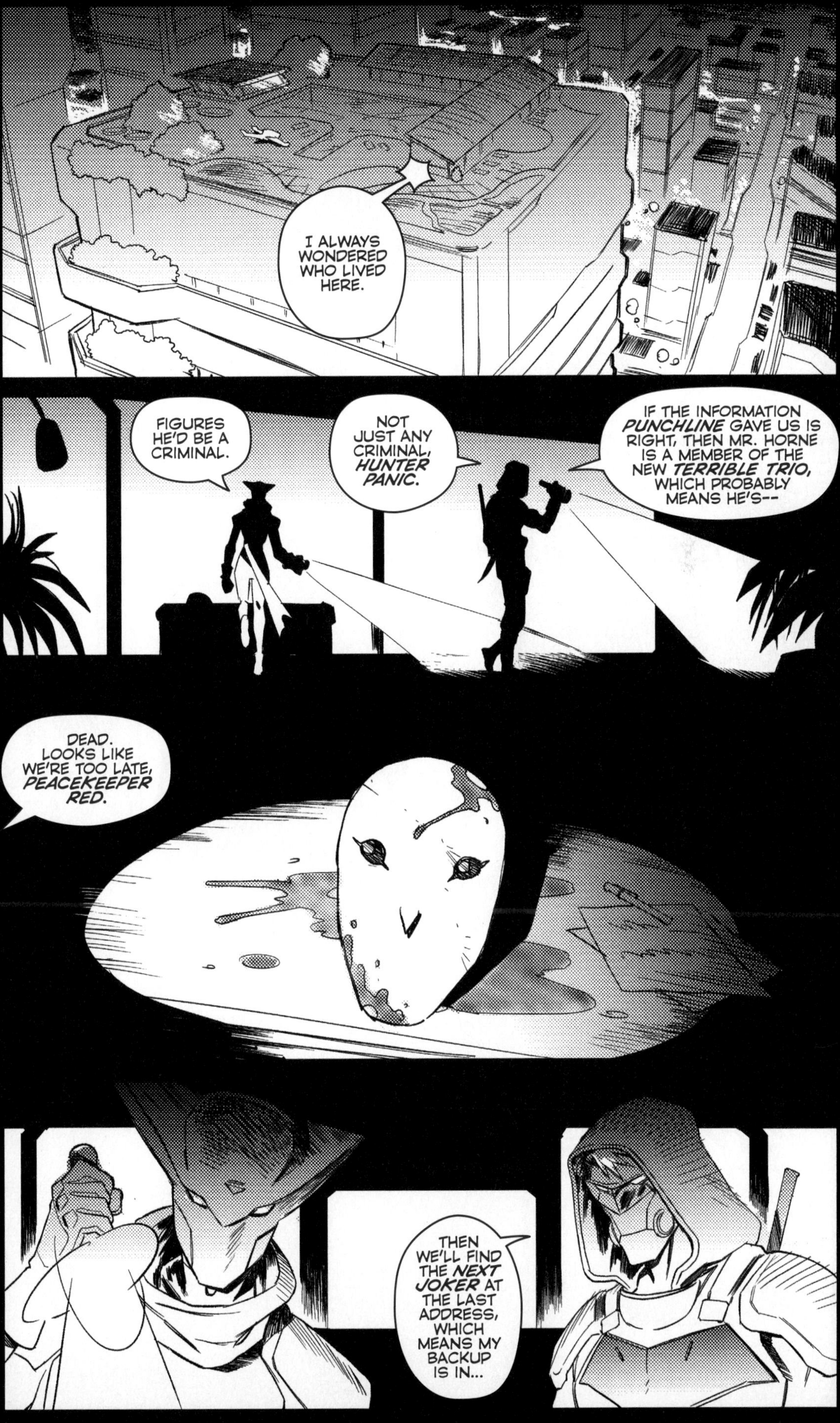
I ALWAYS WONDERED WHO LIVED HERE.
FIGURES HE'D BE A CRIMINAL.
NOT JUST ANY CRIMINAL, *HUNTER PANIC*.
IF THE INFORMATION *PUNCHLINE* GAVE US IS RIGHT, THEN MR. HORNE IS A MEMBER OF THE NEW *TERRIBLE TRIO*, WHICH PROBABLY MEANS HE'S--
DEAD. LOOKS LIKE WE'RE TOO LATE, *PEACEKEEPER RED*.
THEN WE'LL FIND THE *NEXT JOKER* AT THE LAST ADDRESS, WHICH MEANS MY BACKUP IS IN...

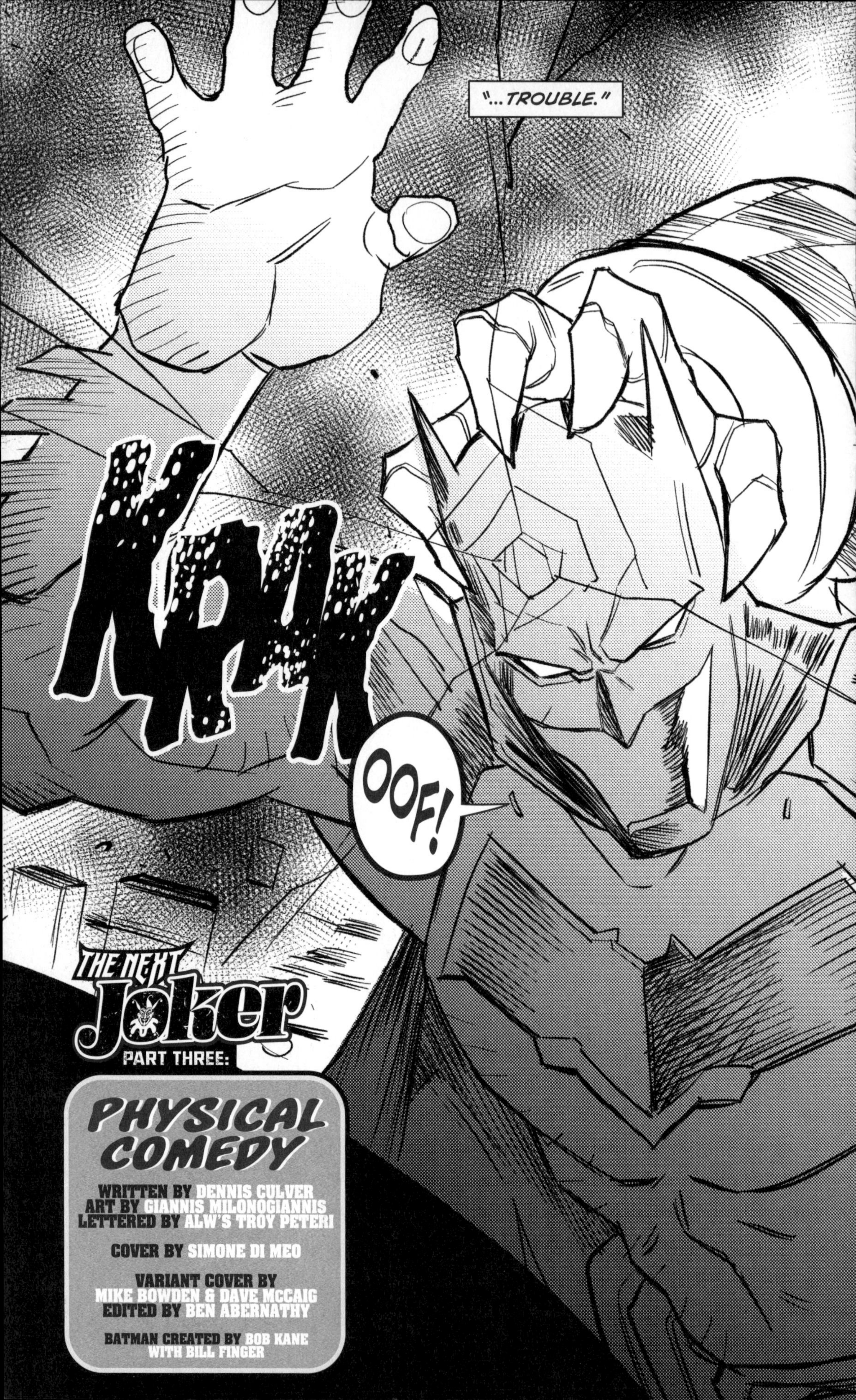
"...TROUBLE."
OOF!
THE NEXT JOKER
PART THREE:
PHYSICAL COMEDY
WRITTEN BY DENNIS CULVER
ART BY GIANNIS MILONOGIANNIS
LETTERED BY ALW'S TROY PETERI
COVER BY SIMONE DI MEO
VARIANT COVER BY
MIKE BOWDEN & DAVE McCAIG
EDITED BY BEN ABERNATHY
BATMAN CREATED BY BOB KANE
WITH BILL FINGER

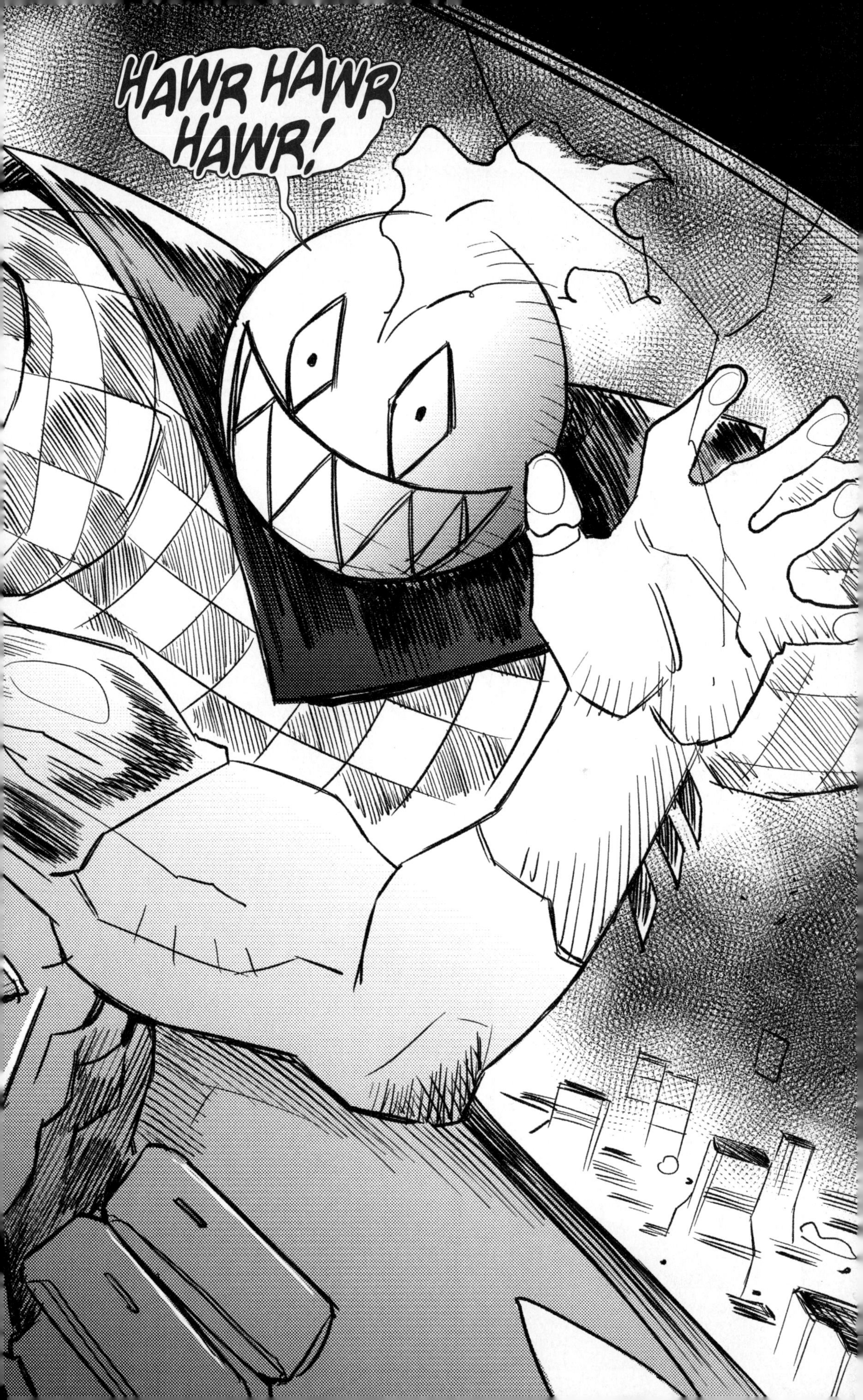
HAWR HAWR HAWR!

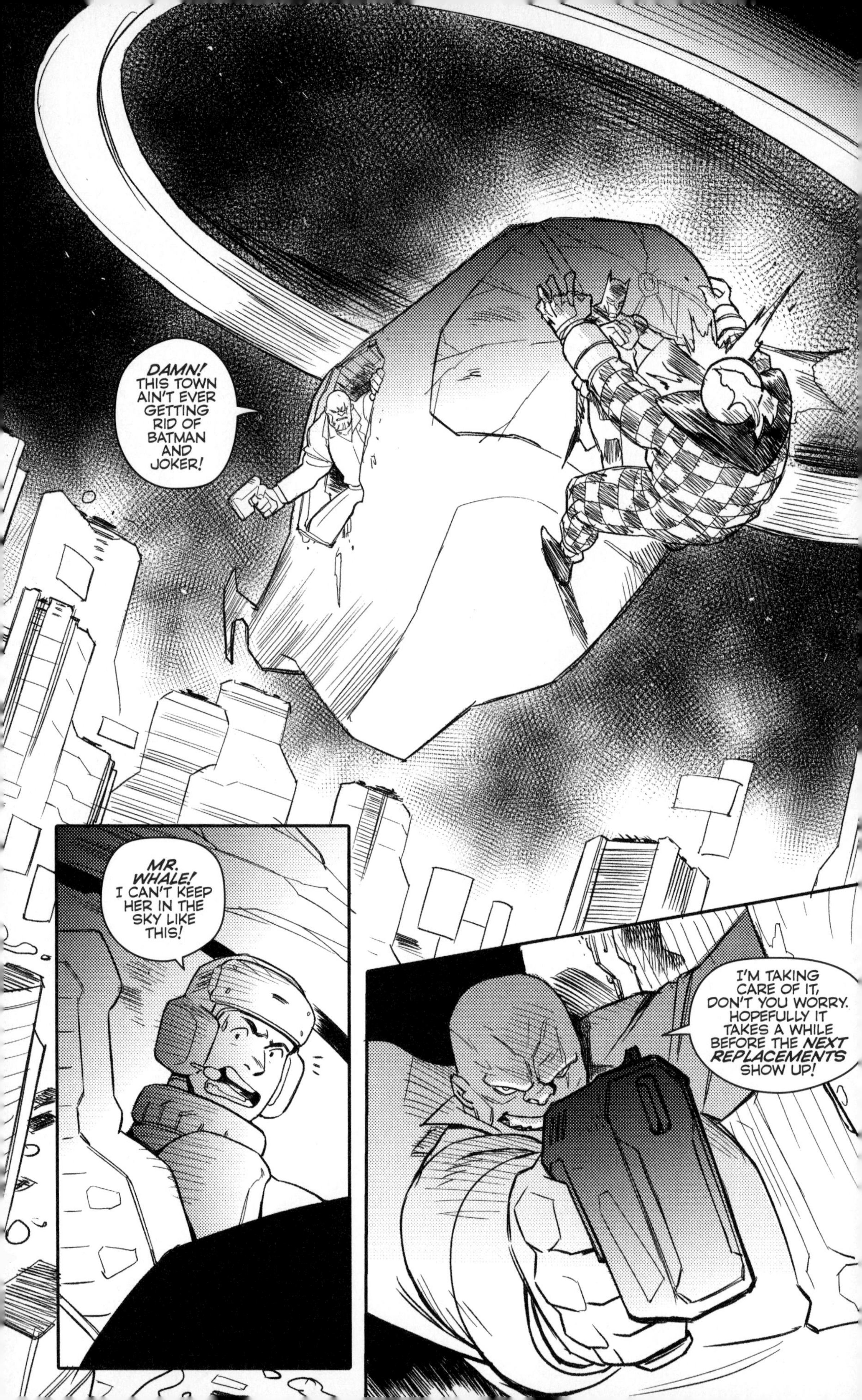
DAMN! THIS TOWN AIN'T EVER GETTING RID OF BATMAN AND JOKER!
MR. WHALE! I CAN'T KEEP HER IN THE SKY LIKE THIS!
I'M TAKING CARE OF IT, DON'T YOU WORRY. HOPEFULLY IT TAKES A WHILE BEFORE THE NEXT REPLACEMENTS SHOW UP!

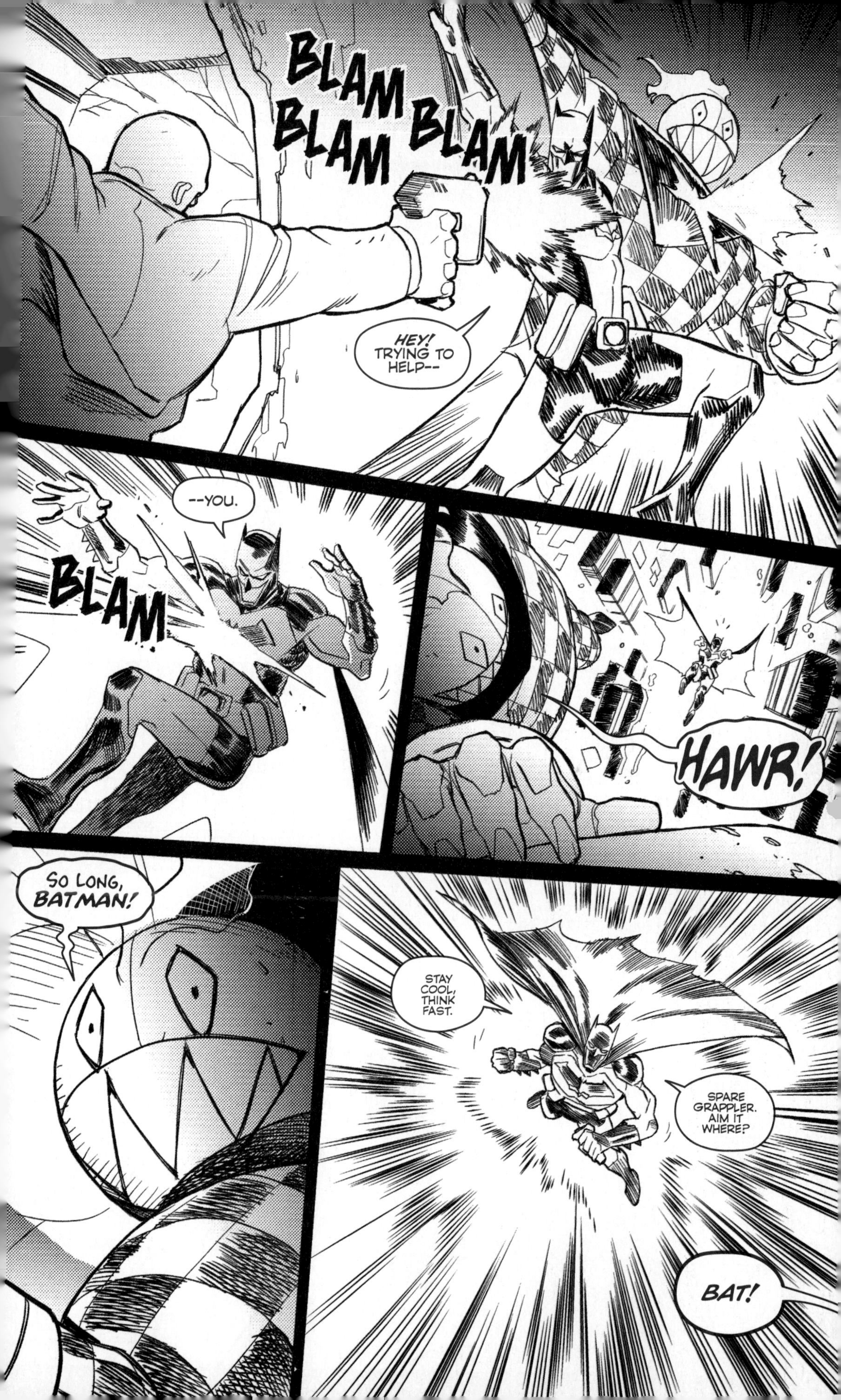
BLAM BLAM BLAM BLAM
HEY! TRYING TO HELP--
--YOU.
BLAM
HAWR!
SO LONG, BATMAN!
STAY COOL, THINK FAST.
SPARE GRAPPLER. AIM IT WHERE?
BAT!

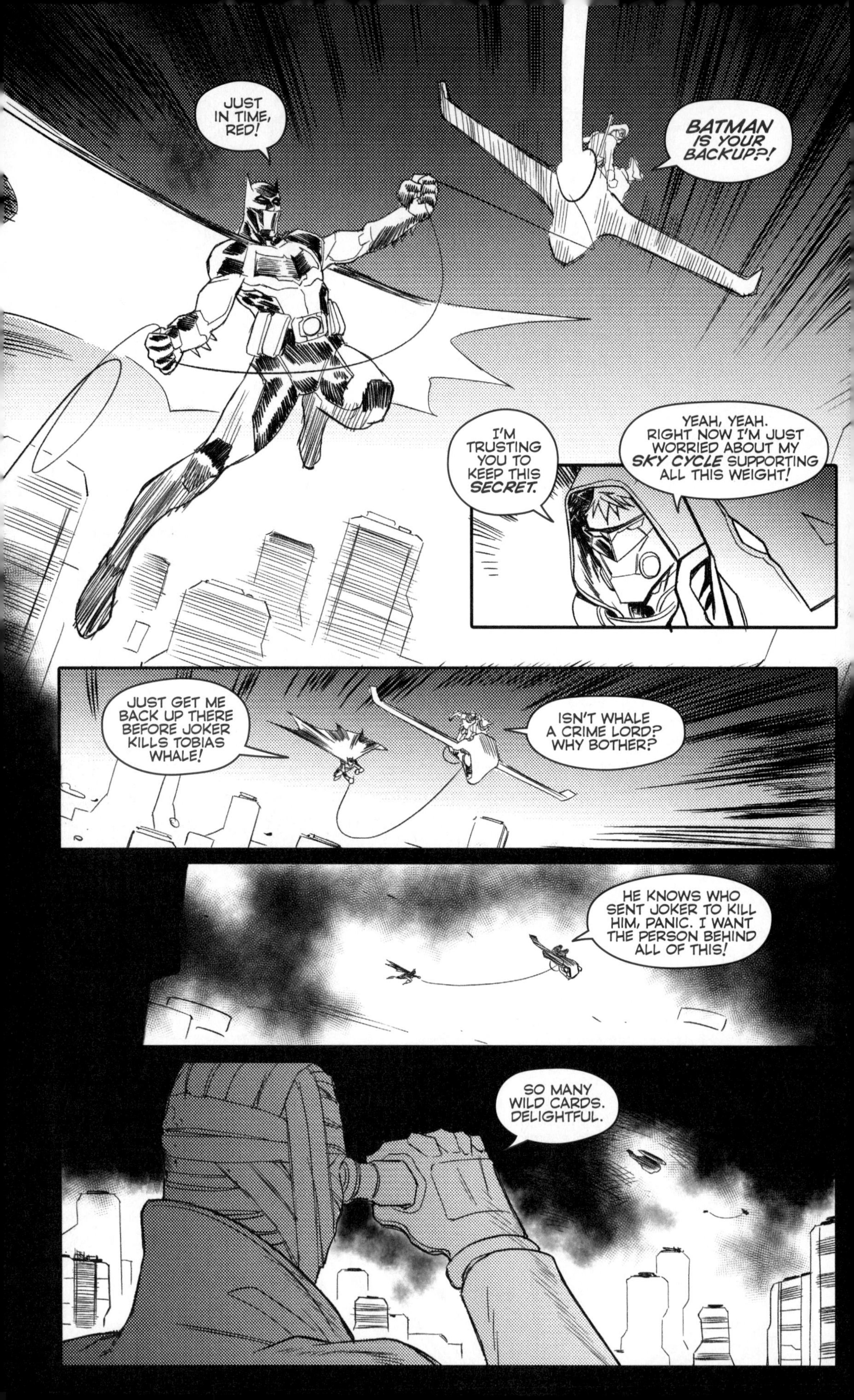
JUST IN TIME, RED!
BATMAN IS YOUR BACKUP?!
I'M TRUSTING YOU TO KEEP THIS SECRET.
YEAH, YEAH. RIGHT NOW I'M JUST WORRIED ABOUT MY SKY CYCLE SUPPORTING ALL THIS WEIGHT!
JUST GET ME BACK UP THERE BEFORE JOKER KILLS TOBIAS WHALE!
ISN'T WHALE A CRIME LORD? WHY BOTHER?
HE KNOWS WHO SENT JOKER TO KILL HIM, PANIC. I WANT THE PERSON BEHIND ALL OF THIS!
SO MANY WILD CARDS. DELIGHTFUL.

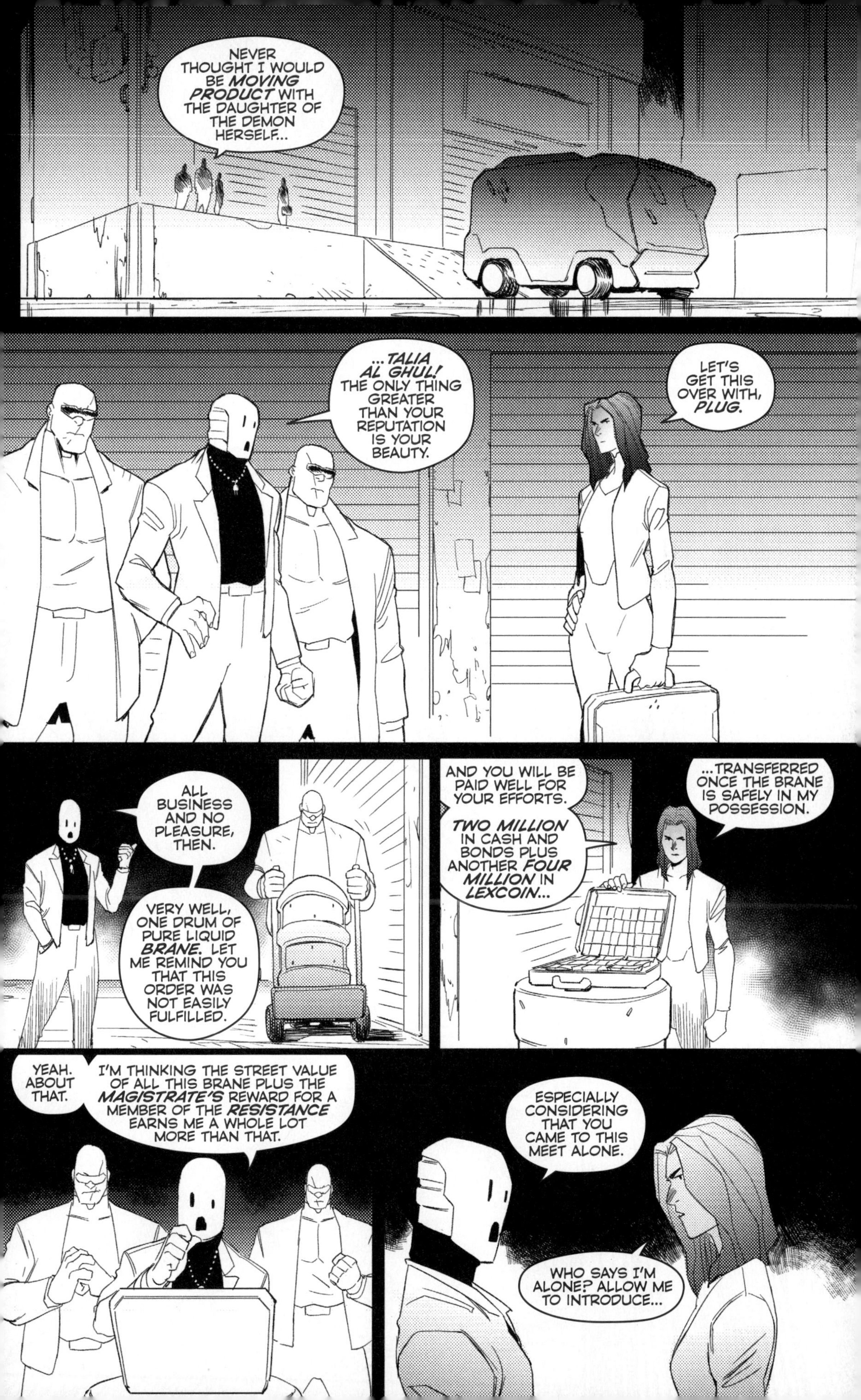
NEVER THOUGHT I WOULD BE MOVING PRODUCT WITH THE DAUGHTER OF THE DEMON HERSELF...
...TALIA AL GHUL! THE ONLY THING GREATER THAN YOUR REPUTATION IS YOUR BEAUTY.
LET'S GET THIS OVER WITH, PLUG.
ALL BUSINESS AND NO PLEASURE, THEN.
VERY WELL, ONE DRUM OF PURE LIQUID BRANE. LET ME REMIND YOU THAT THIS ORDER WAS NOT EASILY FULFILLED.
AND YOU WILL BE PAID WELL FOR YOUR EFFORTS.
TWO MILLION IN CASH AND BONDS PLUS ANOTHER FOUR MILLION IN LEXCOIN...
...TRANSFERRED ONCE THE BRANE IS SAFELY IN MY POSSESSION.
YEAH. ABOUT THAT.
I'M THINKING THE STREET VALUE OF ALL THIS BRANE PLUS THE MAGISTRATE'S REWARD FOR A MEMBER OF THE RESISTANCE EARNS ME A WHOLE LOT MORE THAN THAT.
ESPECIALLY CONSIDERING THAT YOU CAME TO THIS MEET ALONE.
WHO SAYS I'M ALONE? ALLOW ME TO INTRODUCE...

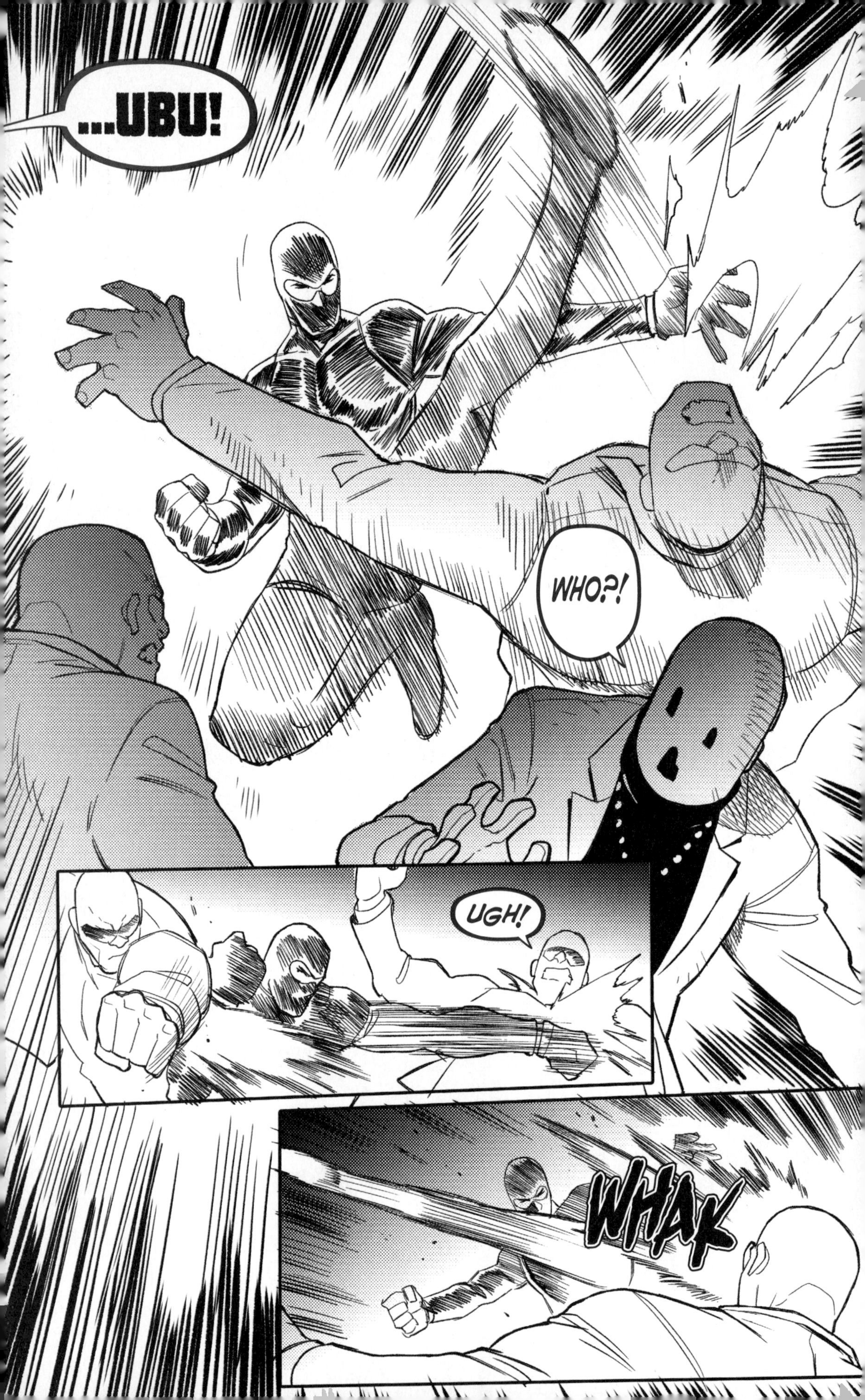
...UBU!
WHO?!
UGH!
WHAK

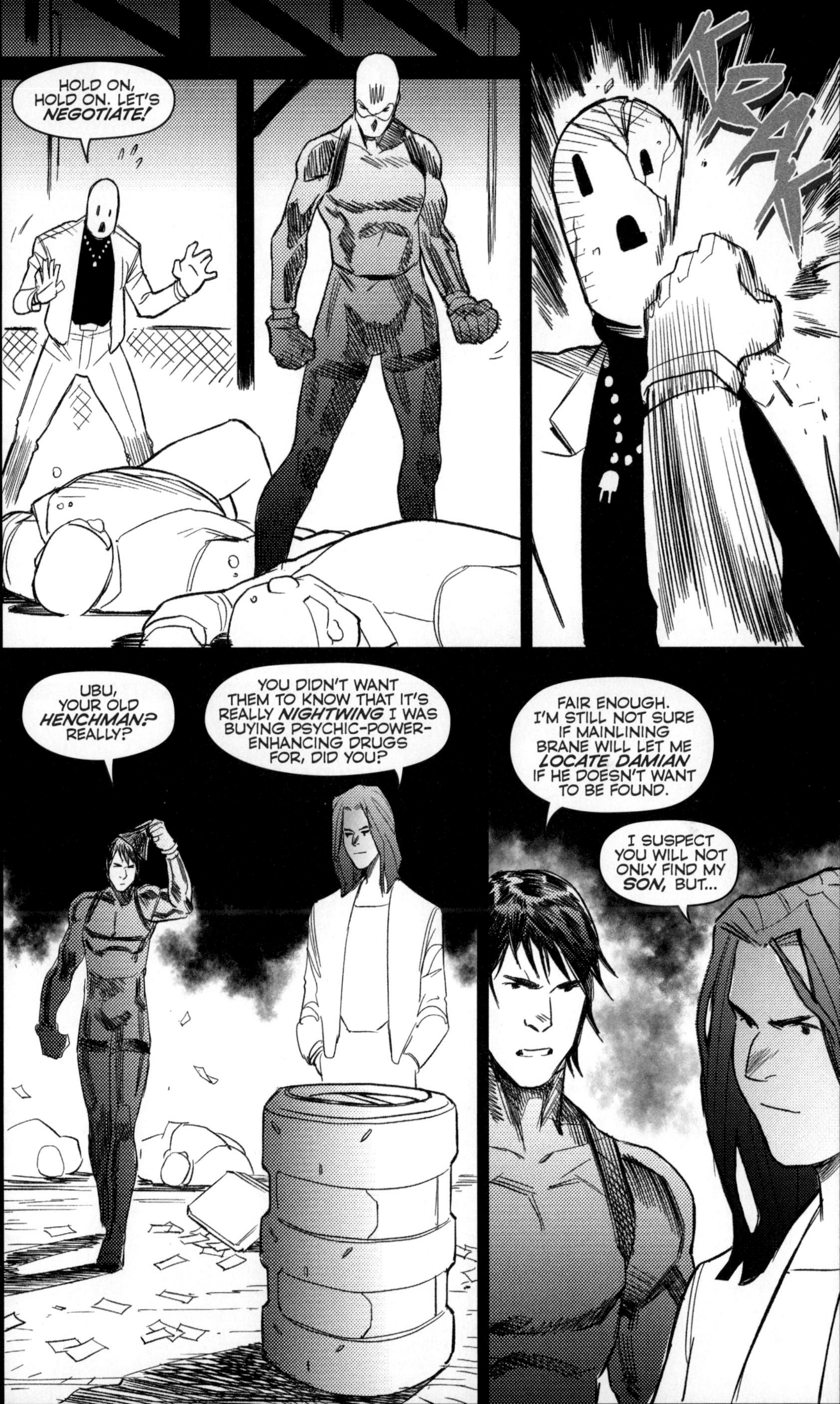
HOLD ON, HOLD ON. LET'S NEGOTIATE!
KRAK
UBU, YOUR OLD HENCHMAN? REALLY?
YOU DIDN'T WANT THEM TO KNOW THAT IT'S REALLY NIGHTWING I WAS BUYING PSYCHIC-POWER-ENHANCING DRUGS FOR, DID YOU?
FAIR ENOUGH. I'M STILL NOT SURE IF MAINLINING BRANE WILL LET ME LOCATE DAMIAN IF HE DOESN'T WANT TO BE FOUND.
I SUSPECT YOU WILL NOT ONLY FIND MY SON, BUT...

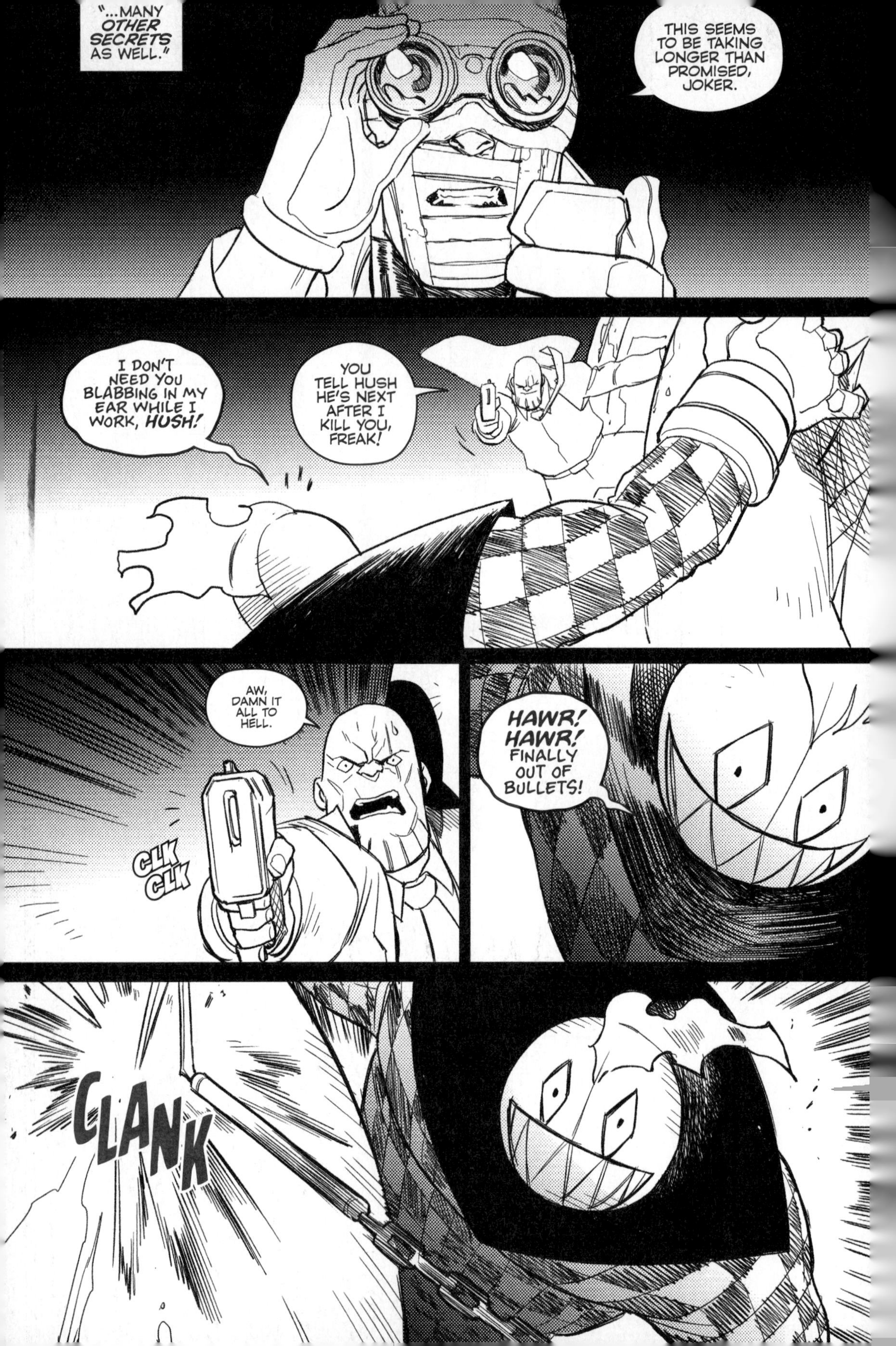
"...MANY *OTHER SECRETS* AS WELL."
THIS SEEMS TO BE TAKING LONGER THAN PROMISED, JOKER.
I DON'T NEED YOU BLABBING IN MY EAR WHILE I WORK, *HUSH!*
YOU TELL HUSH HE'S NEXT AFTER I KILL YOU, FREAK!
AW, DAMN IT ALL TO HELL.
CLK CLK
HAWR! HAWR! FINALLY OUT OF BULLETS!
CLANK

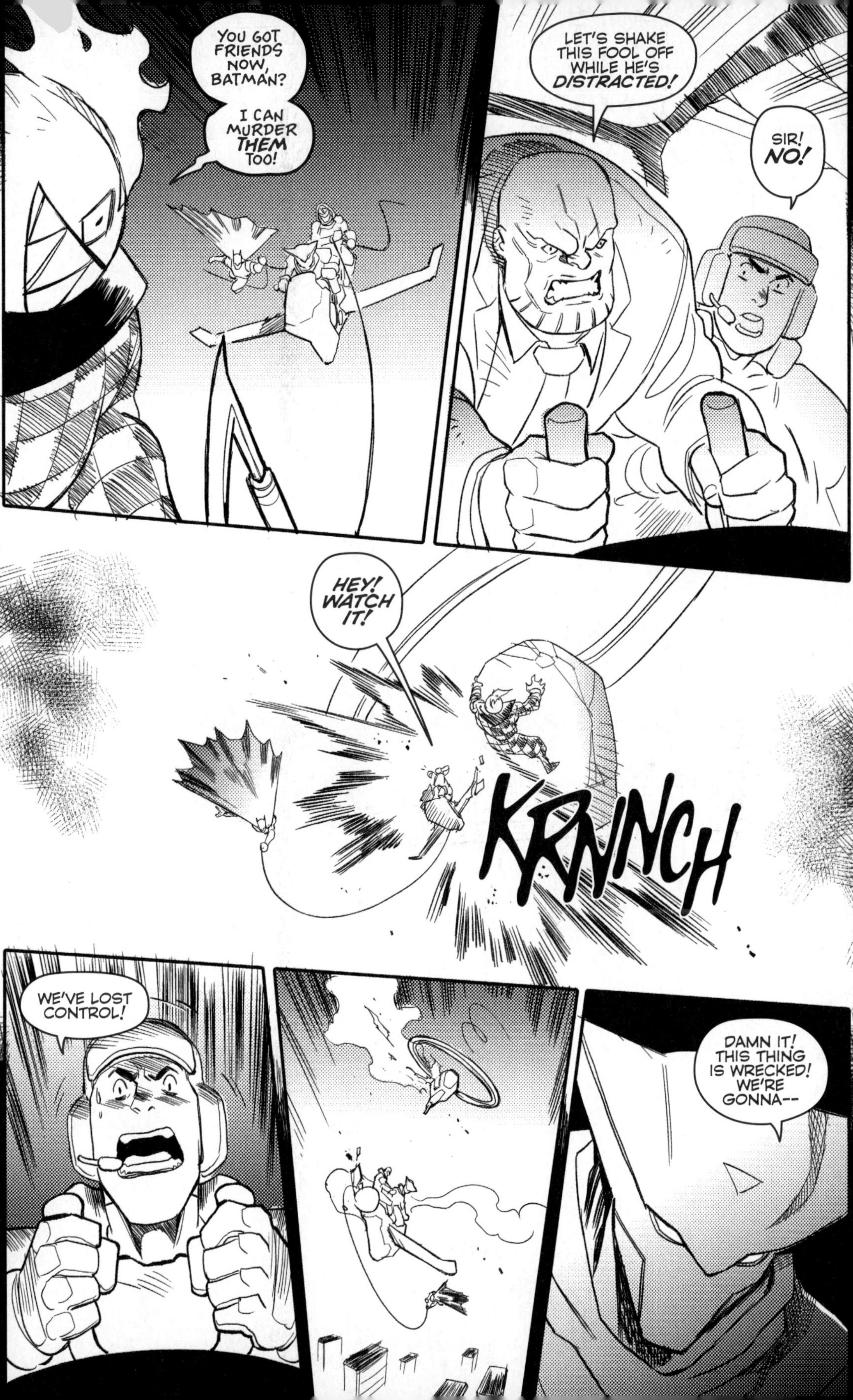
YOU GOT FRIENDS NOW, BATMAN?
I CAN MURDER THEM TOO!
LET'S SHAKE THIS FOOL OFF WHILE HE'S DISTRACTED!
SIR! NO!
HEY! WATCH IT!
KRNNCH
WE'VE LOST CONTROL!
DAMN IT! THIS THING IS WRECKED! WE'RE GONNA--

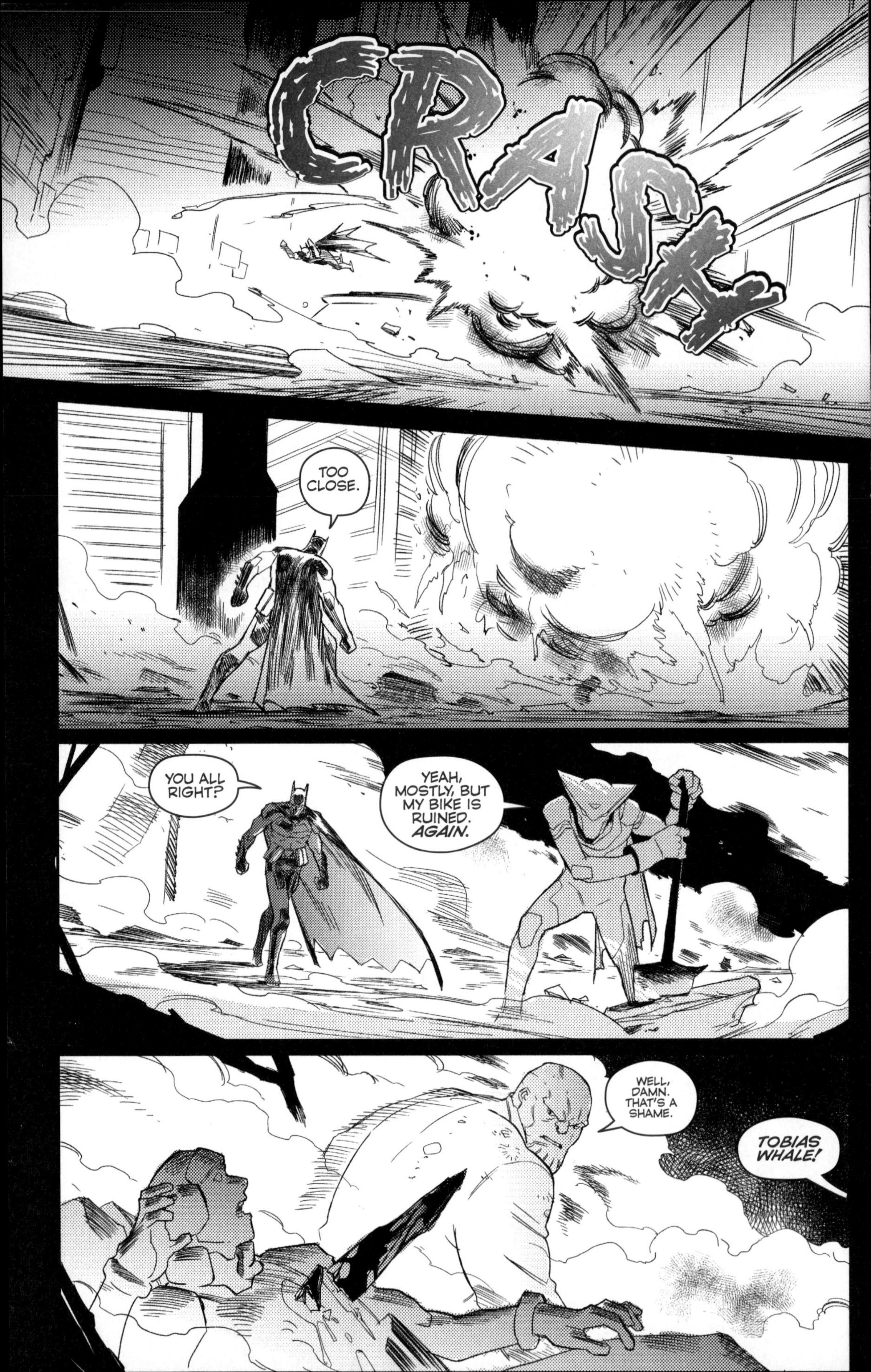
CRASH
TOO CLOSE.
YOU ALL RIGHT?
YEAH, MOSTLY, BUT MY BIKE IS RUINED. *AGAIN.*
WELL, DAMN. THAT'S A SHAME.
TOBIAS WHALE!

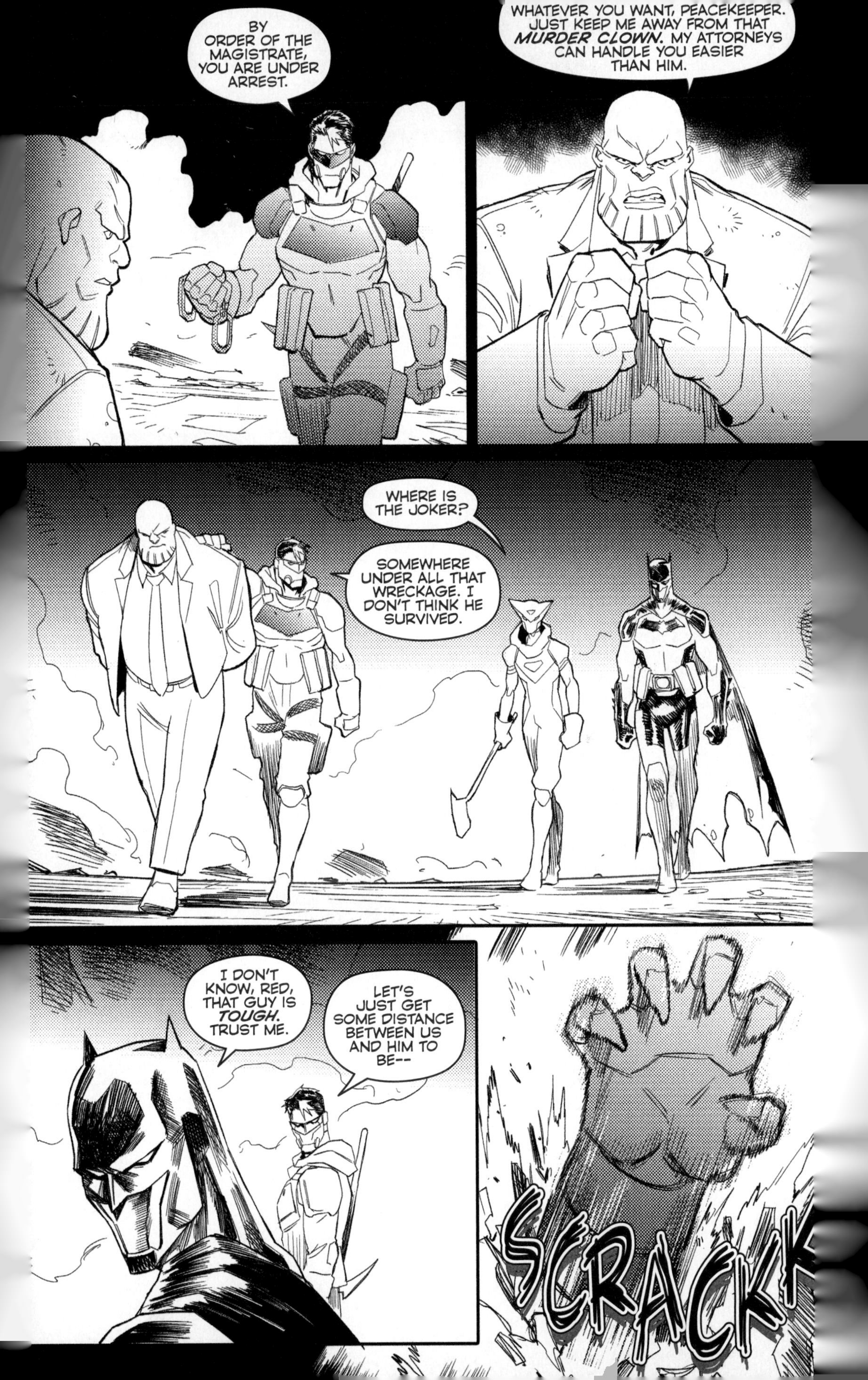
BY ORDER OF THE MAGISTRATE, YOU ARE UNDER ARREST.
WHATEVER YOU WANT, PEACEKEEPER. JUST KEEP ME AWAY FROM THAT *MURDER CLOWN.* MY ATTORNEYS CAN HANDLE YOU EASIER THAN HIM.
WHERE IS THE JOKER?
SOMEWHERE UNDER ALL THAT WRECKAGE. I DON'T THINK HE SURVIVED.
I DON'T KNOW, RED, THAT GUY IS *TOUGH*. TRUST ME.
LET'S JUST GET SOME DISTANCE BETWEEN US AND HIM TO BE--
SCRACKK

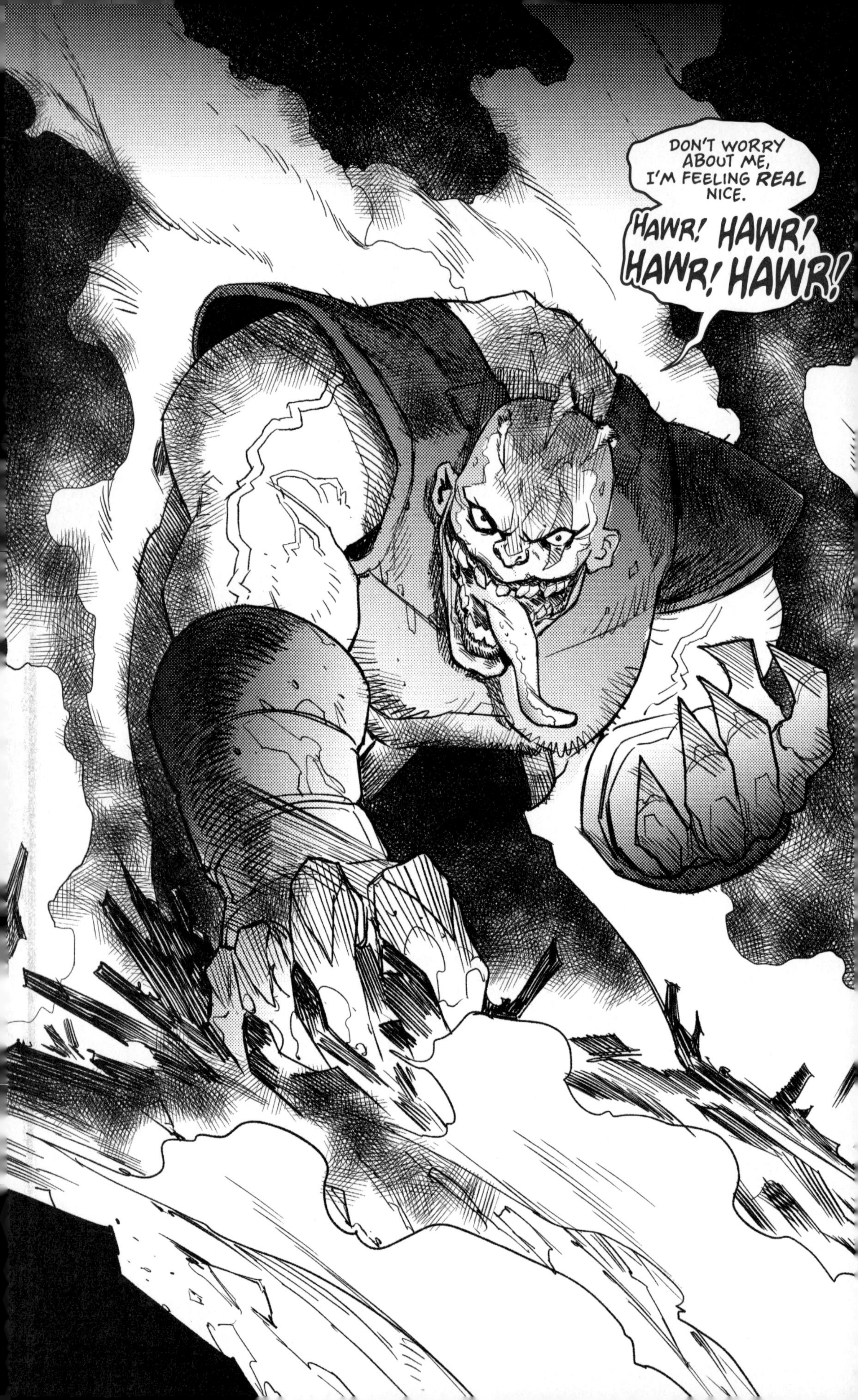
DON'T WORRY ABOUT ME, I'M FEELING REAL NICE.
HAWR! HAWR! HAWR! HAWR!

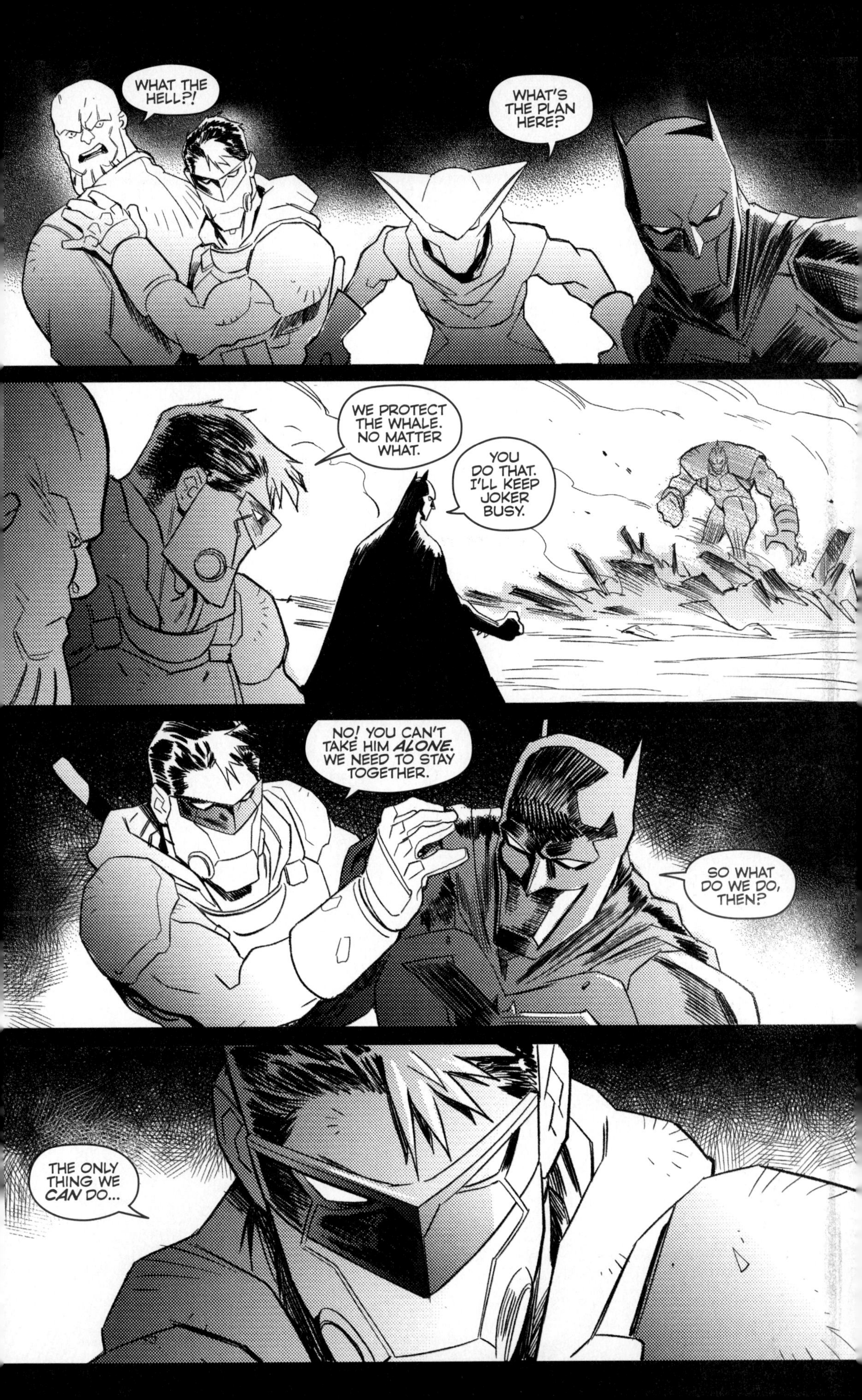
WHAT THE HELL?!
WHAT'S THE PLAN HERE?
WE PROTECT THE WHALE. NO MATTER WHAT.
YOU DO THAT. I'LL KEEP JOKER BUSY.
NO! YOU CAN'T TAKE HIM ALONE. WE NEED TO STAY TOGETHER.
SO WHAT DO WE DO, THEN?
THE ONLY THING WE CAN DO...

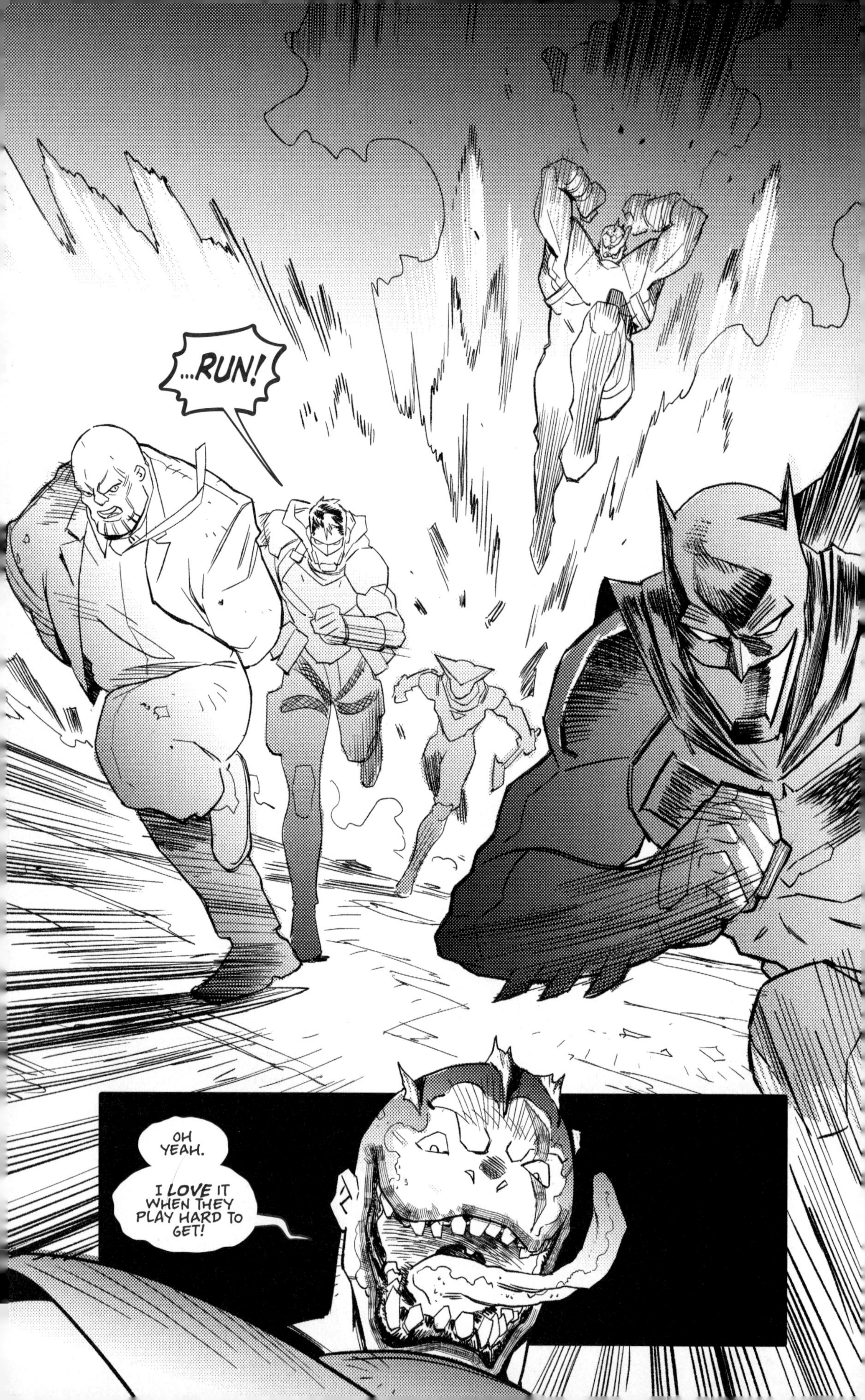
...RUN!
OH YEAH.
I LOVE IT WHEN THEY PLAY HARD TO GET!

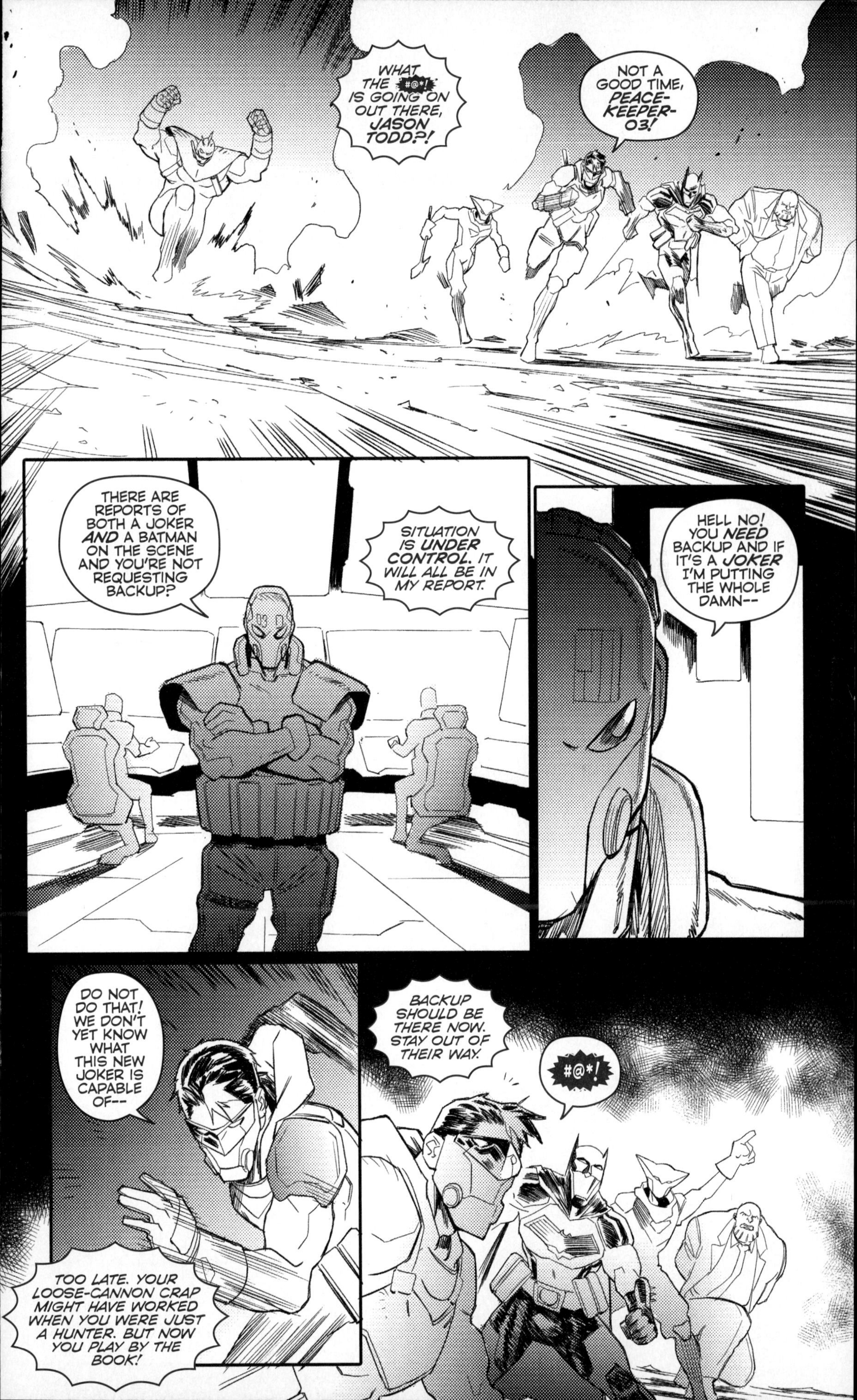
WHAT THE #@*! IS GOING ON OUT THERE, JASON TODD?!
NOT A GOOD TIME, PEACE-KEEPER-03!
THERE ARE REPORTS OF BOTH A JOKER AND A BATMAN ON THE SCENE AND YOU'RE NOT REQUESTING BACKUP?
SITUATION IS UNDER CONTROL. IT WILL ALL BE IN MY REPORT.
HELL NO! YOU NEED BACKUP AND IF IT'S A JOKER I'M PUTTING THE WHOLE DAMN--
DO NOT DO THAT! WE DON'T YET KNOW WHAT THIS NEW JOKER IS CAPABLE OF--
TOO LATE. YOUR LOOSE-CANNON CRAP MIGHT HAVE WORKED WHEN YOU WERE JUST A HUNTER. BUT NOW YOU PLAY BY THE BOOK!
BACKUP SHOULD BE THERE NOW. STAY OUT OF THEIR WAY.
#@*!

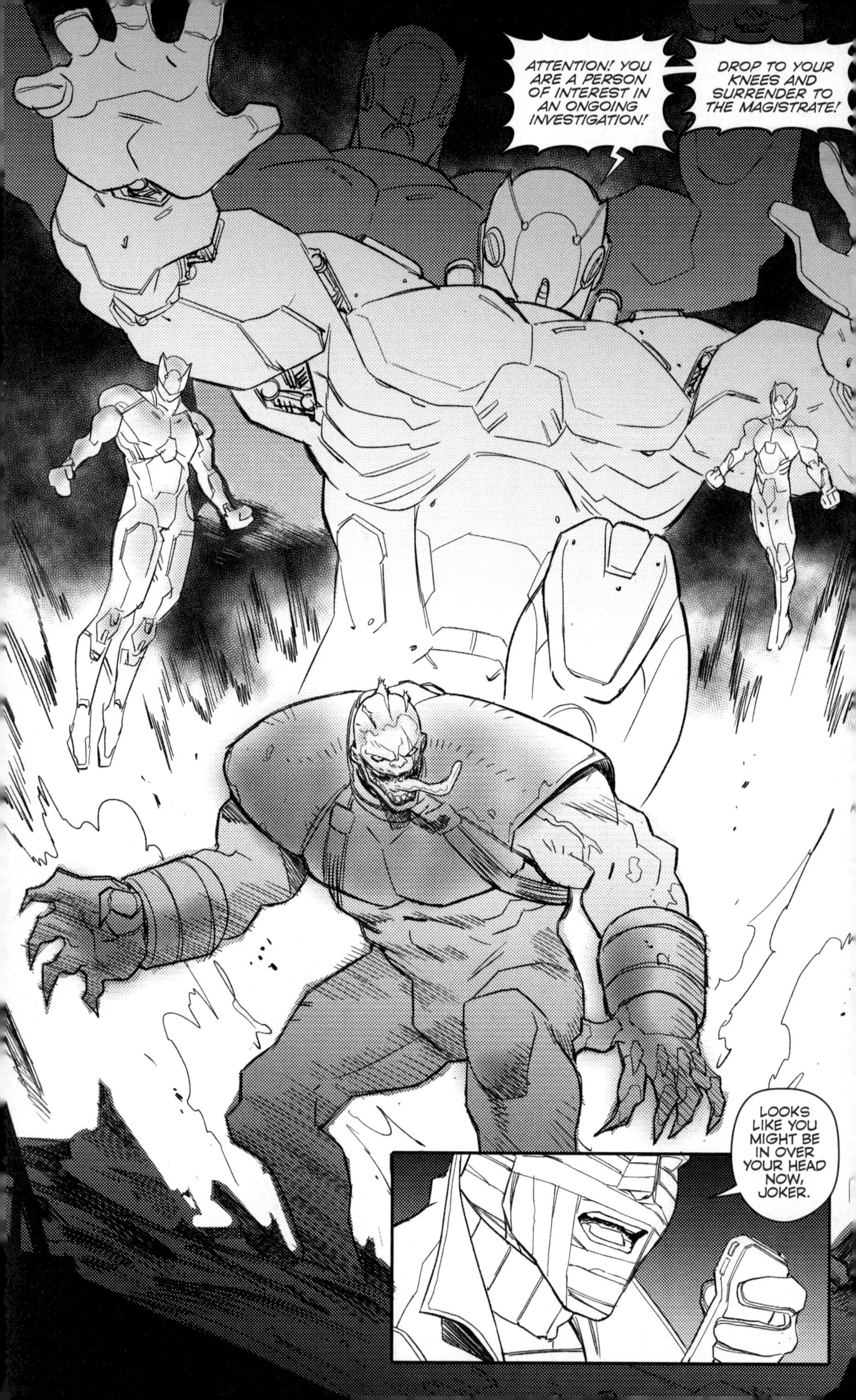
ATTENTION! YOU ARE A PERSON OF INTEREST IN AN ONGOING INVESTIGATION!
DROP TO YOUR KNEES AND SURRENDER TO THE MAGISTRATE!
LOOKS LIKE YOU MIGHT BE IN OVER YOUR HEAD NOW, JOKER.

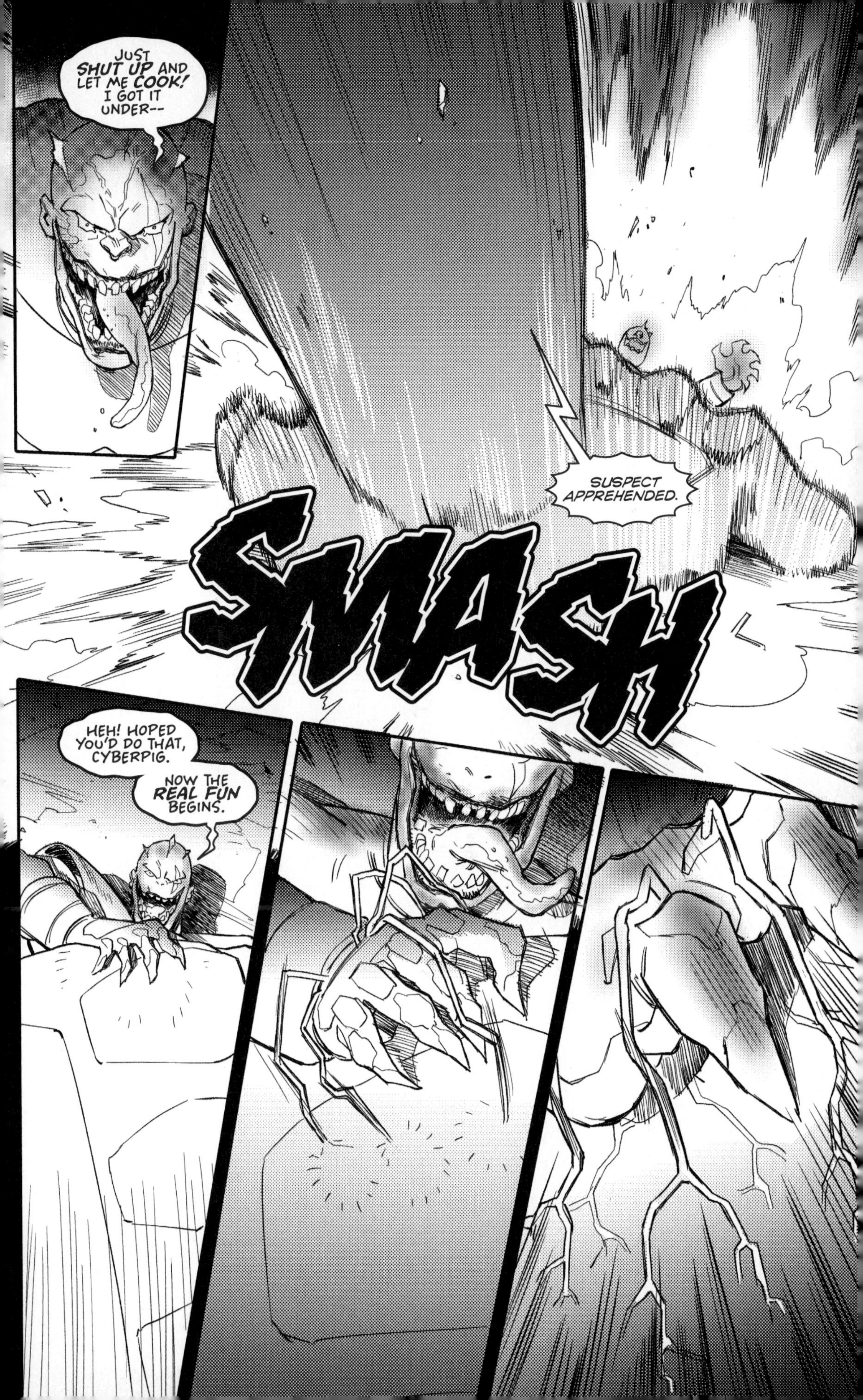
JUST SHUT UP AND LET ME COOK! I GOT IT UNDER--
SUSPECT APPREHENDED.
SMASH
HEH! HOPED YOU'D DO THAT, CYBERPIG.
NOW THE REAL FUN BEGINS.

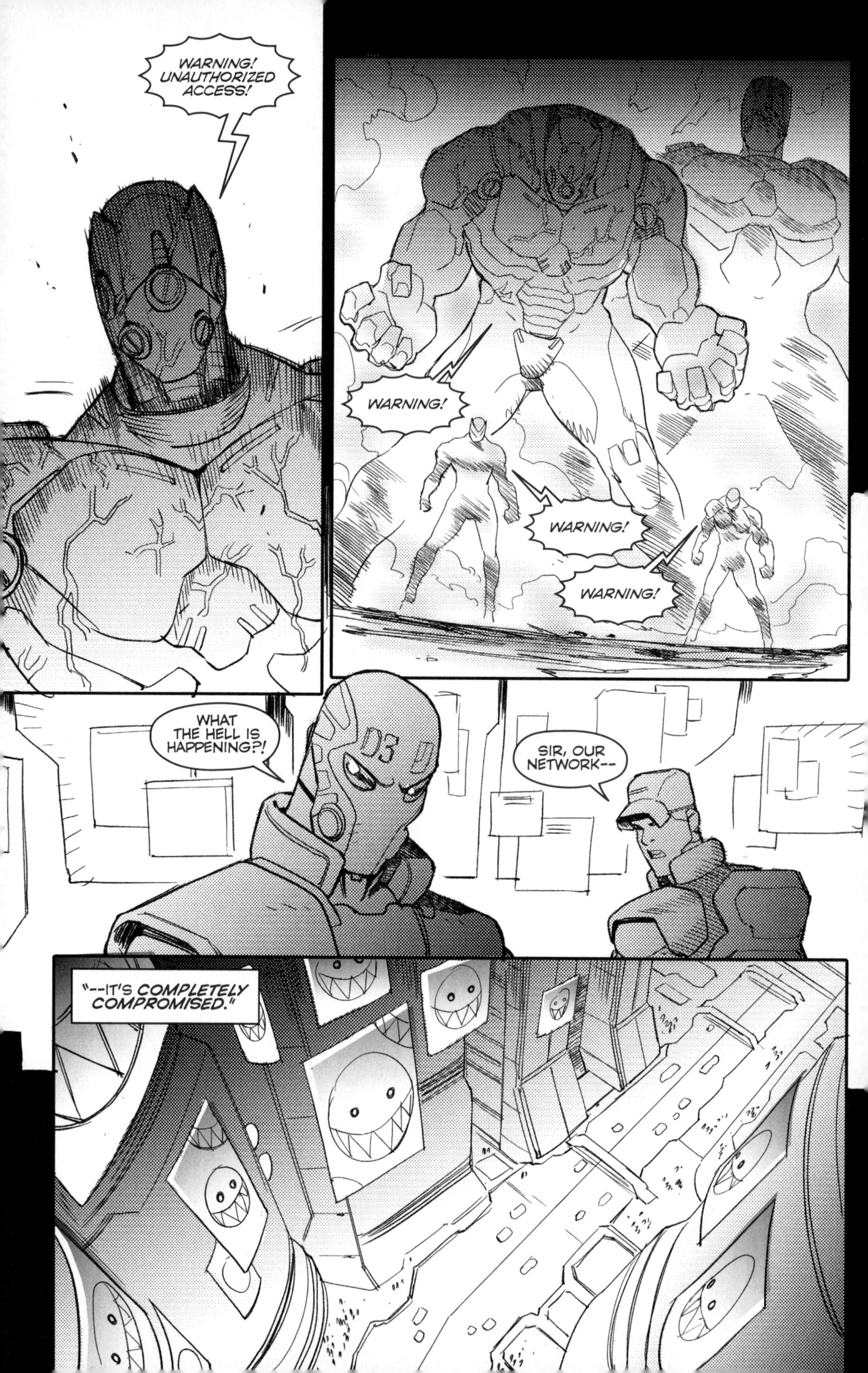
WARNING! UNAUTHORIZED ACCESS!
WARNING!
WARNING!
WARNING!
WHAT THE HELL IS HAPPENING?!
SIR, OUR NETWORK--
"--IT'S COMPLETELY COMPROMISED."

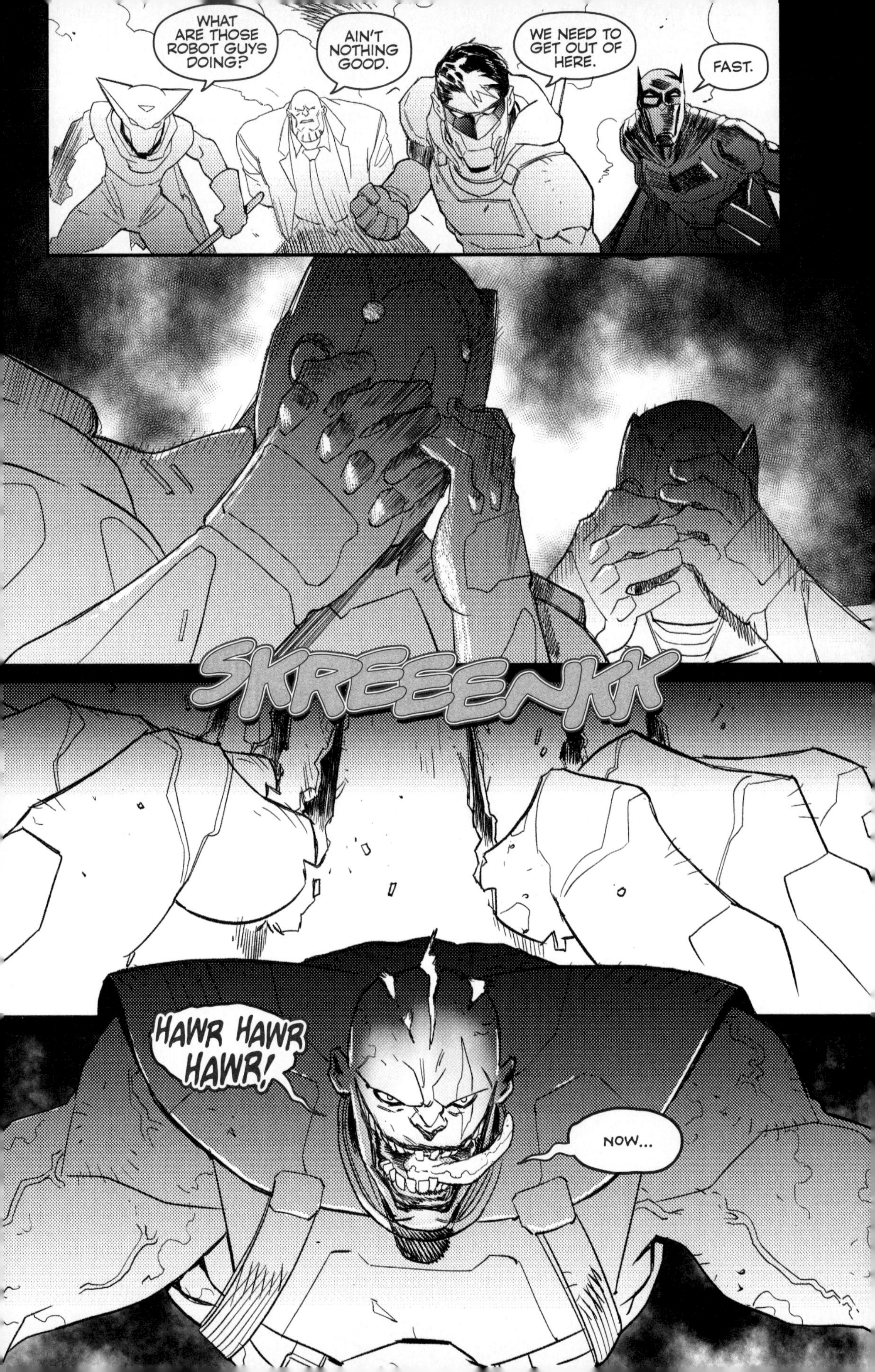
WHAT ARE THOSE ROBOT GUYS DOING?
AIN'T NOTHING GOOD.
WE NEED TO GET OUT OF HERE.
FAST.
SKREEENKK
HAWR HAWR HAWR!
NOW...

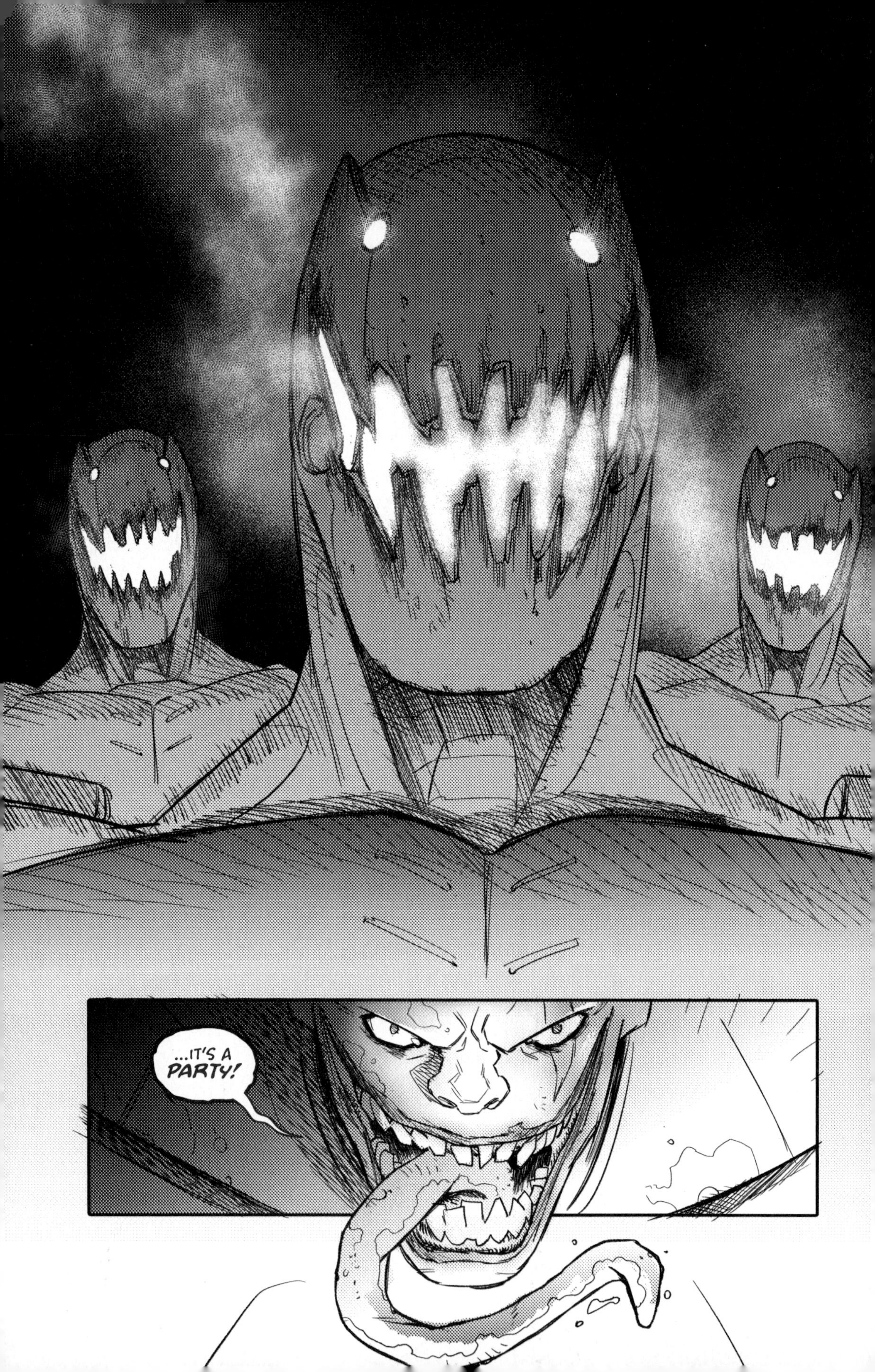
...IT'S A PARTY!

Future State: Gotham #11
cover art by SIMONE DI MEO

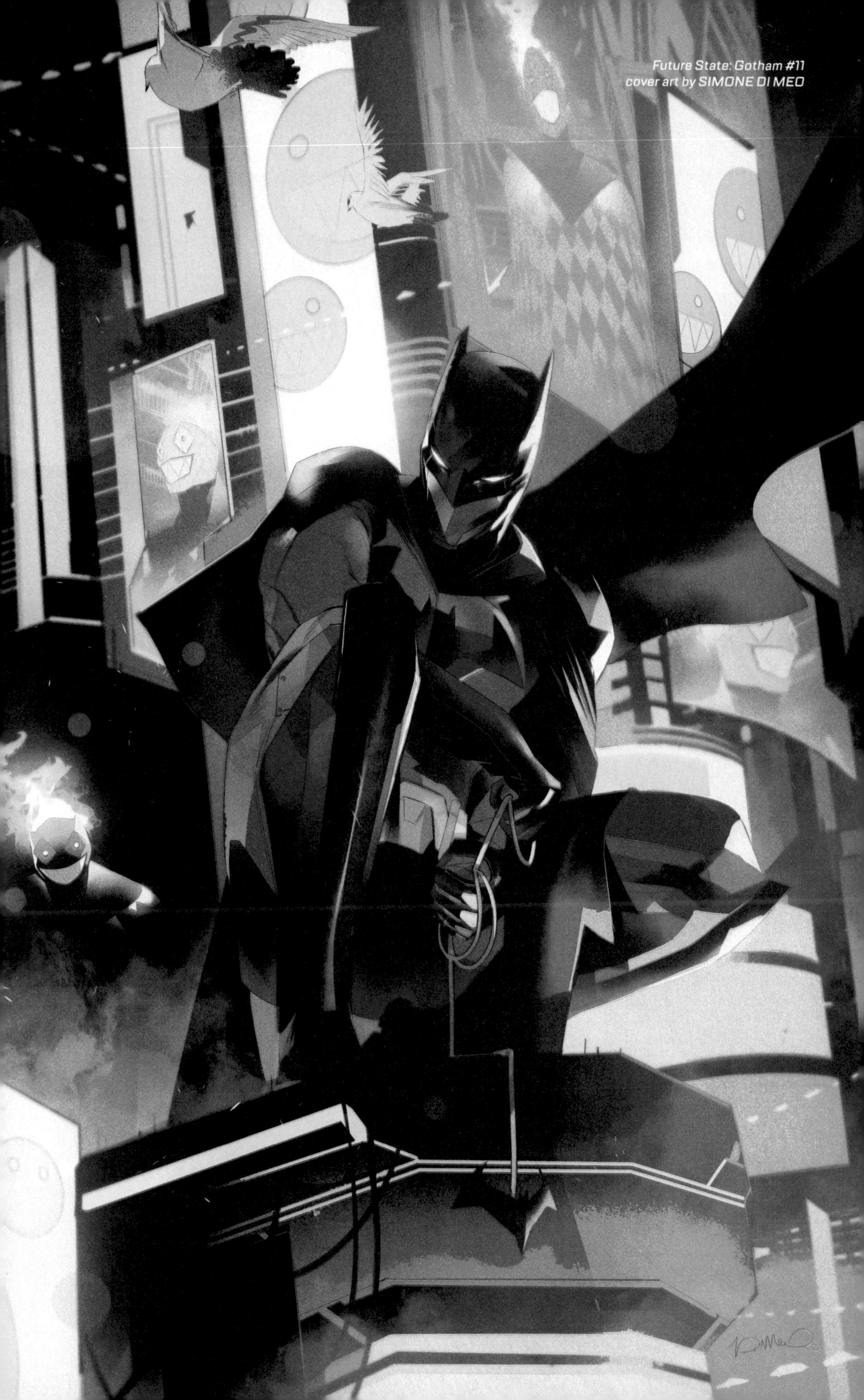

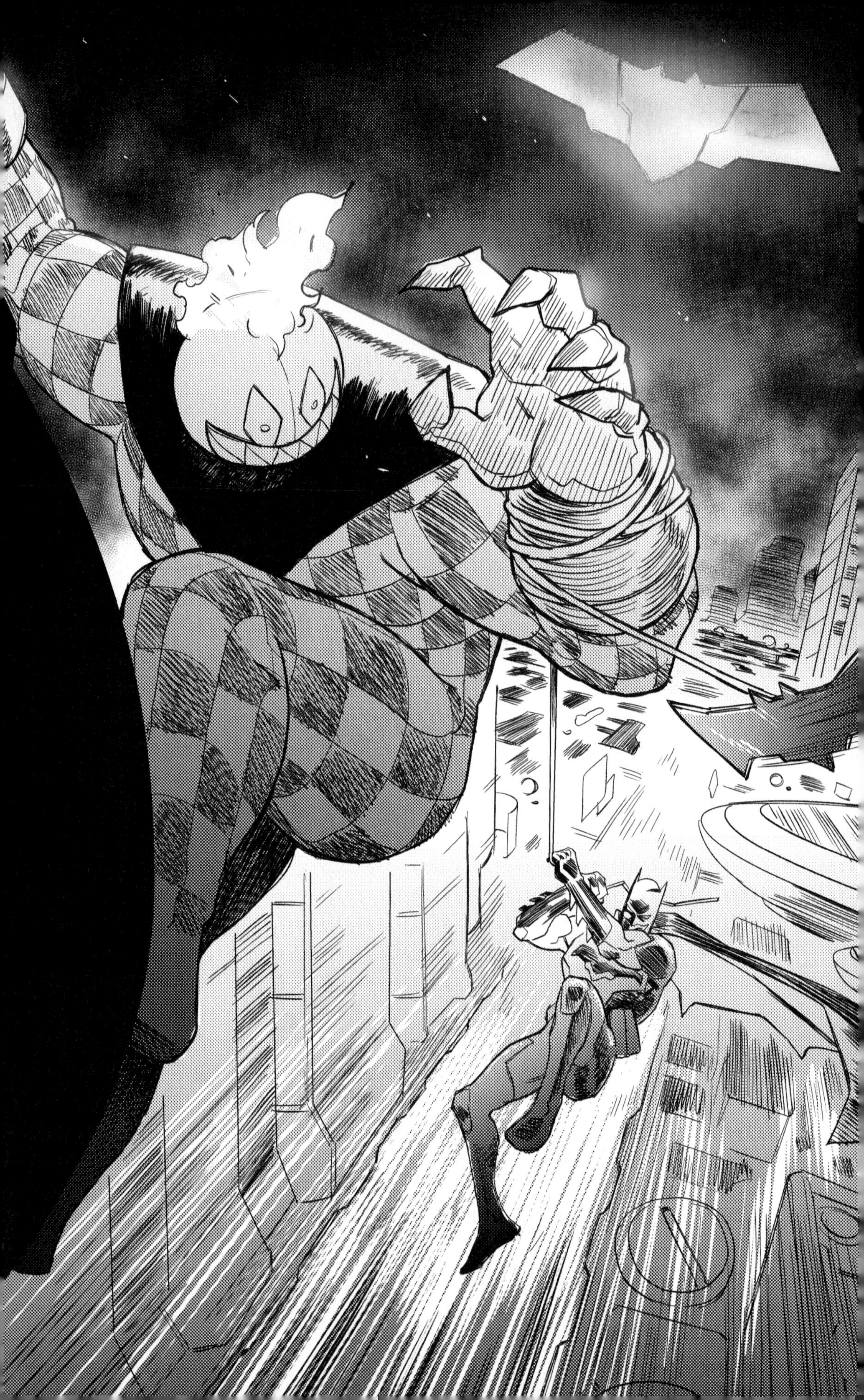

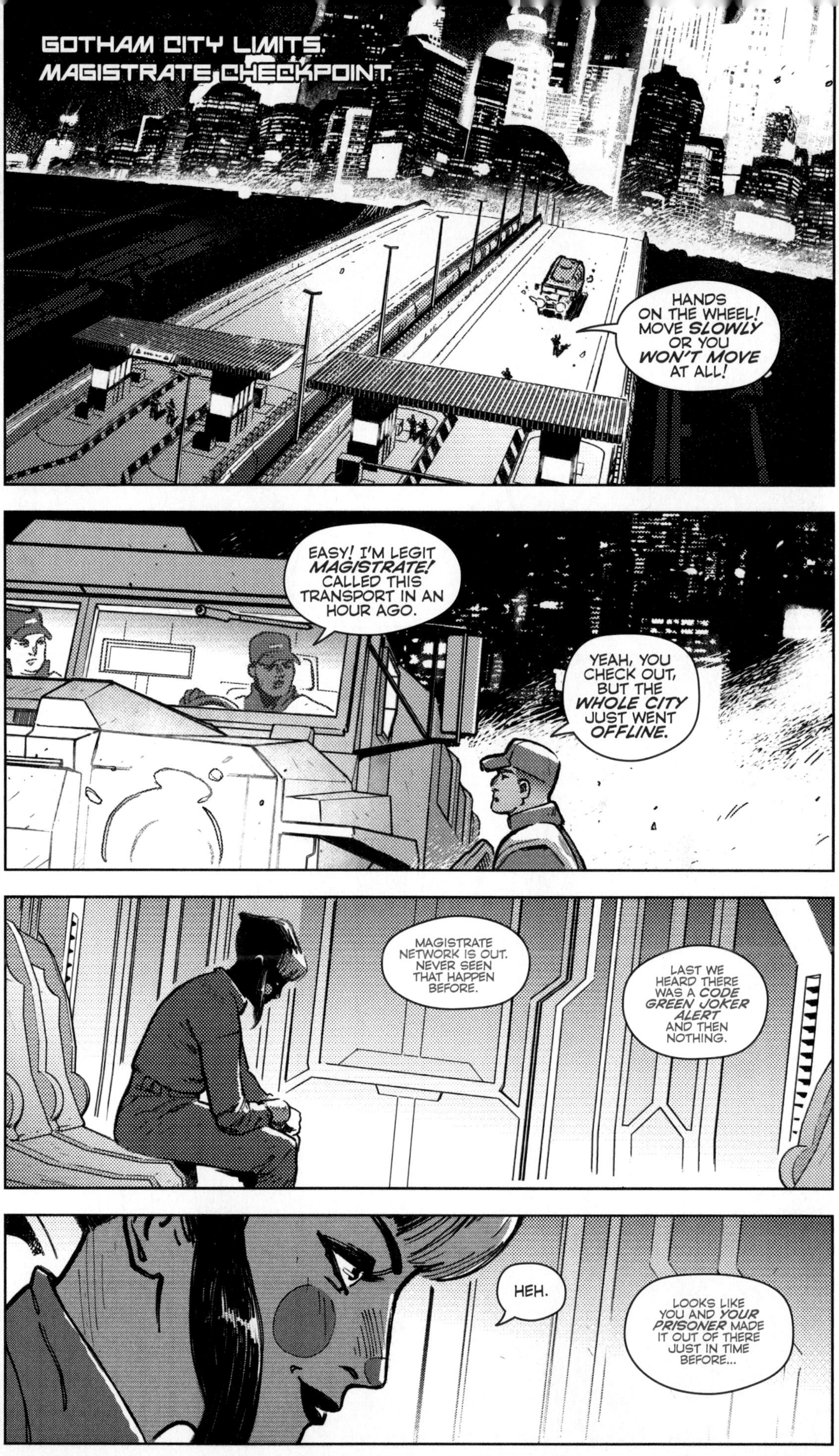
GOTHAM CITY LIMITS. MAGISTRATE CHECKPOINT.
HANDS ON THE WHEEL! MOVE SLOWLY OR YOU WON'T MOVE AT ALL!
EASY! I'M LEGIT MAGISTRATE! CALLED THIS TRANSPORT IN AN HOUR AGO.
YEAH, YOU CHECK OUT, BUT THE WHOLE CITY JUST WENT OFFLINE.
MAGISTRATE NETWORK IS OUT. NEVER SEEN THAT HAPPEN BEFORE.
LAST WE HEARD THERE WAS A CODE GREEN JOKER ALERT AND THEN NOTHING.
HEH.
LOOKS LIKE YOU AND YOUR PRISONER MADE IT OUT OF THERE JUST IN TIME BEFORE...

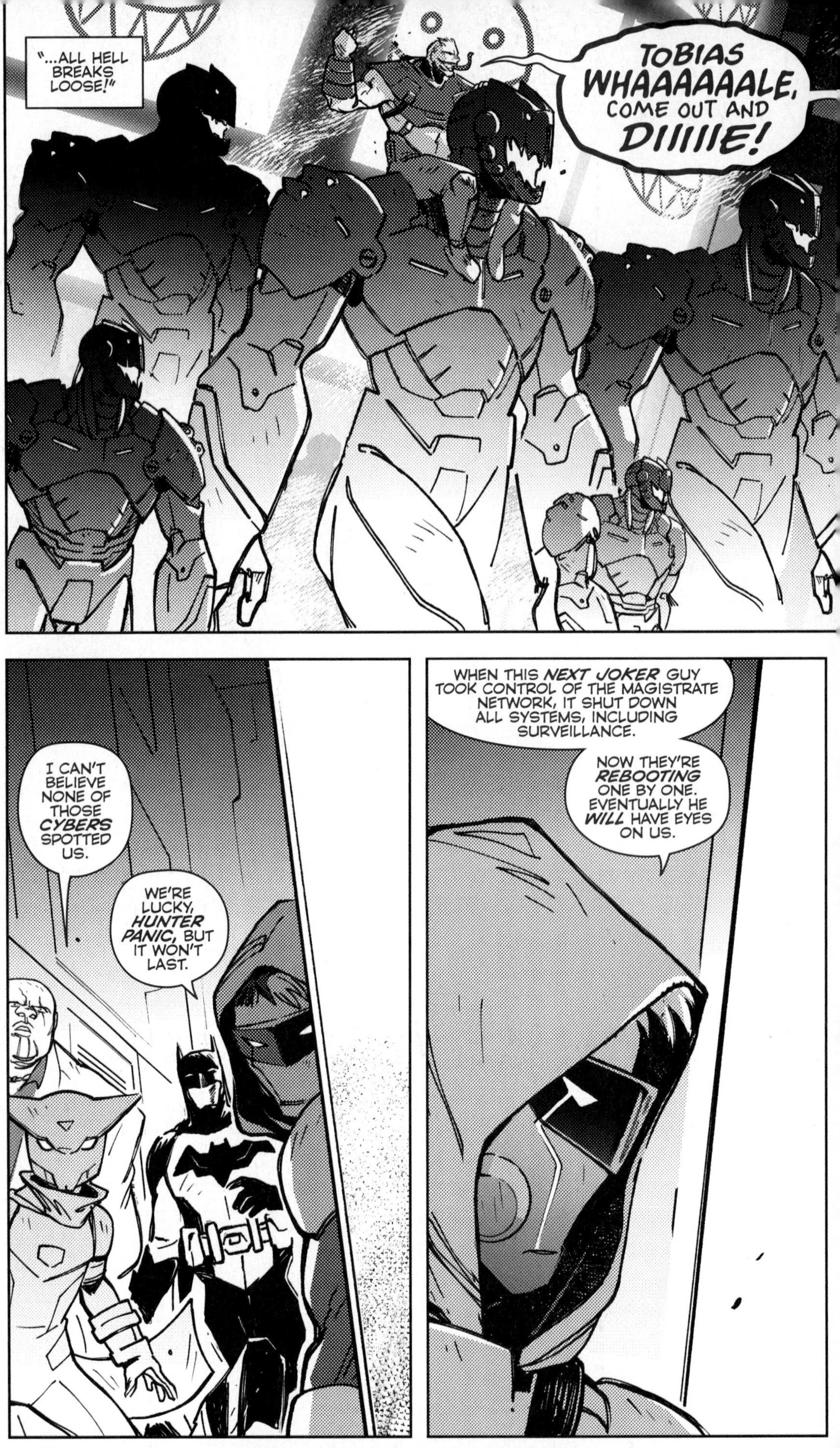
"...ALL HELL BREAKS LOOSE!"
TOBIAS WHAAAAAALE, COME OUT AND DIIIIIE!
I CAN'T BELIEVE NONE OF THOSE CYBERS SPOTTED US.
WE'RE LUCKY, HUNTER PANIC, BUT IT WON'T LAST.
WHEN THIS NEXT JOKER GUY TOOK CONTROL OF THE MAGISTRATE NETWORK, IT SHUT DOWN ALL SYSTEMS, INCLUDING SURVEILLANCE.
NOW THEY'RE REBOOTING ONE BY ONE. EVENTUALLY HE WILL HAVE EYES ON US.

HAWR! HAWR! HAWR! HAWR! HAWR!

THE NEXT Joker
PART FOUR:
JOKE POLICE

WRITTEN BY DENNIS CULVER ART BY GEOFFO
LETTERED BY ALW'S TROY PETERI
COVER BY SIMONE DI MEO
VARIANT COVER BY MIKE BOWDEN AND REX LOKUS
EDITED BY BEN ABERNATHY
BATMAN CREATED BY BOB KANE
WITH BILL FINGER

SO WE NEED TO GET *TOBIAS WHALE* SOMEWHERE SAFE BEFORE THAT HAPPENS.

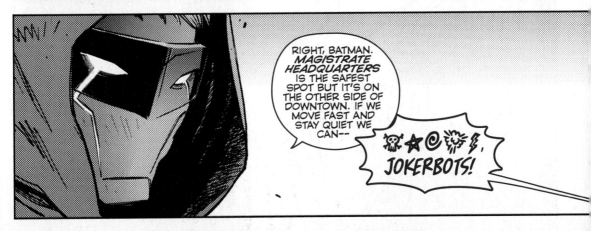

RIGHT, BATMAN. *MAGISTRATE HEADQUARTERS* IS THE SAFEST SPOT BUT IT'S ON THE OTHER SIDE OF DOWNTOWN. IF WE MOVE FAST AND STAY QUIET WE CAN--

※☆©✺⚡, JOKERBOTS!

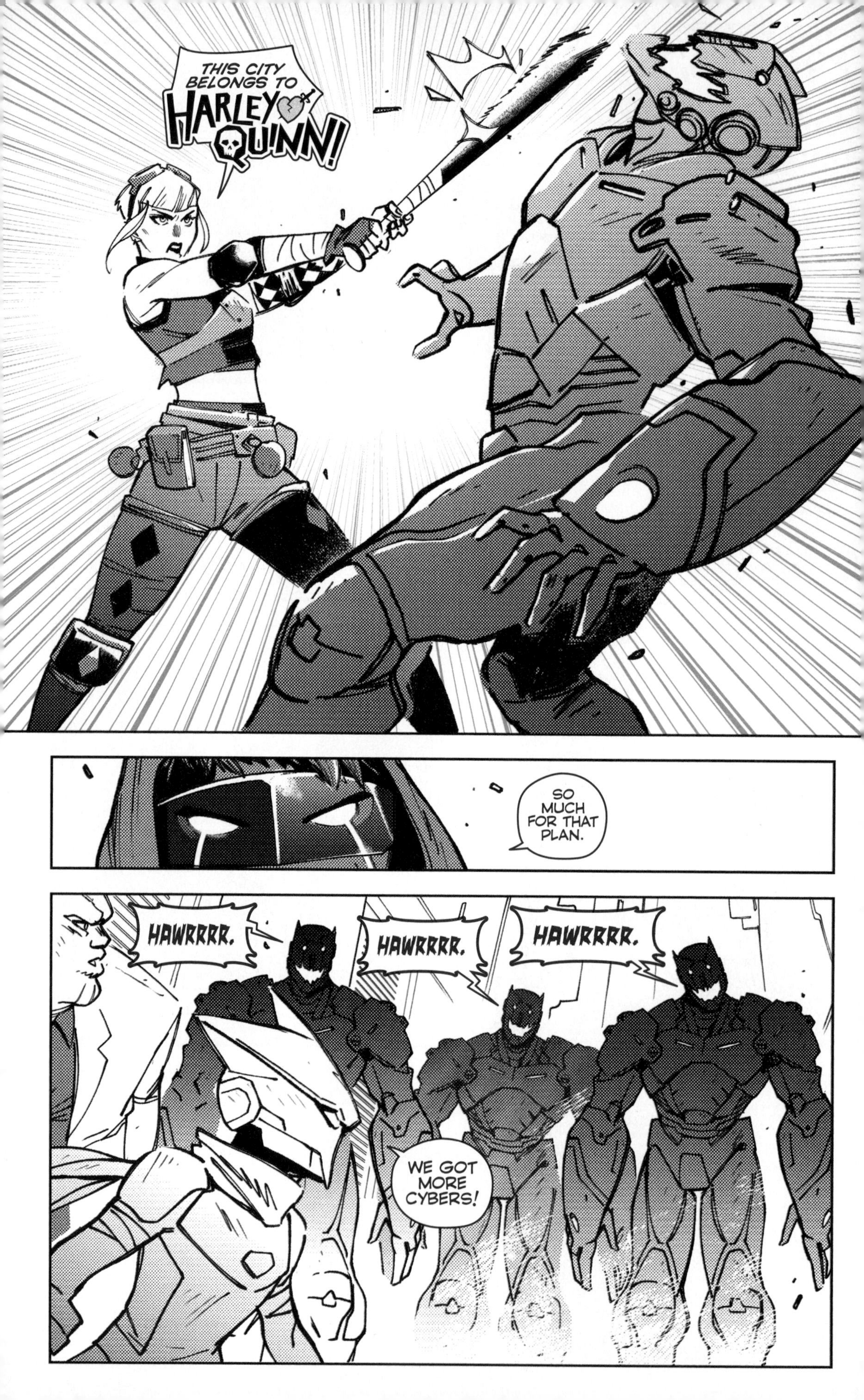
THIS CITY BELONGS TO HARLEY QUINN!
SO MUCH FOR THAT PLAN.
HAWRRRR.
HAWRRRR.
HAWRRRR.
WE GOT MORE CYBERS!

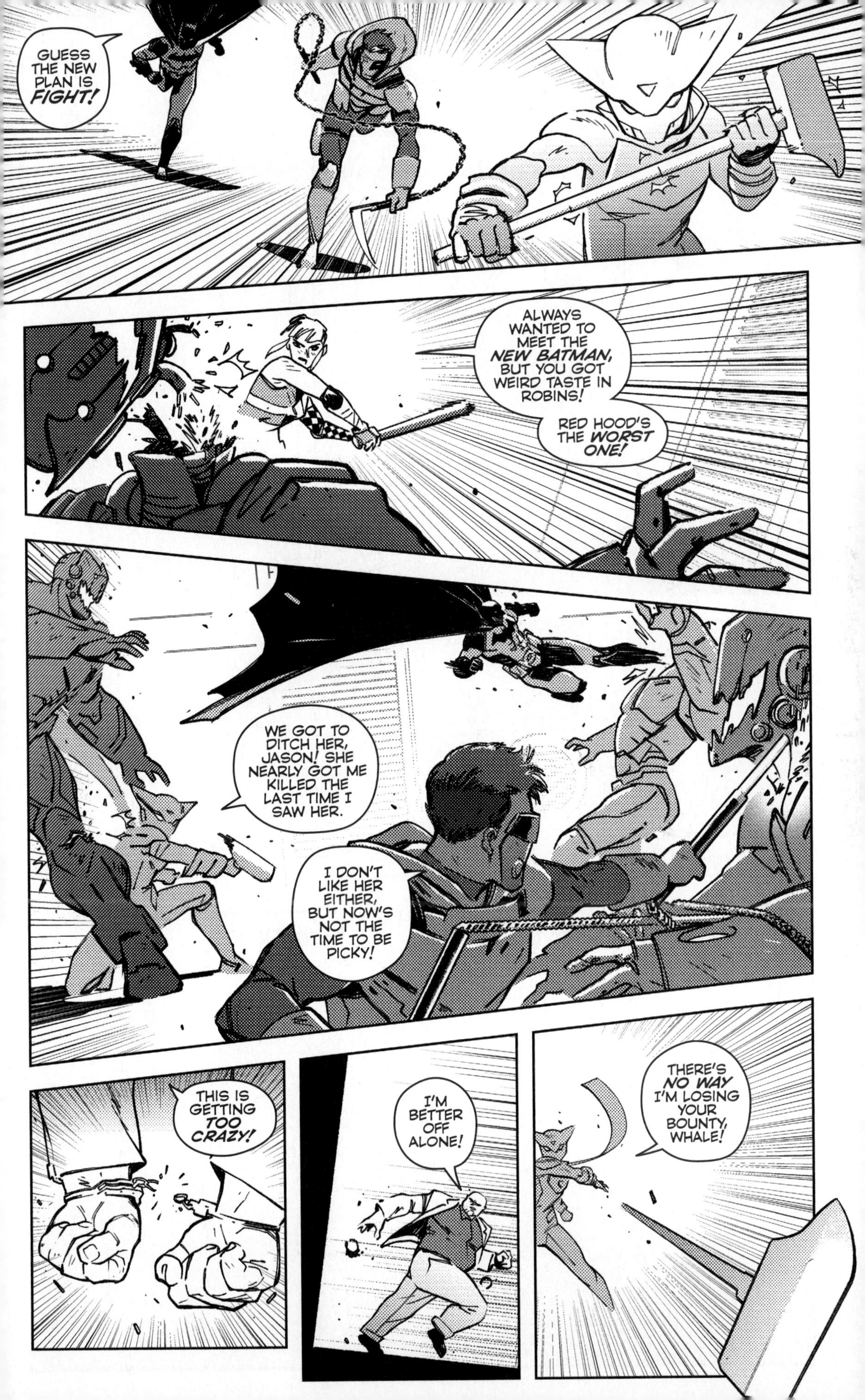
GUESS THE NEW PLAN IS *FIGHT!*
ALWAYS WANTED TO MEET THE *NEW BATMAN,* BUT YOU GOT WEIRD TASTE IN ROBINS!
RED HOOD'S THE *WORST ONE!*
WE GOT TO DITCH HER, JASON! SHE NEARLY GOT ME KILLED THE LAST TIME I SAW HER.
I DON'T LIKE HER EITHER, BUT NOW'S NOT THE TIME TO BE PICKY!
THIS IS GETTING *TOO CRAZY!*
I'M BETTER OFF ALONE!
THERE'S *NO WAY* I'M LOSING YOUR BOUNTY, WHALE!

AW, *DAMN!*

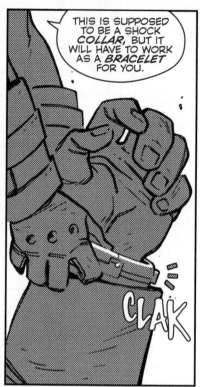

THIS IS SUPPOSED TO BE A SHOCK *COLLAR,* BUT IT WILL HAVE TO WORK AS A *BRACELET* FOR YOU.

CLAK

YOU GET TOO FAR AWAY FROM ME AND THERE'S ENOUGH *VOLTAGE* TO KNOCK EVEN *YOU* ON YOUR BUTT, WHALE.

AIN'T GONNA MATTER WHEN Y'ALL GET ME KILLED.

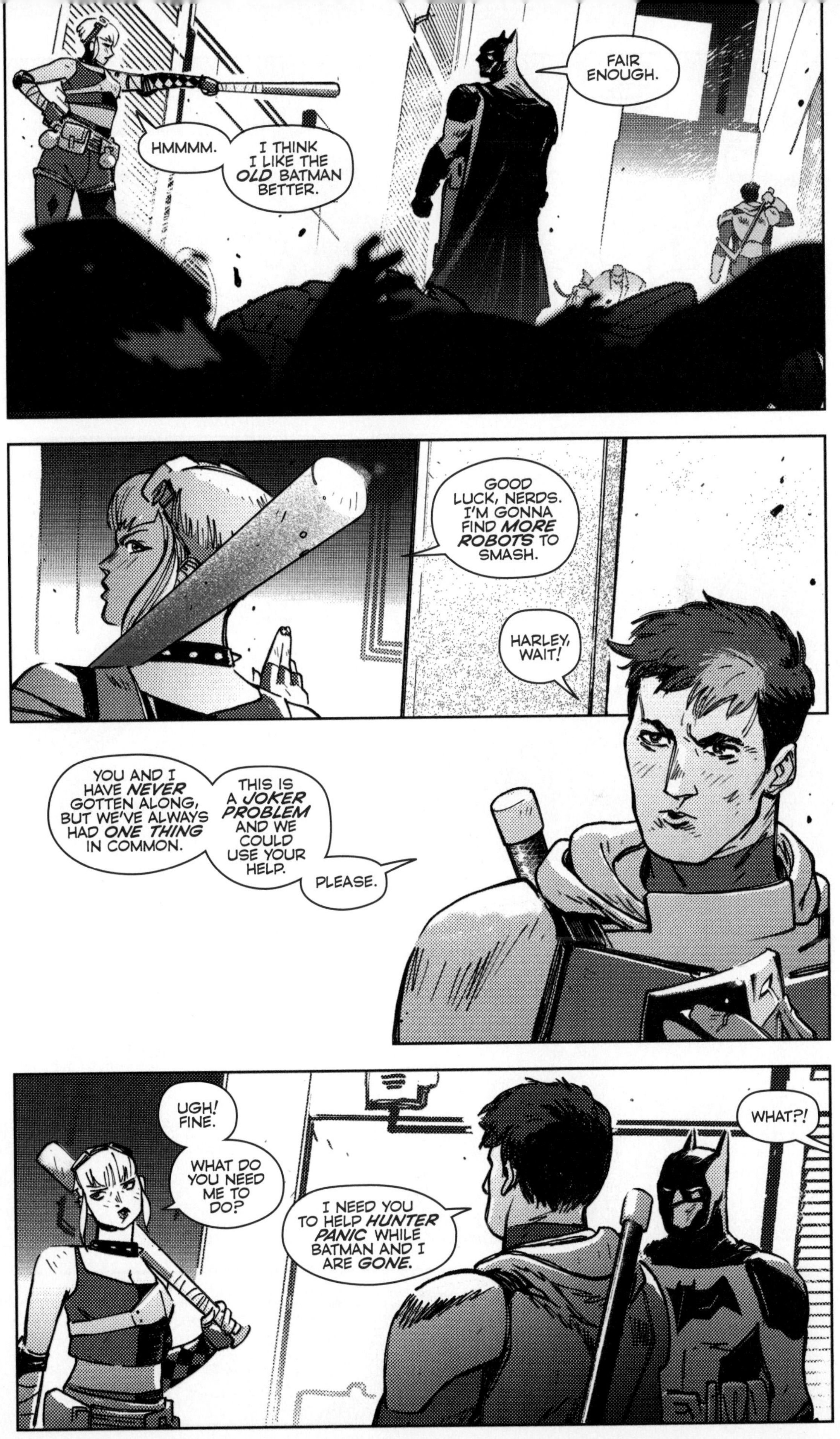

HMMMM.
I THINK I LIKE THE OLD BATMAN BETTER.
FAIR ENOUGH.
GOOD LUCK, NERDS. I'M GONNA FIND MORE ROBOTS TO SMASH.
HARLEY, WAIT!
YOU AND I HAVE NEVER GOTTEN ALONG, BUT WE'VE ALWAYS HAD ONE THING IN COMMON.
THIS IS A JOKER PROBLEM AND WE COULD USE YOUR HELP.
PLEASE.
UGH! FINE.
WHAT DO YOU NEED ME TO DO?
I NEED YOU TO HELP HUNTER PANIC WHILE BATMAN AND I ARE GONE.
WHAT?!

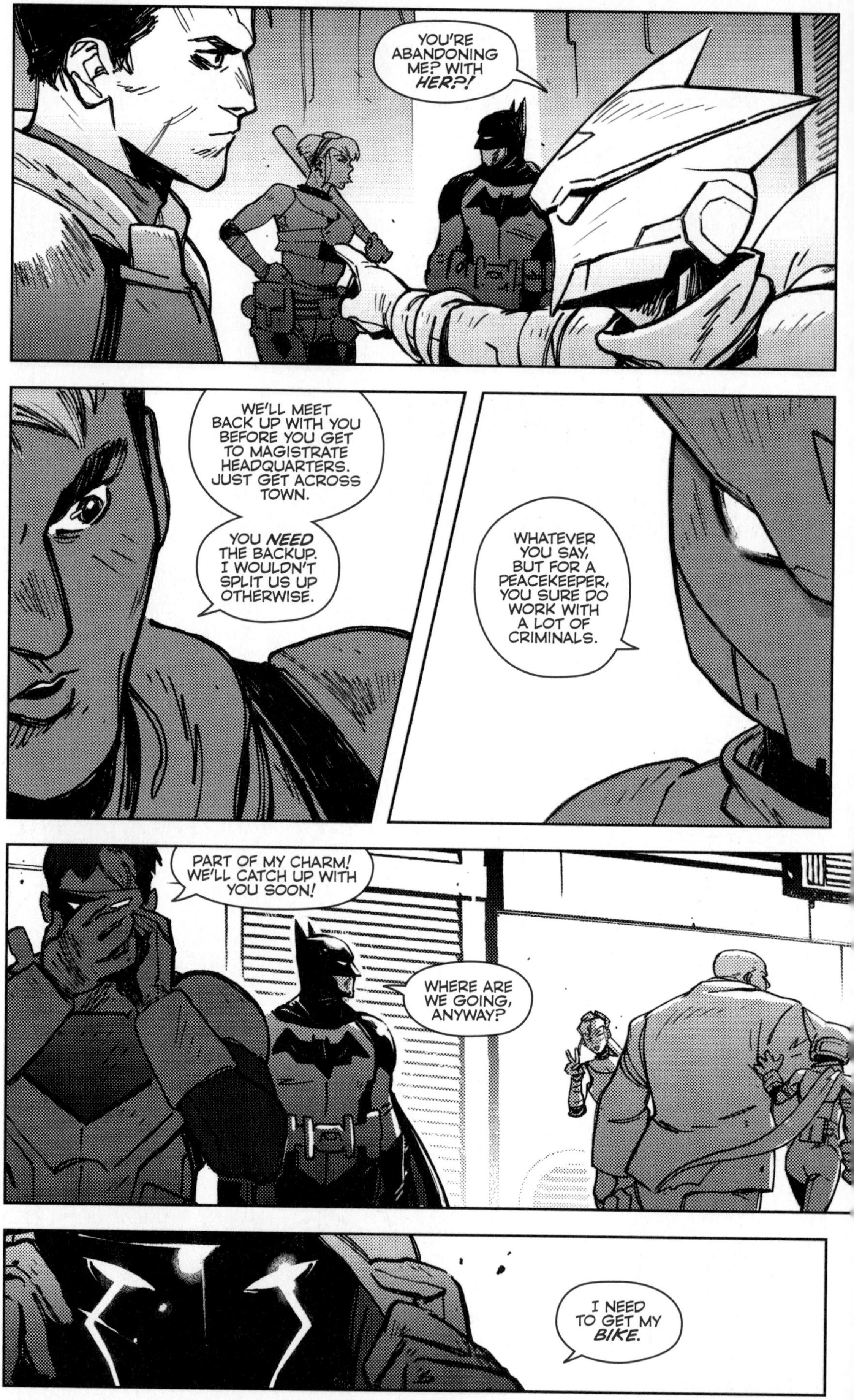
YOU'RE ABANDONING ME? WITH *HER?!*
WE'LL MEET BACK UP WITH YOU BEFORE YOU GET TO MAGISTRATE HEADQUARTERS. JUST GET ACROSS TOWN.
YOU *NEED* THE BACKUP. I WOULDN'T SPLIT US UP OTHERWISE.
WHATEVER YOU SAY, BUT FOR A PEACEKEEPER, YOU SURE DO WORK WITH A LOT OF CRIMINALS.
PART OF MY CHARM! WE'LL CATCH UP WITH YOU SOON!
WHERE ARE WE GOING, ANYWAY?
I NEED TO GET MY *BIKE*.

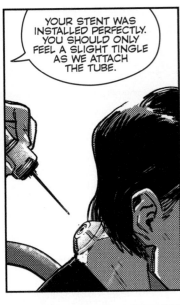

YOUR STENT WAS INSTALLED PERFECTLY. YOU SHOULD ONLY FEEL A SLIGHT TINGLE AS WE ATTACH THE TUBE.

THIS GAUNTLET WILL ALLOW YOU TO CONTROL THE DOSE AND FLOW OF *BRANE* THAT ENTERS YOUR SYSTEM.

EACH CARTRIDGE SHOULD GIVE YOU TWENTY MINUTES OF MAXIMUM DOSE. YOU CAN LOAD UP TO THREE AT A TIME.

THERE'S AN *OVERRIDE BUTTON* IF YOU WANT TO EXCEED THAT DOSE, BUT THAT IS...*NOT RECOMMENDED.*

SO YOU'RE ALL SET, UH...MR. NIGHTWING.

THANKS, DOC. I CAN TAKE IT FROM HERE.

REMEMBER, YOUR PRIORITY THIS FIRST TIME IS *DAMIAN.*

FIND MY SON AND THEN YOU CAN USE YOUR ENHANCED *PSYCHIC ABILITIES* FROM THE DRUG HOWEVER YOU SEE FIT.

ASSUMING MY HEAD DOESN'T POP OFF FROM MAINLINING AN *EXPERIMENTAL STREET DRUG.*

INDEED. TRY NOT TO DO THAT, NIGHTWING.

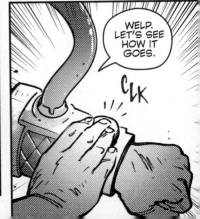

WELP. LET'S SEE HOW IT GOES.

CLK

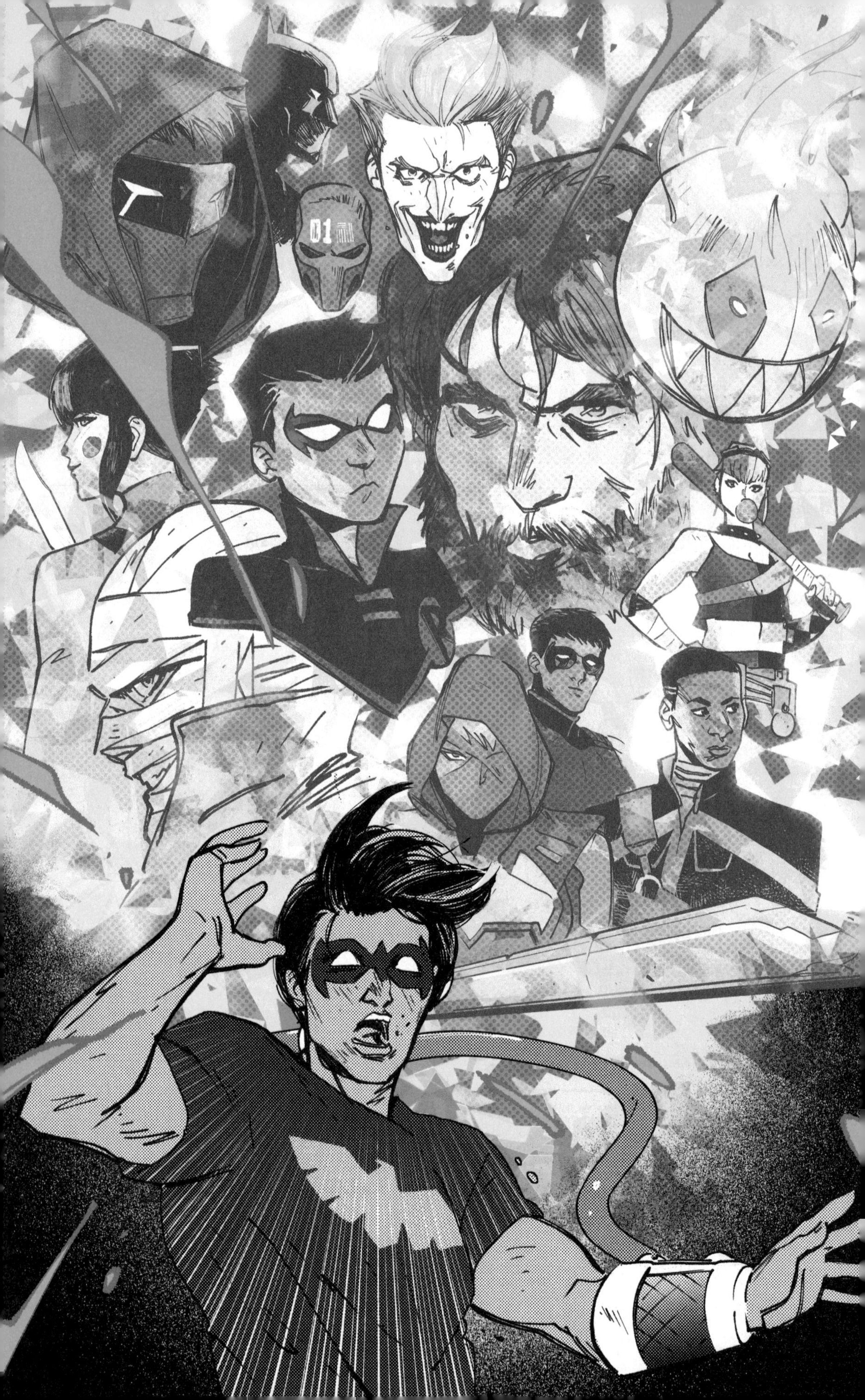
01

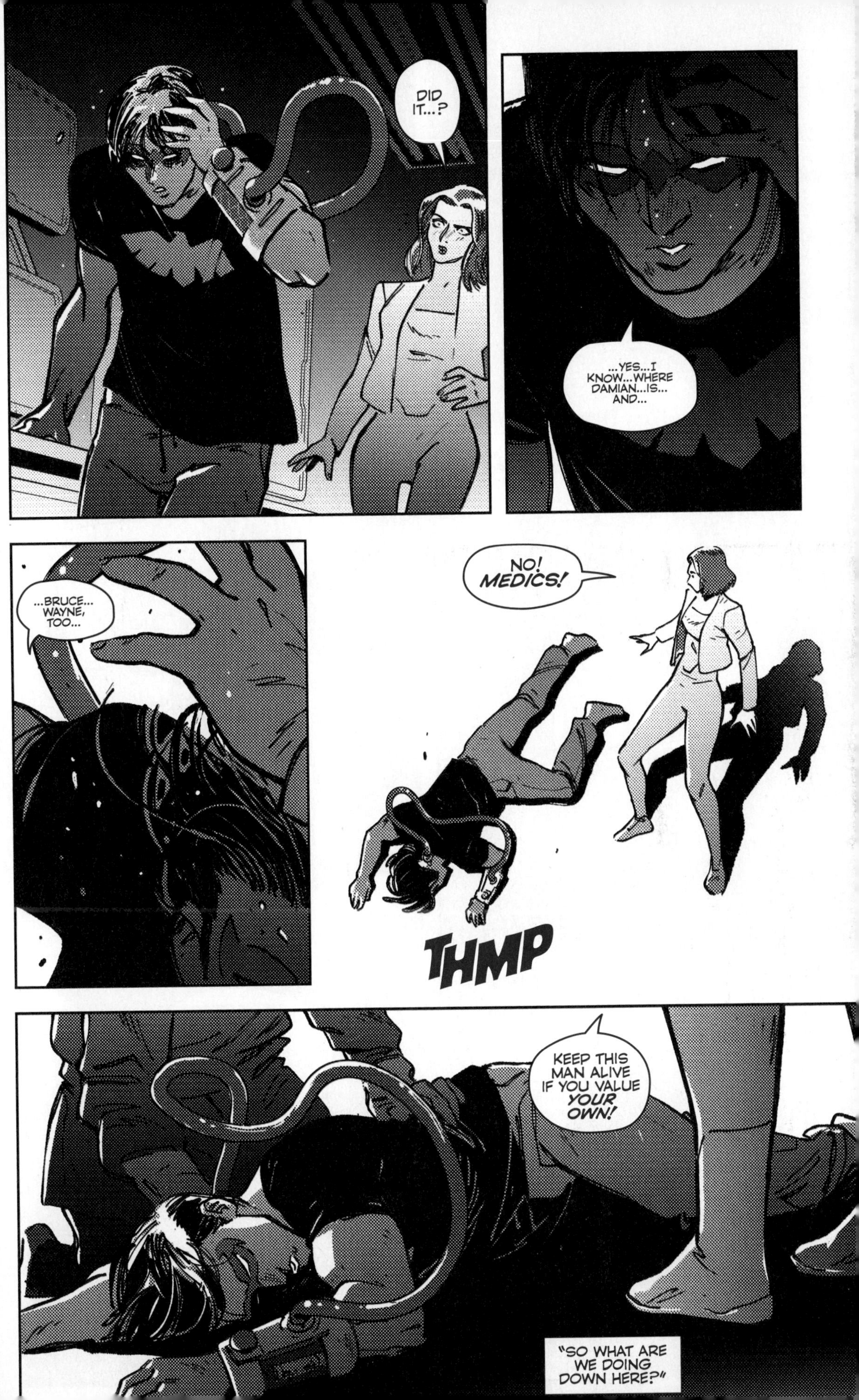
DID IT...?
...YES...I KNOW...WHERE DAMIAN...IS... AND...
...BRUCE... WAYNE, TOO...
NO! MEDICS!
THMP
KEEP THIS MAN ALIVE IF YOU VALUE YOUR OWN!
"SO WHAT ARE WE DOING DOWN HERE?"

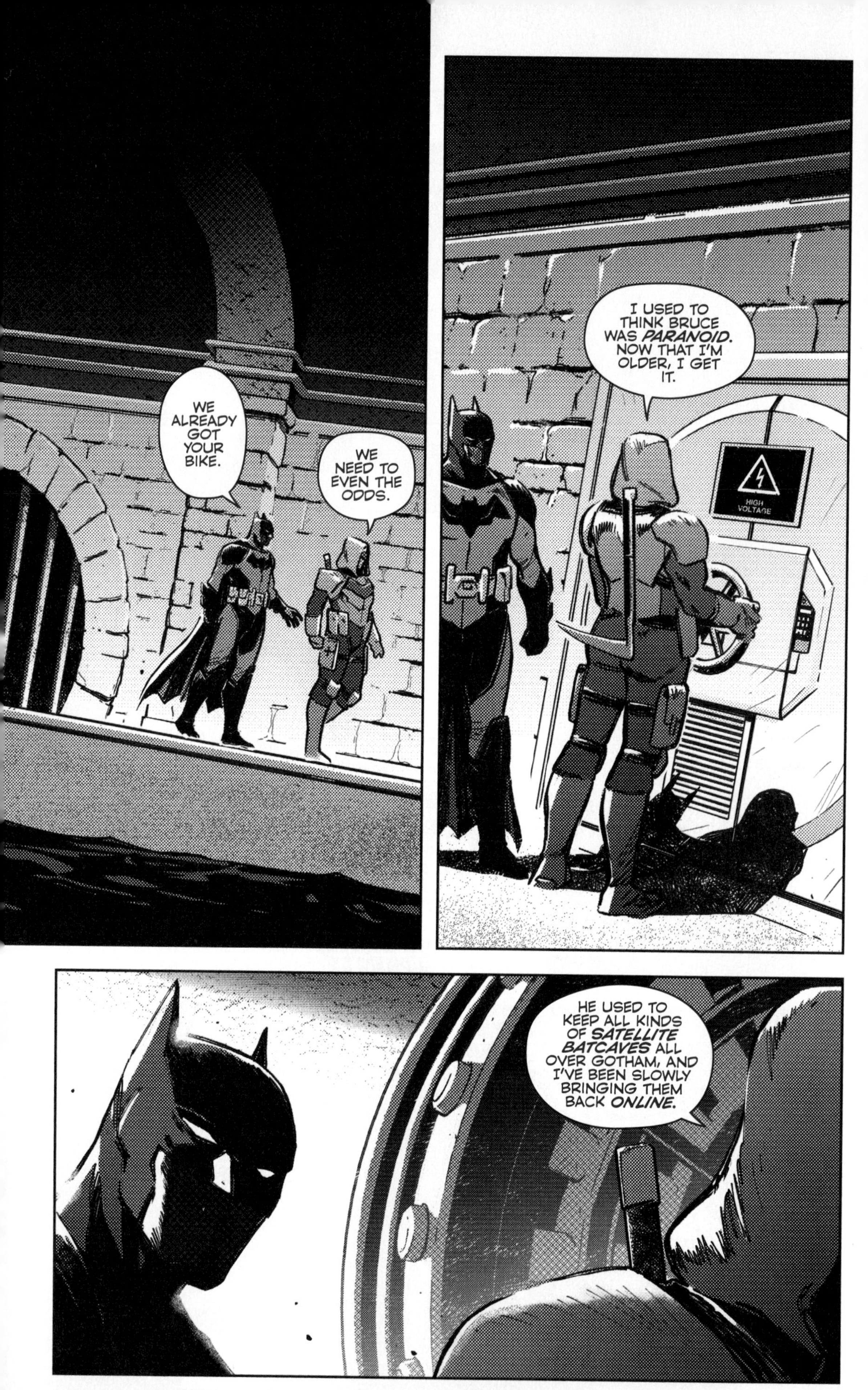
WE ALREADY GOT YOUR BIKE.
WE NEED TO EVEN THE ODDS.
I USED TO THINK BRUCE WAS *PARANOID*. NOW THAT I'M OLDER, I GET IT.
HIGH VOLTAGE
HE USED TO KEEP ALL KINDS OF ***SATELLITE BATCAVES*** ALL OVER GOTHAM, AND I'VE BEEN SLOWLY BRINGING THEM BACK ***ONLINE***.

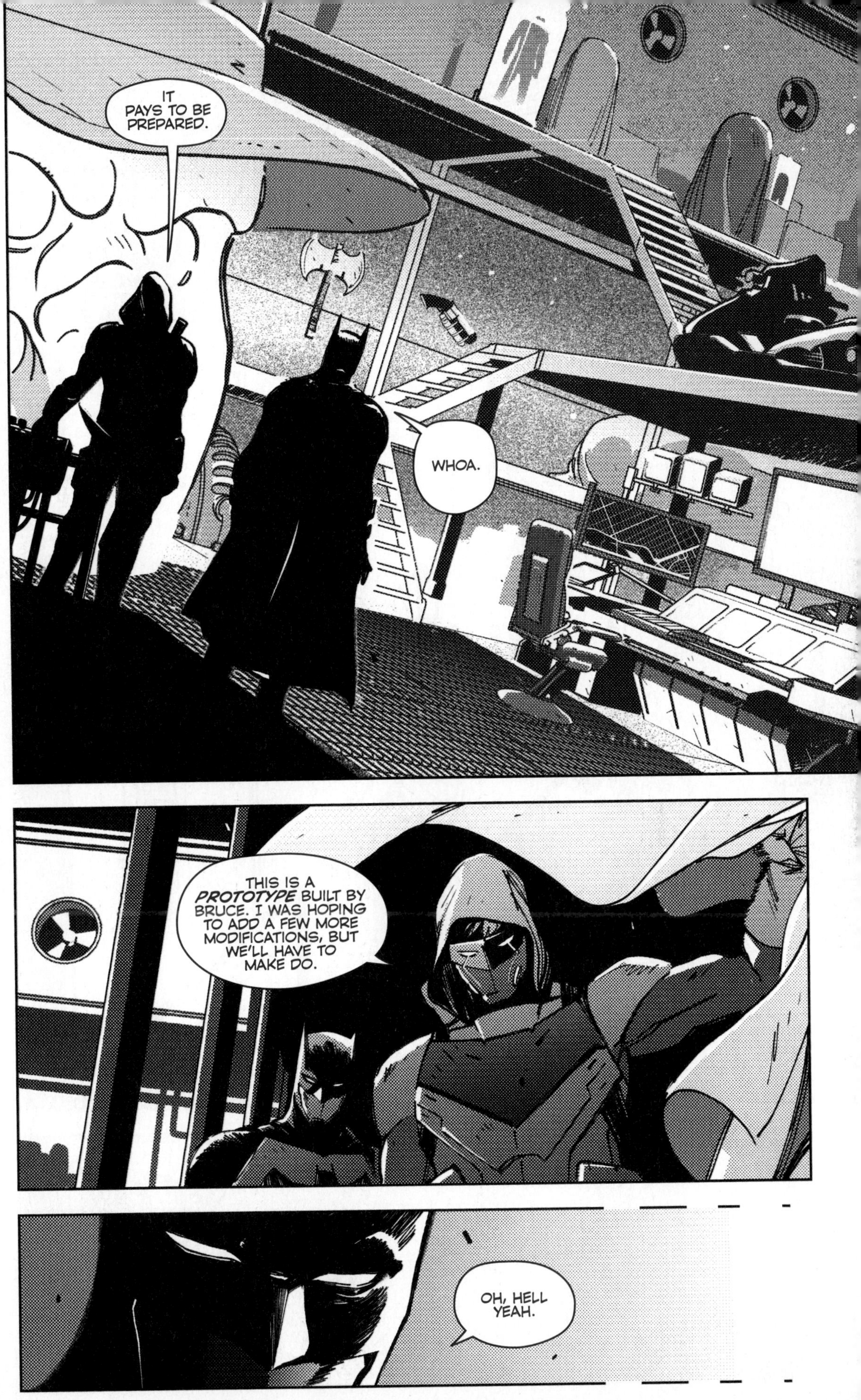
IT PAYS TO BE PREPARED.
WHOA.
THIS IS A *PROTOTYPE* BUILT BY BRUCE. I WAS HOPING TO ADD A FEW MORE MODIFICATIONS, BUT WE'LL HAVE TO MAKE DO.
OH, HELL YEAH.

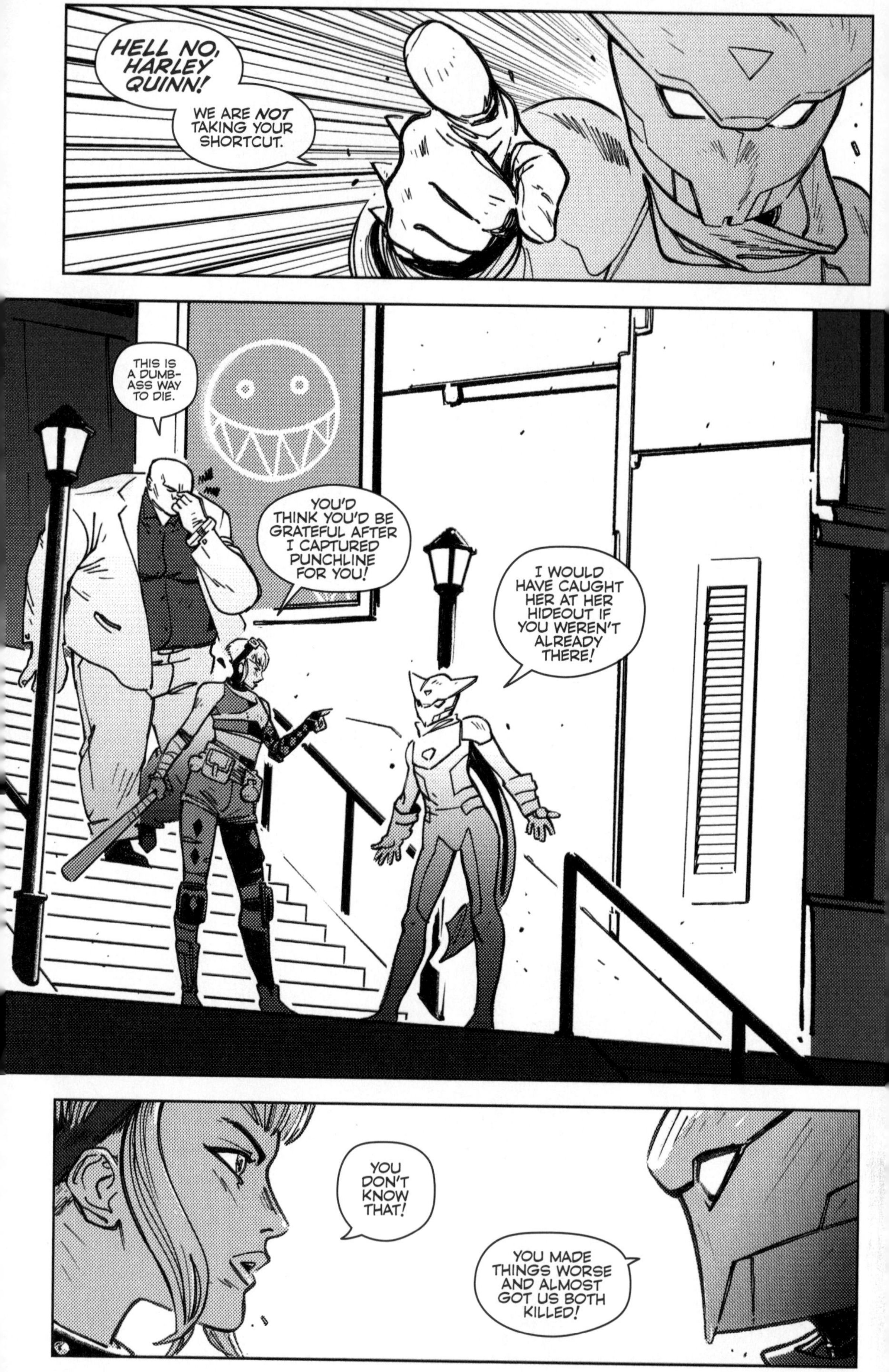
HELL NO, HARLEY QUINN!
WE ARE NOT TAKING YOUR SHORTCUT.
THIS IS A DUMB-ASS WAY TO DIE.
YOU'D THINK YOU'D BE GRATEFUL AFTER I CAPTURED PUNCHLINE FOR YOU!
I WOULD HAVE CAUGHT HER AT HER HIDEOUT IF YOU WEREN'T ALREADY THERE!
YOU DON'T KNOW THAT!
YOU MADE THINGS WORSE AND ALMOST GOT US BOTH KILLED!

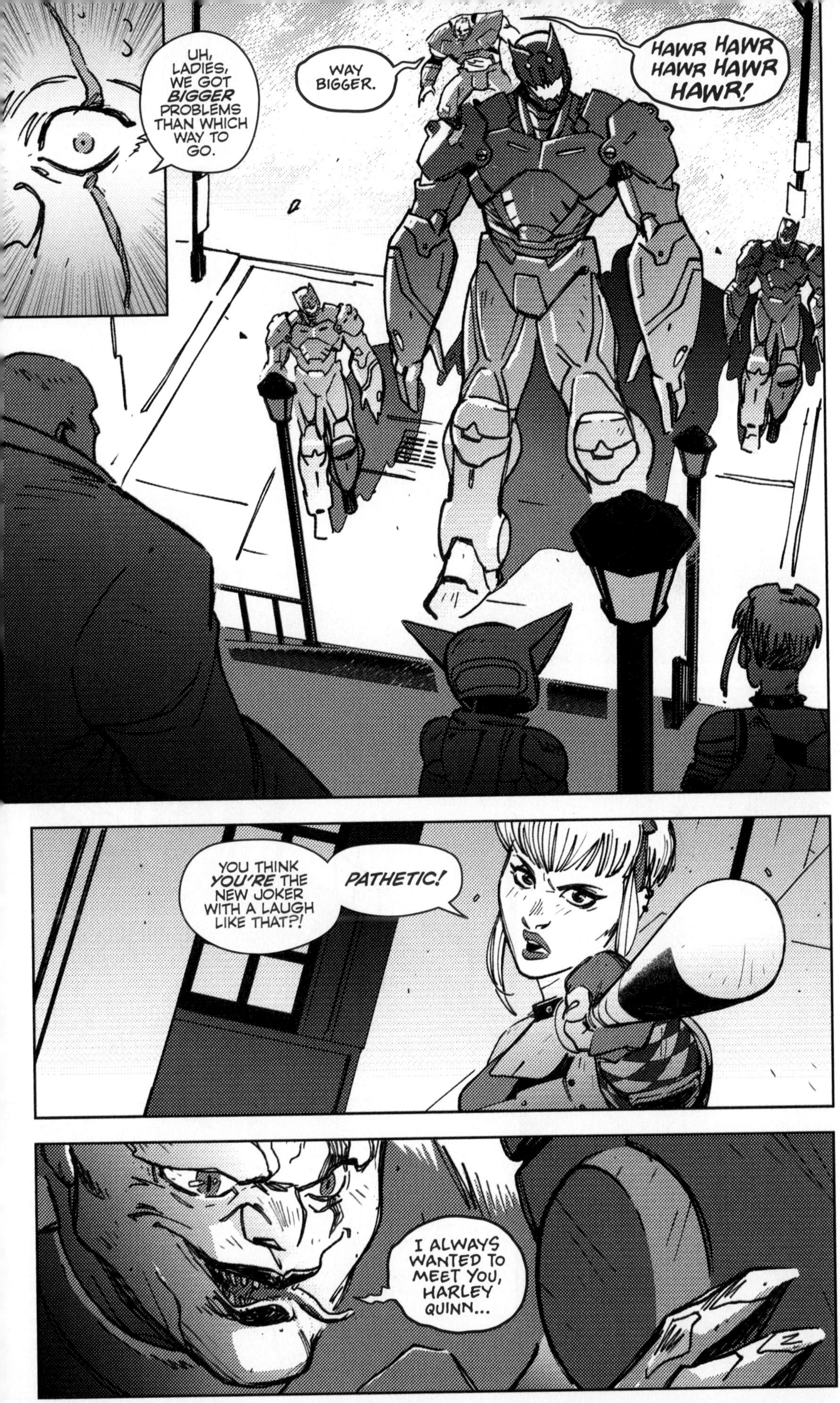

UH, LADIES, WE GOT BIGGER PROBLEMS THAN WHICH WAY TO GO.
WAY BIGGER.
HAWR HAWR HAWR HAWR HAWR!
YOU THINK YOU'RE THE NEW JOKER WITH A LAUGH LIKE THAT?!
PATHETIC!
I ALWAYS WANTED TO MEET YOU, HARLEY QUINN...

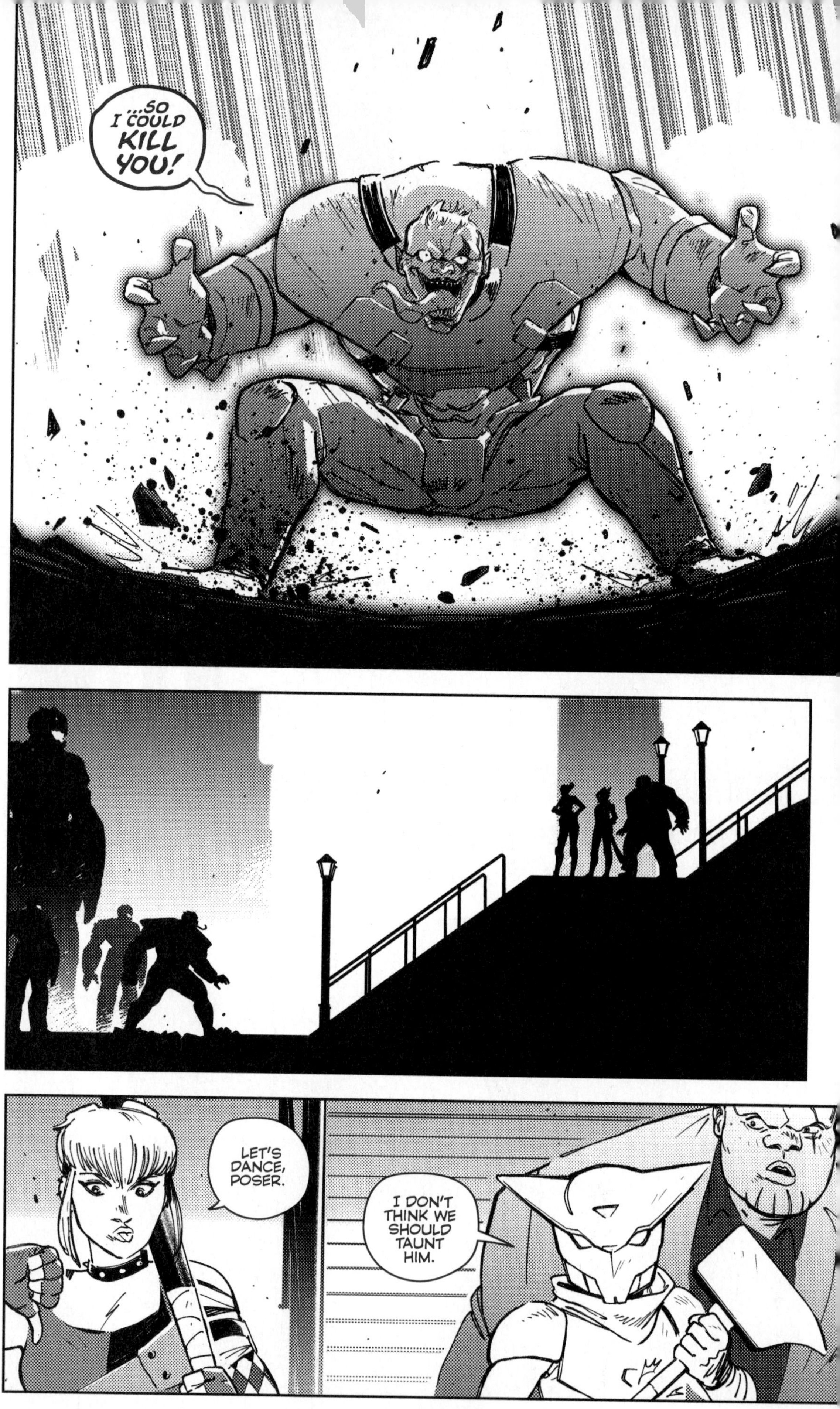
...SO I COULD KILL YOU!
LET'S DANCE, POSER.
I DON'T THINK WE SHOULD TAUNT HIM.

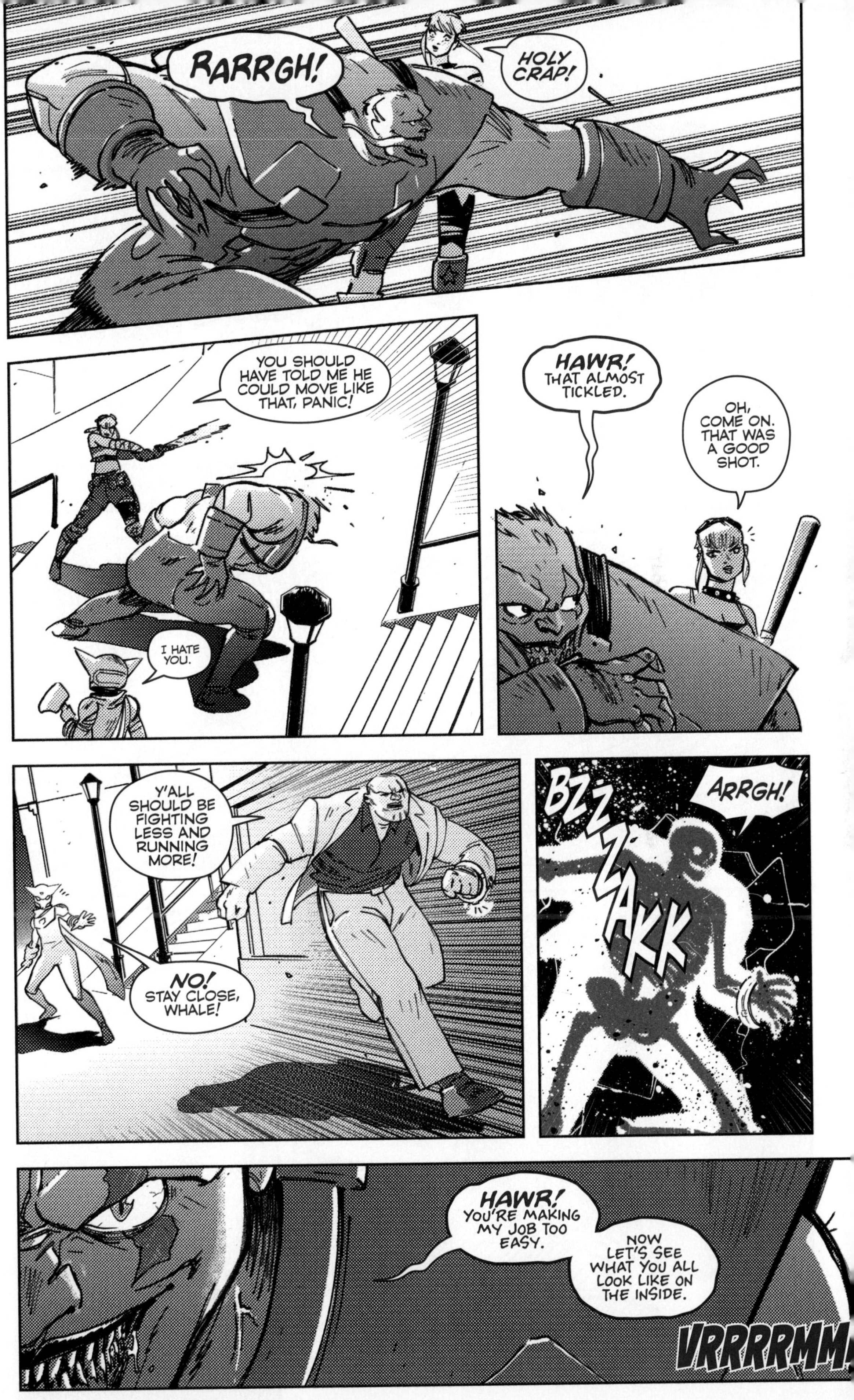
RARRGH!
HOLY CRAP!
YOU SHOULD HAVE TOLD ME HE COULD MOVE LIKE THAT, PANIC!
I HATE YOU.
HAWR! THAT ALMOST TICKLED.
OH, COME ON. THAT WAS A GOOD SHOT.
Y'ALL SHOULD BE FIGHTING LESS AND RUNNING MORE!
NO! STAY CLOSE, WHALE!
BZZZAKK
ARRGH!
HAWR! YOU'RE MAKING MY JOB TOO EASY.
NOW LET'S SEE WHAT YOU ALL LOOK LIKE ON THE INSIDE.
VRRRRMM

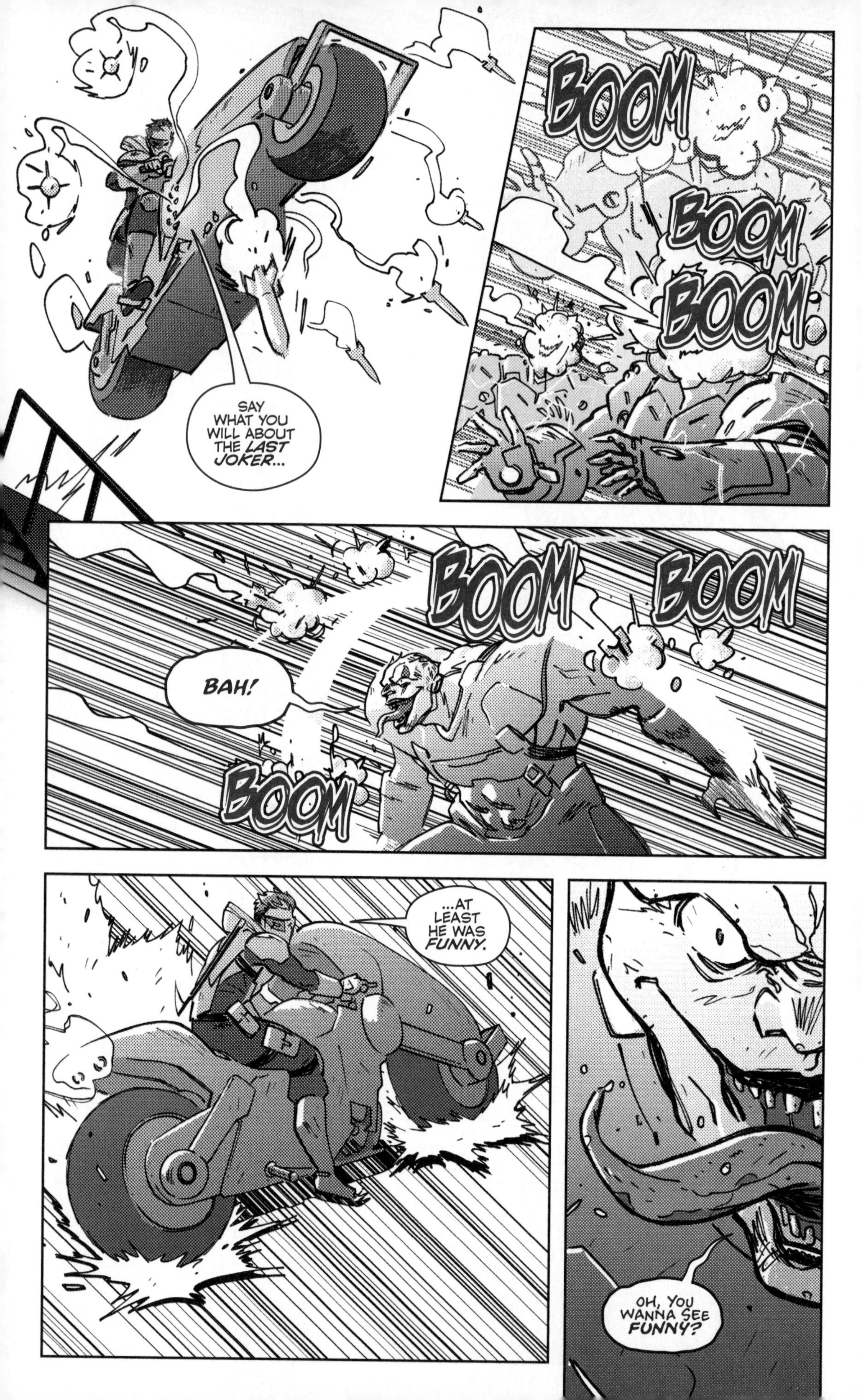

SAY WHAT YOU WILL ABOUT THE LAST JOKER...
BOOM
BOOM
BOOM
BOOM
BOOM
BAH!
BOOM
...AT LEAST HE WAS FUNNY.
OH, YOU WANNA SEE FUNNY?

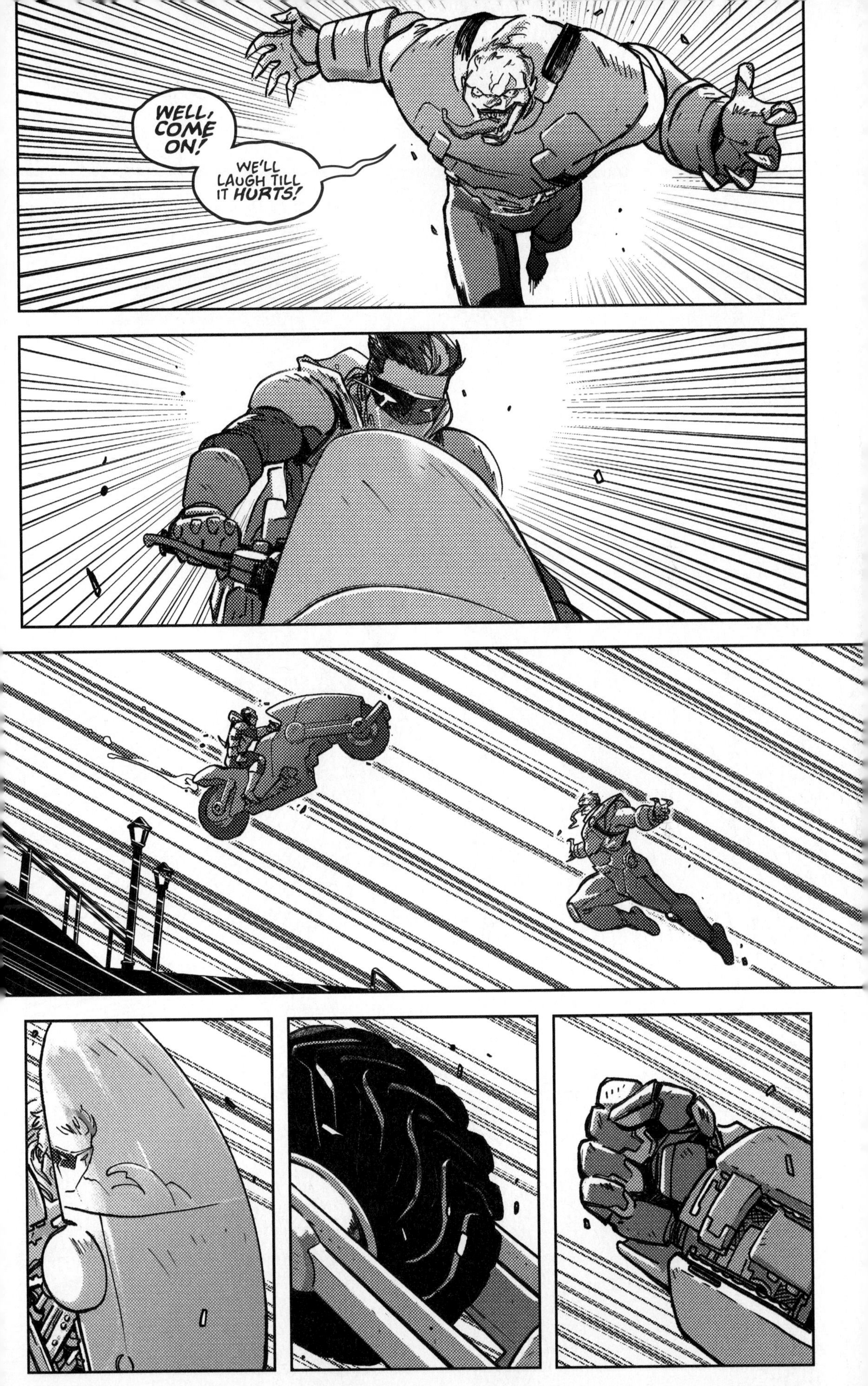
WELL, COME ON!
WE'LL LAUGH TILL IT HURTS!

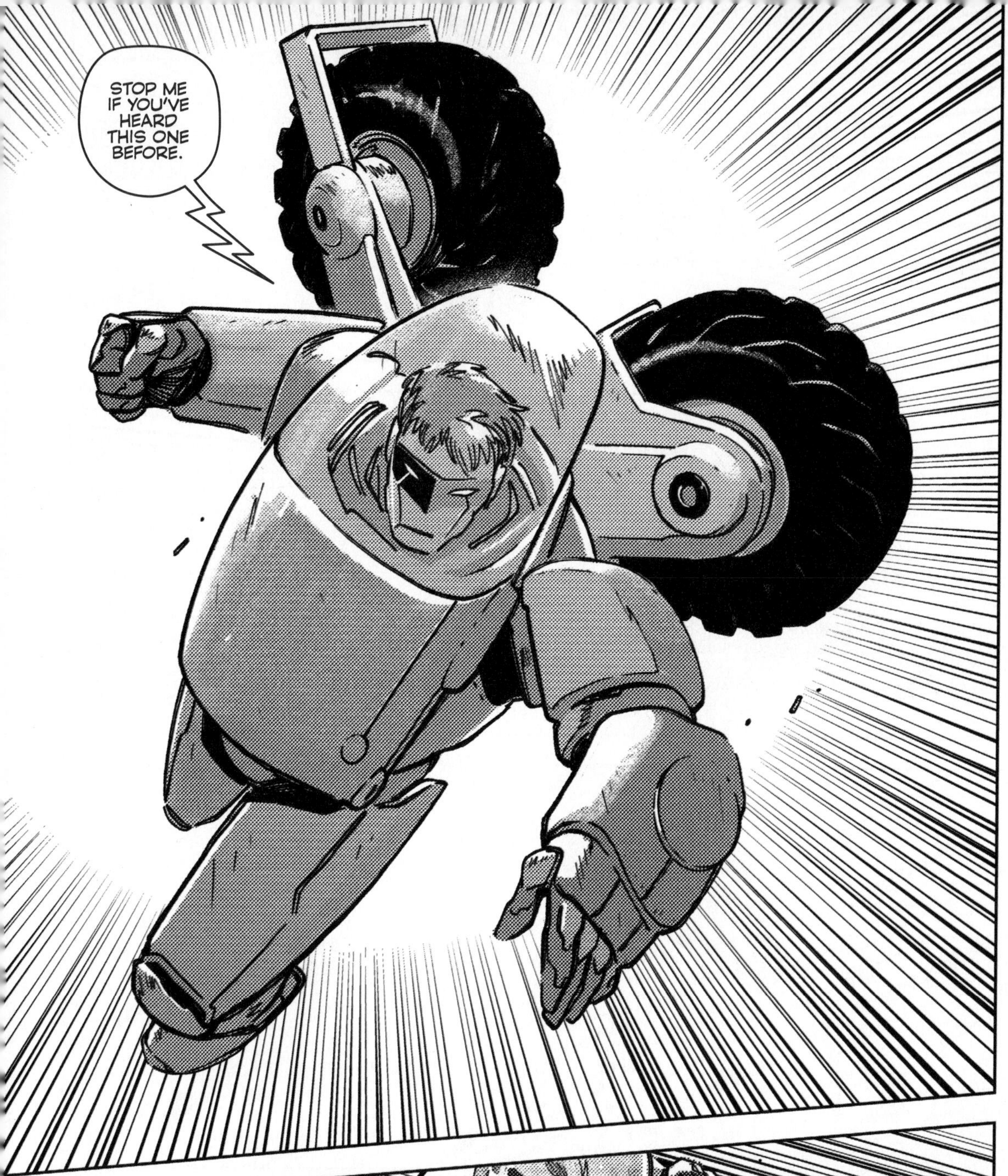
STOP ME IF YOU'VE HEARD THIS ONE BEFORE.

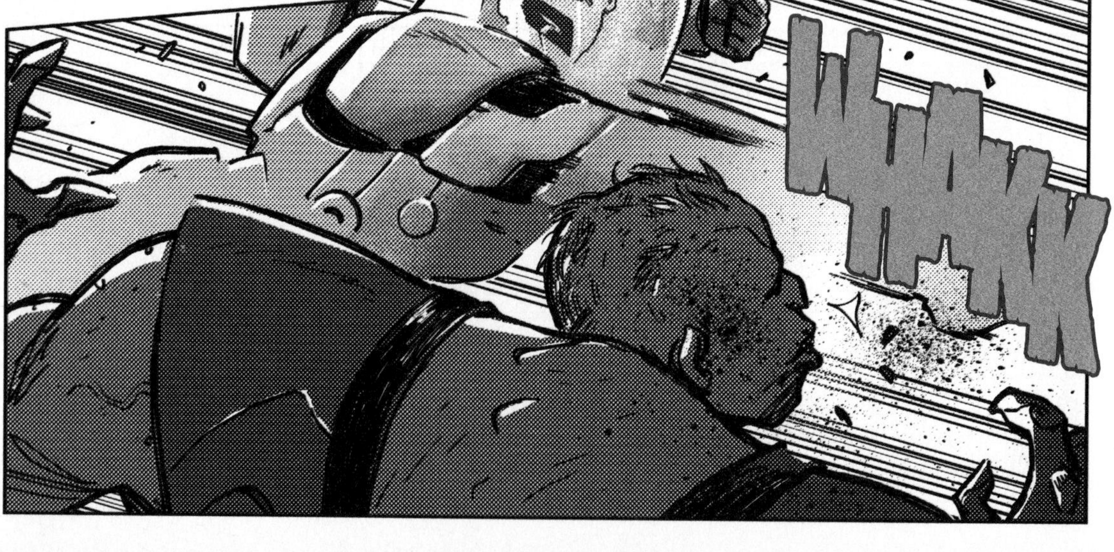
WHAKK

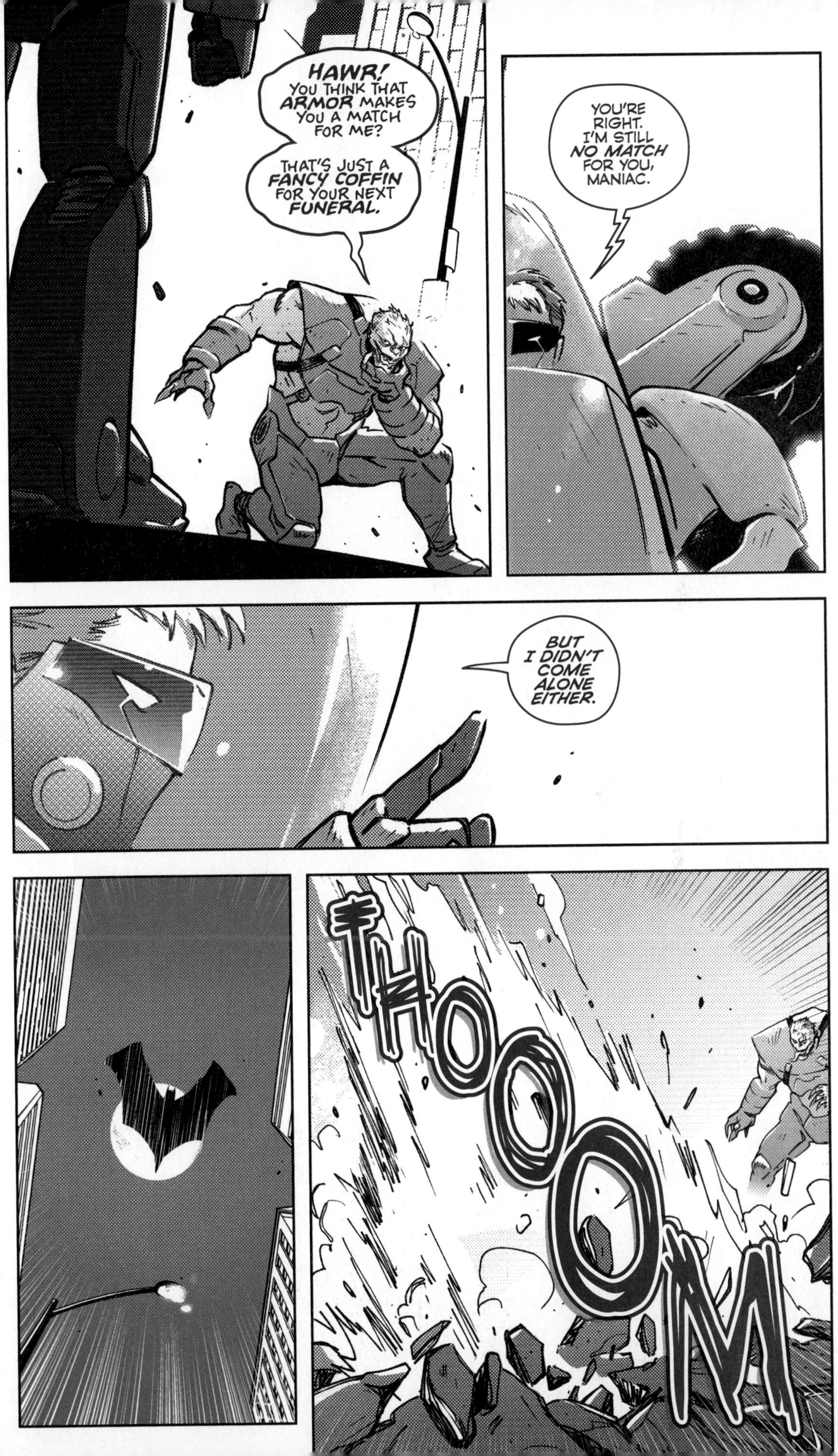
HAWR! YOU THINK THAT ARMOR MAKES YOU A MATCH FOR ME?
THAT'S JUST A FANCY COFFIN FOR YOUR NEXT FUNERAL.
YOU'RE RIGHT. I'M STILL NO MATCH FOR YOU, MANIAC.
BUT I DIDN'T COME ALONE EITHER.
THOOOOOM

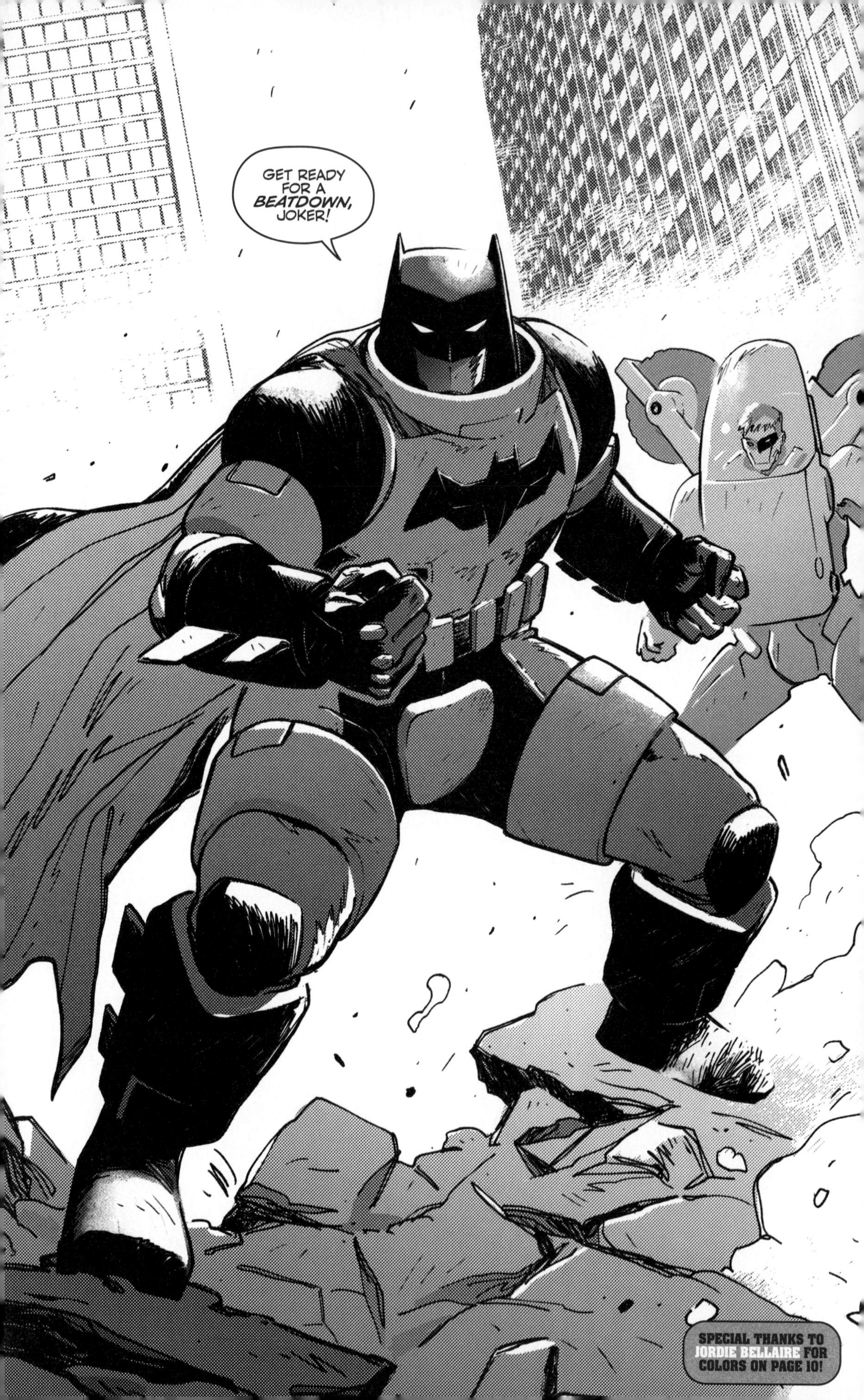
GET READY FOR A *BEATDOWN,* JOKER!
SPECIAL THANKS TO JORDIE BELLAIRE FOR COLORS ON PAGE 10!

Future State: Gotham #12
cover art by SIMONE DI MEO

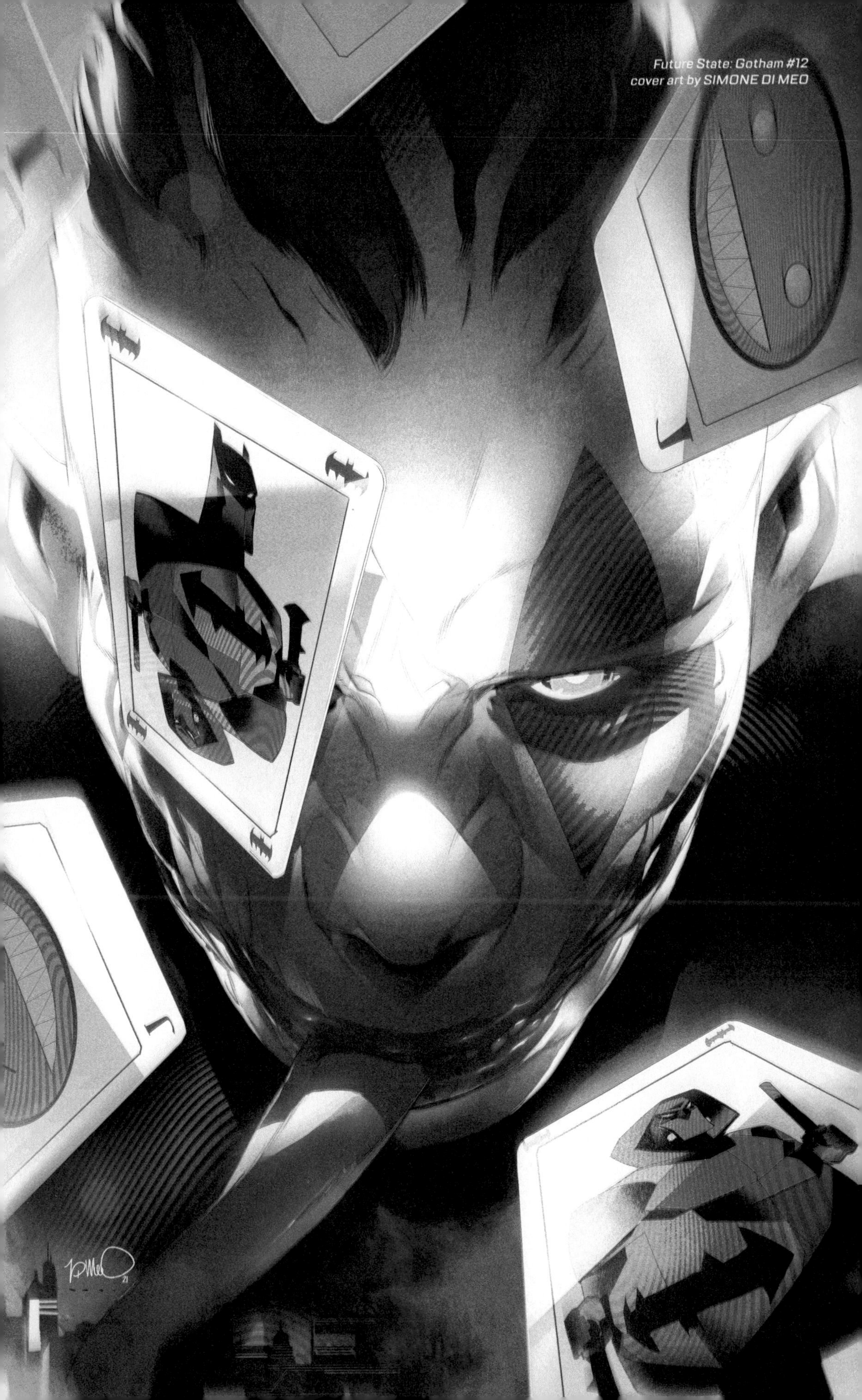

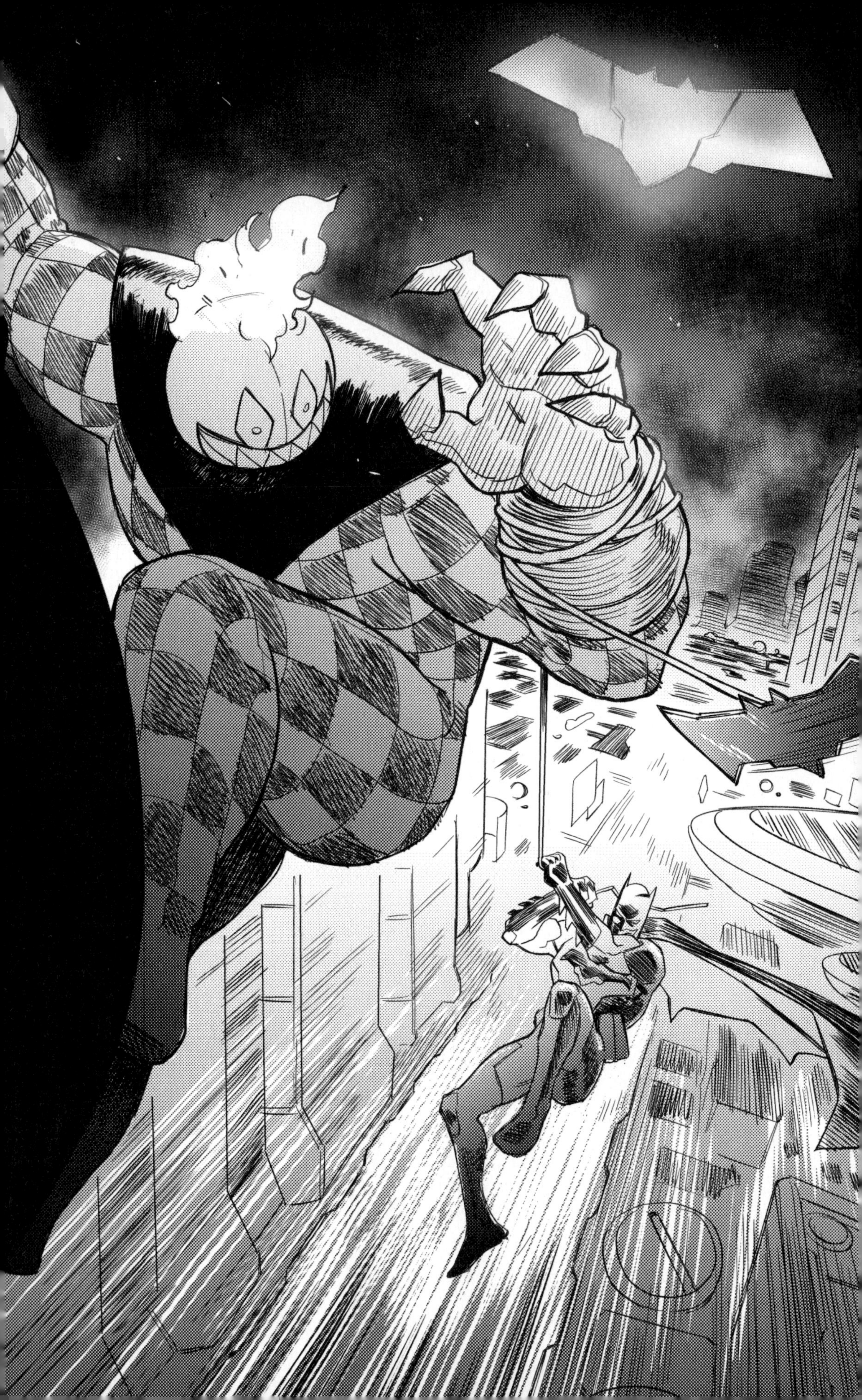

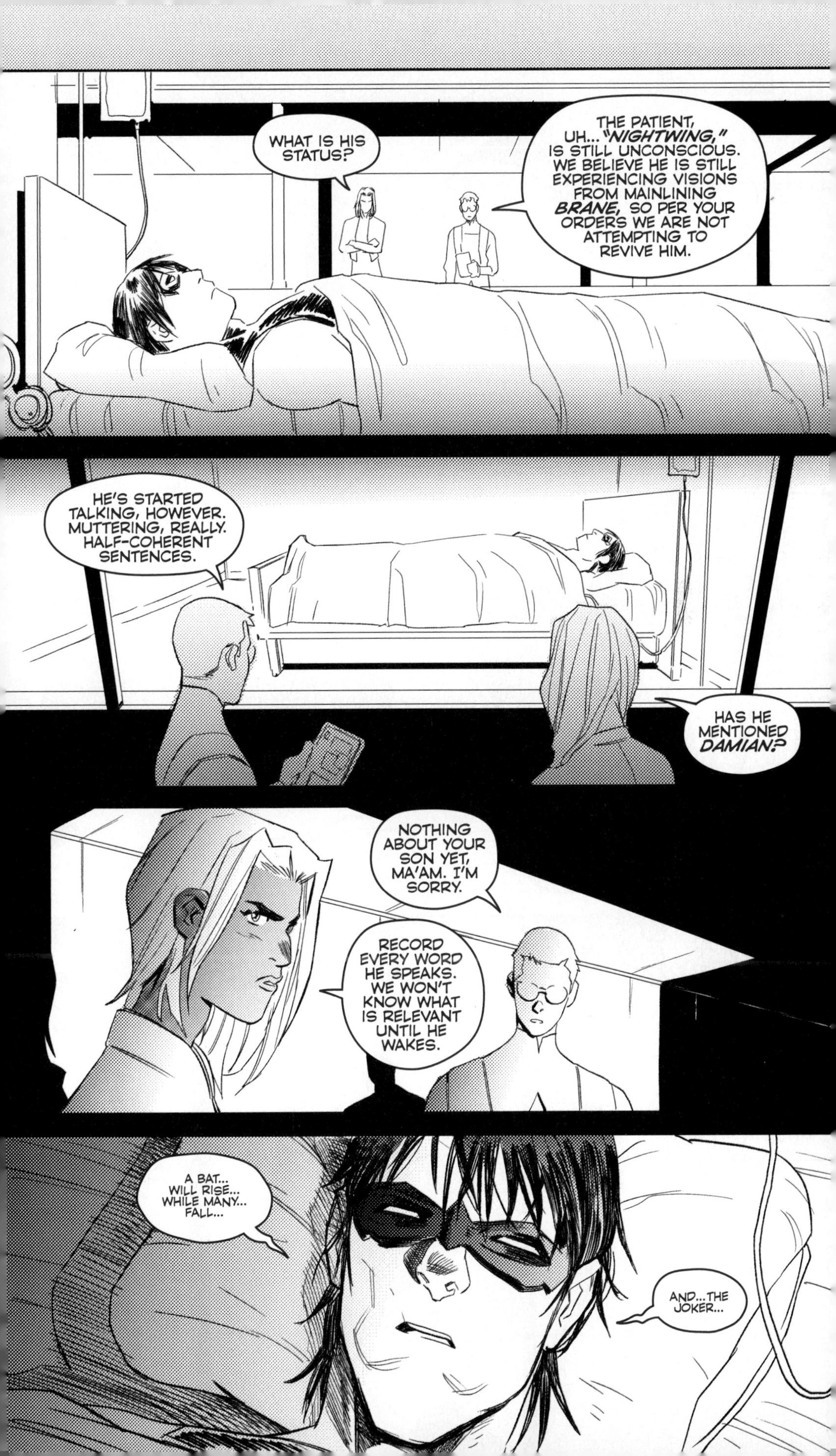
WHAT IS HIS STATUS?
THE PATIENT, UH... "NIGHTWING," IS STILL UNCONSCIOUS. WE BELIEVE HE IS STILL EXPERIENCING VISIONS FROM MAINLINING BRANE, SO PER YOUR ORDERS WE ARE NOT ATTEMPTING TO REVIVE HIM.
HE'S STARTED TALKING, HOWEVER. MUTTERING, REALLY. HALF-COHERENT SENTENCES.
HAS HE MENTIONED DAMIAN?
NOTHING ABOUT YOUR SON YET, MA'AM. I'M SORRY.
RECORD EVERY WORD HE SPEAKS. WE WON'T KNOW WHAT IS RELEVANT UNTIL HE WAKES.
A BAT... WILL RISE... WHILE MANY... FALL...
AND...THE JOKER...

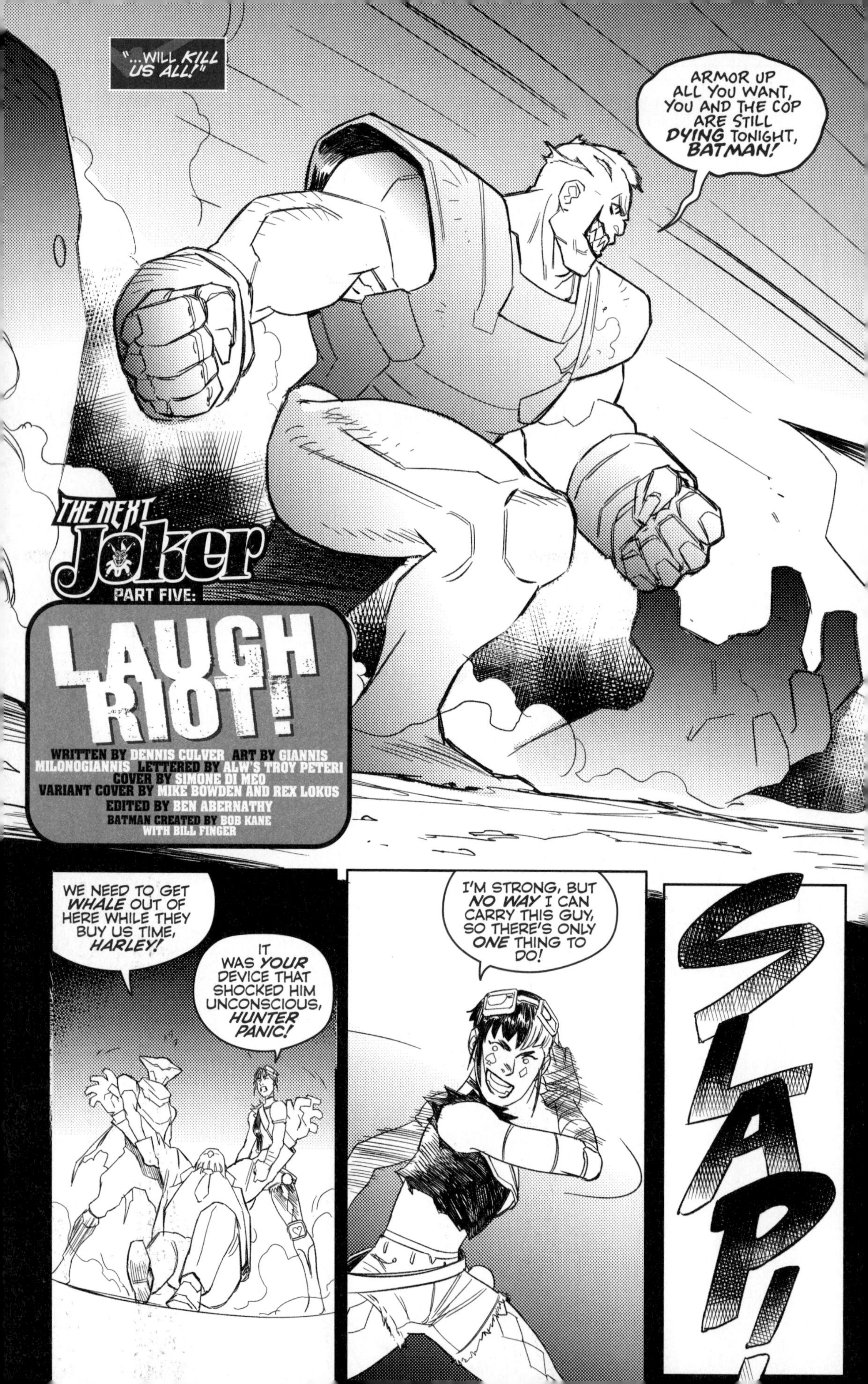
"...WILL KILL US ALL!"
ARMOR UP ALL YOU WANT, YOU AND THE COP ARE STILL DYING TONIGHT, BATMAN!
THE NEXT JOKER
PART FIVE:
LAUGH RIOT!
WRITTEN BY DENNIS CULVER ART BY GIANNIS MILONOGIANNIS LETTERED BY ALW'S TROY PETERI
COVER BY SIMONE DI MEO
VARIANT COVER BY MIKE BOWDEN AND REX LOKUS
EDITED BY BEN ABERNATHY
BATMAN CREATED BY BOB KANE WITH BILL FINGER
WE NEED TO GET WHALE OUT OF HERE WHILE THEY BUY US TIME, HARLEY!
IT WAS YOUR DEVICE THAT SHOCKED HIM UNCONSCIOUS, HUNTER PANIC!
I'M STRONG, BUT NO WAY I CAN CARRY THIS GUY, SO THERE'S ONLY ONE THING TO DO!
SLAP!

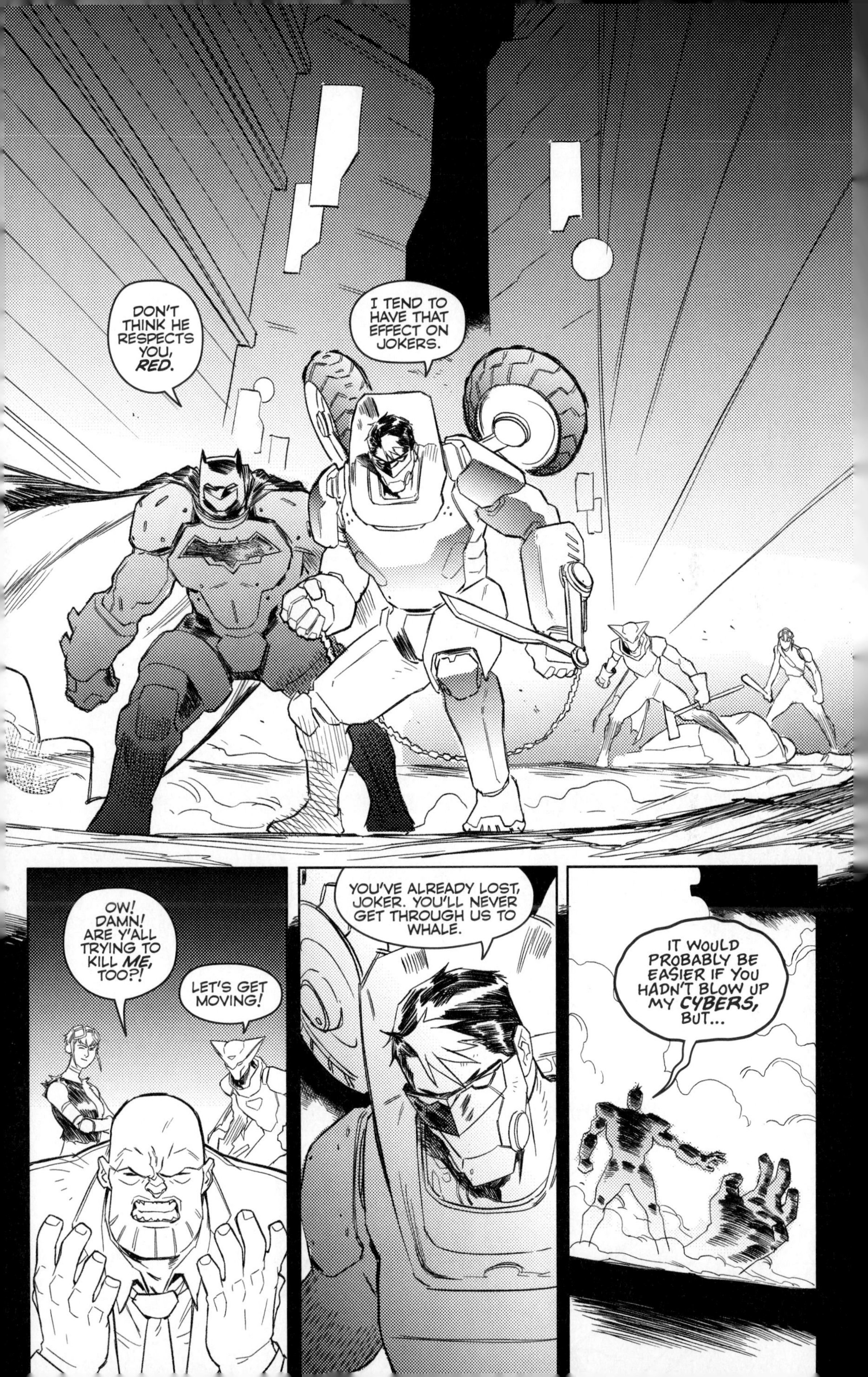
DON'T THINK HE RESPECTS YOU, RED.
I TEND TO HAVE THAT EFFECT ON JOKERS.
OW! DAMN! ARE Y'ALL TRYING TO KILL ME, TOO?!
LET'S GET MOVING!
YOU'VE ALREADY LOST, JOKER. YOU'LL NEVER GET THROUGH US TO WHALE.
IT WOULD PROBABLY BE EASIER IF YOU HADN'T BLOW UP MY CYBERS, BUT...

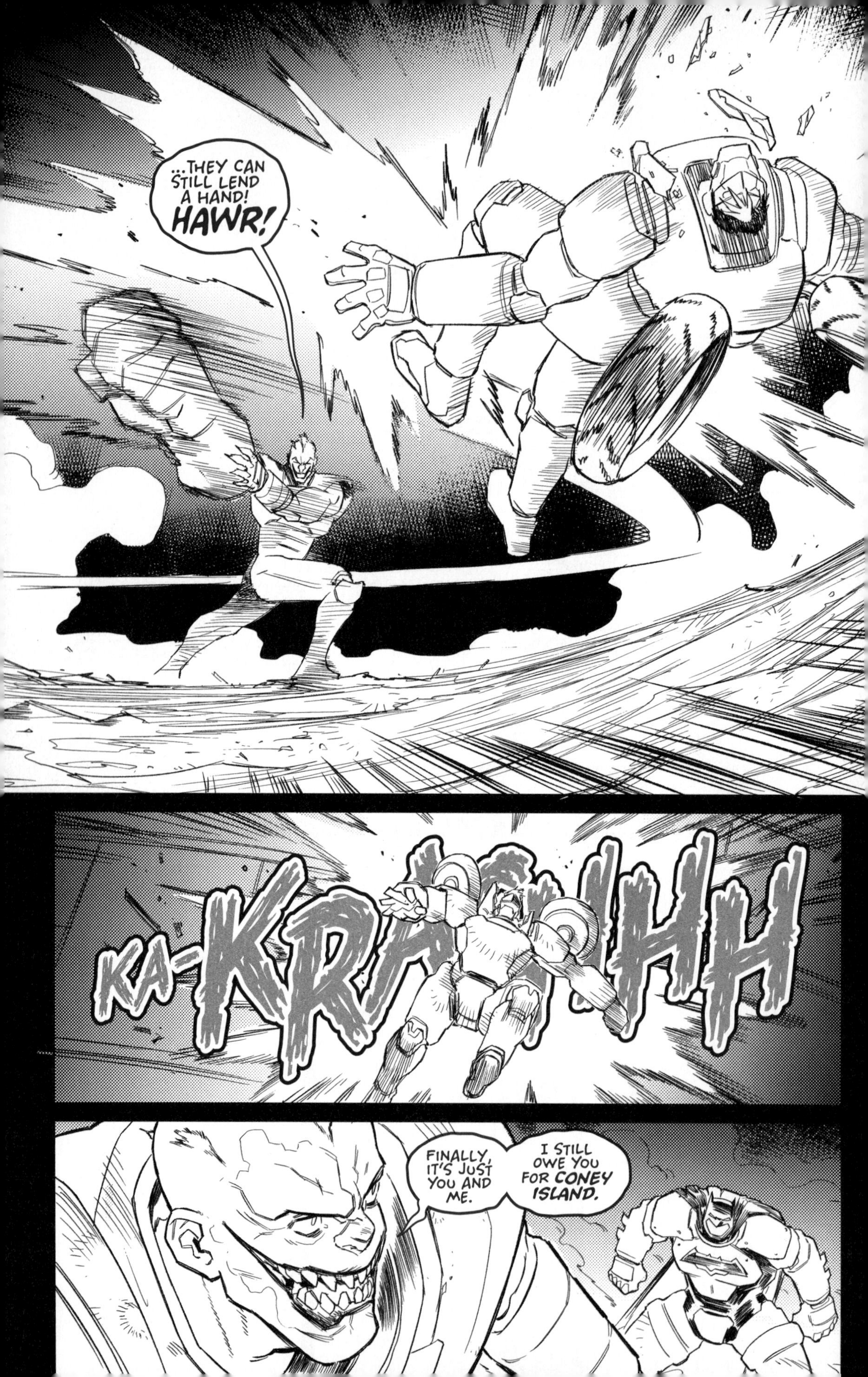
...THEY CAN STILL LEND A HAND! HAWR!
KA-KR
HH
FINALLY, IT'S JUST YOU AND ME.
I STILL OWE YOU FOR CONEY ISLAND.

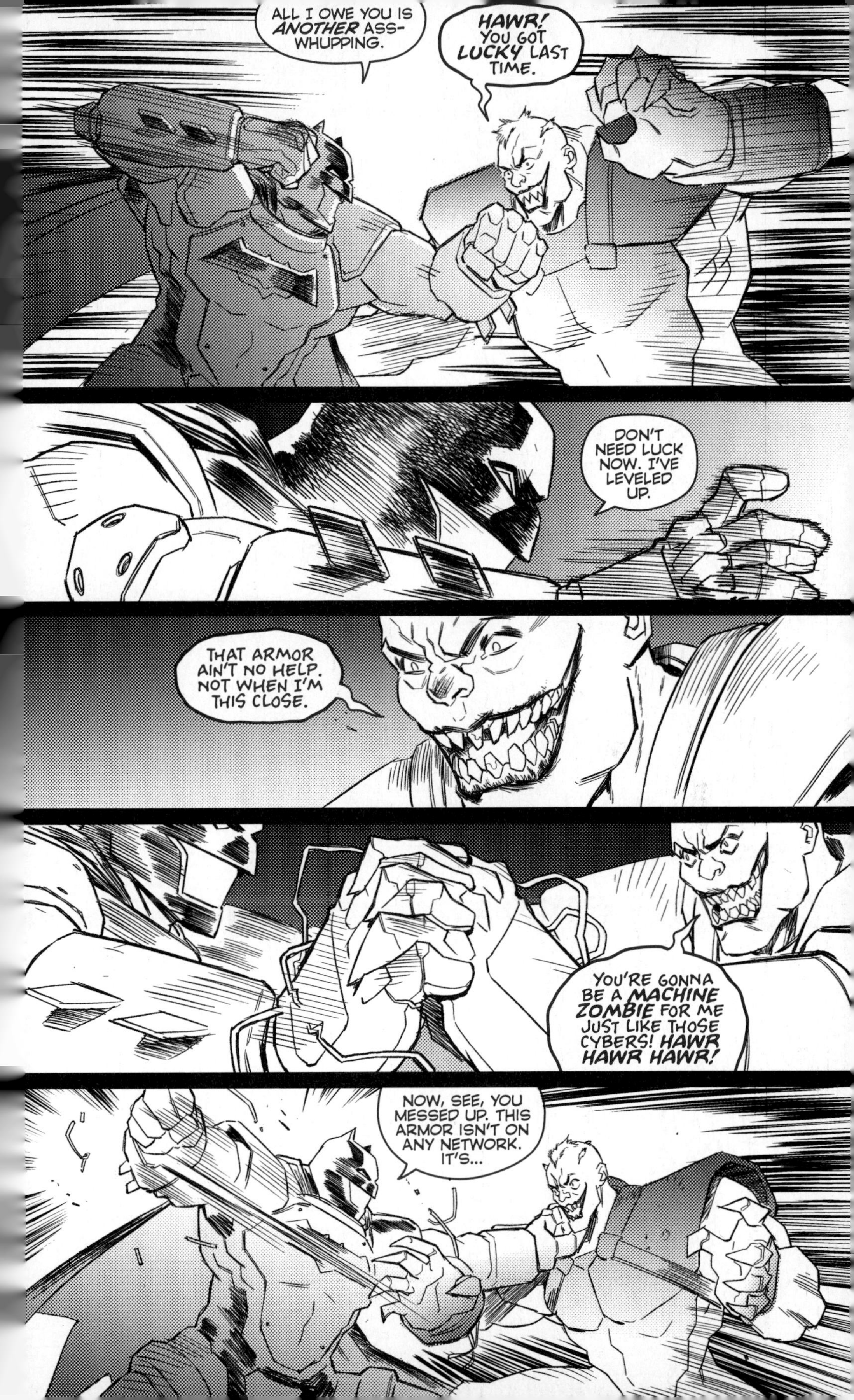
ALL I OWE YOU IS ANOTHER ASS-WHUPPING.
HAWR! YOU GOT LUCKY LAST TIME.
DON'T NEED LUCK NOW. I'VE LEVELED UP.
THAT ARMOR AIN'T NO HELP. NOT WHEN I'M THIS CLOSE.
YOU'RE GONNA BE A MACHINE ZOMBIE FOR ME JUST LIKE THOSE CYBERS! HAWR HAWR HAWR!
NOW, SEE, YOU MESSED UP. THIS ARMOR ISN'T ON ANY NETWORK. IT'S...

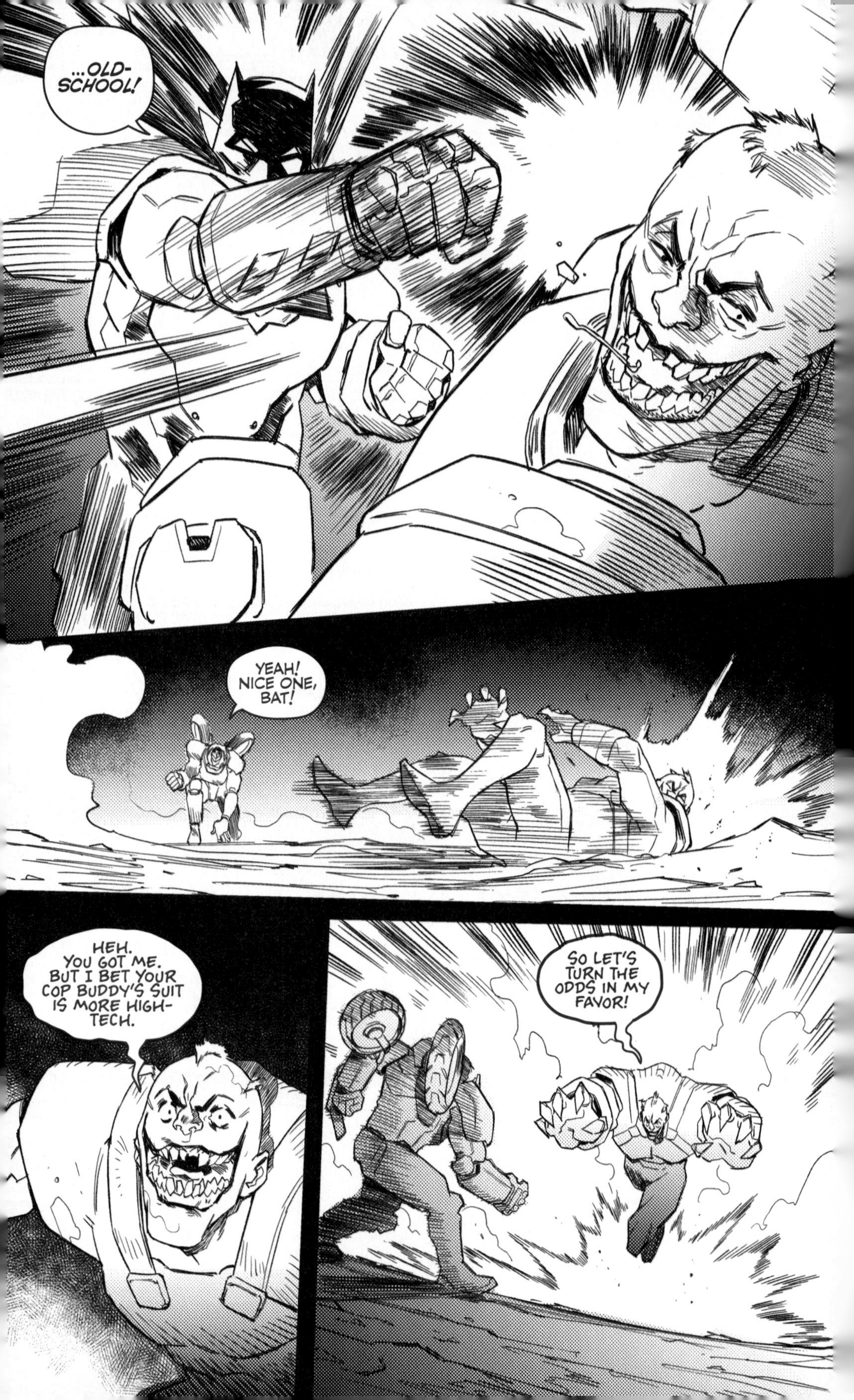
...OLD-SCHOOL!
YEAH! NICE ONE, BAT!
HEH. YOU GOT ME. BUT I BET YOUR COP BUDDY'S SUIT IS MORE HIGH-TECH.
SO LET'S TURN THE ODDS IN MY FAVOR!

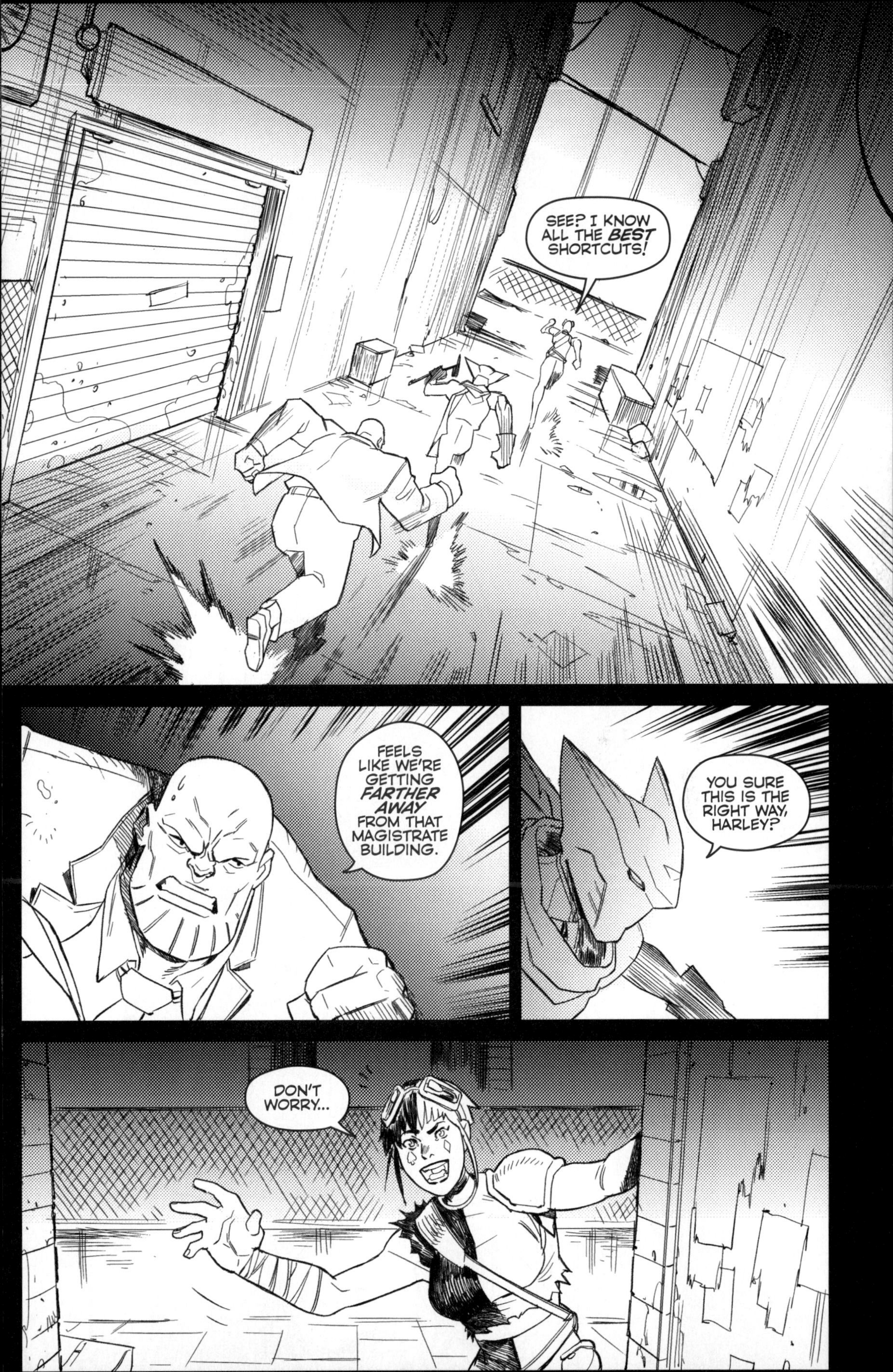
SEE? I KNOW ALL THE BEST SHORTCUTS!
FEELS LIKE WE'RE GETTING FARTHER AWAY FROM THAT MAGISTRATE BUILDING.
YOU SURE THIS IS THE RIGHT WAY, HARLEY?
DON'T WORRY...

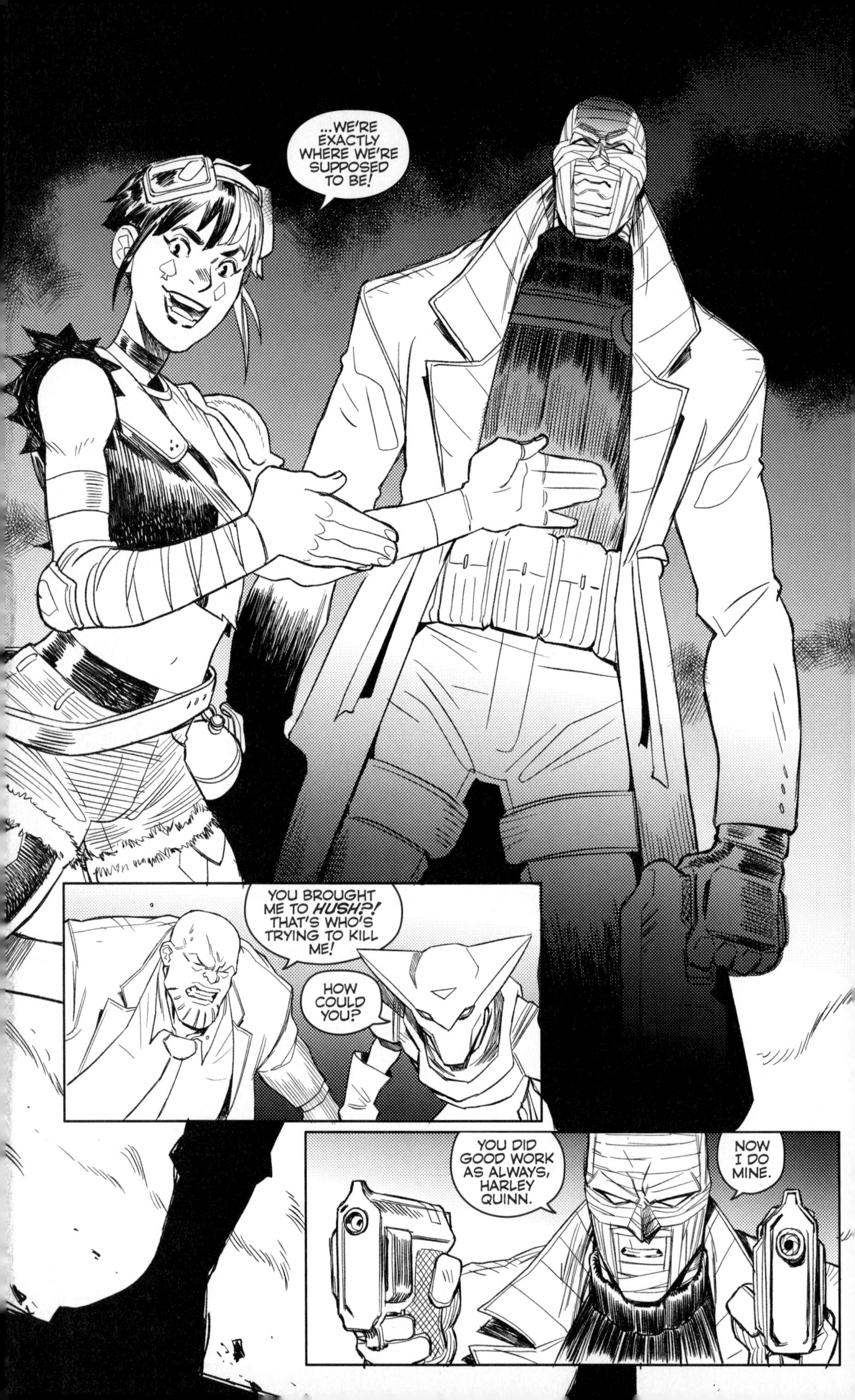
...WE'RE EXACTLY WHERE WE'RE SUPPOSED TO BE!
YOU BROUGHT ME TO HUSH?! THAT'S WHO'S TRYING TO KILL ME!
HOW COULD YOU?
YOU DID GOOD WORK AS ALWAYS, HARLEY QUINN.
NOW I DO MINE.

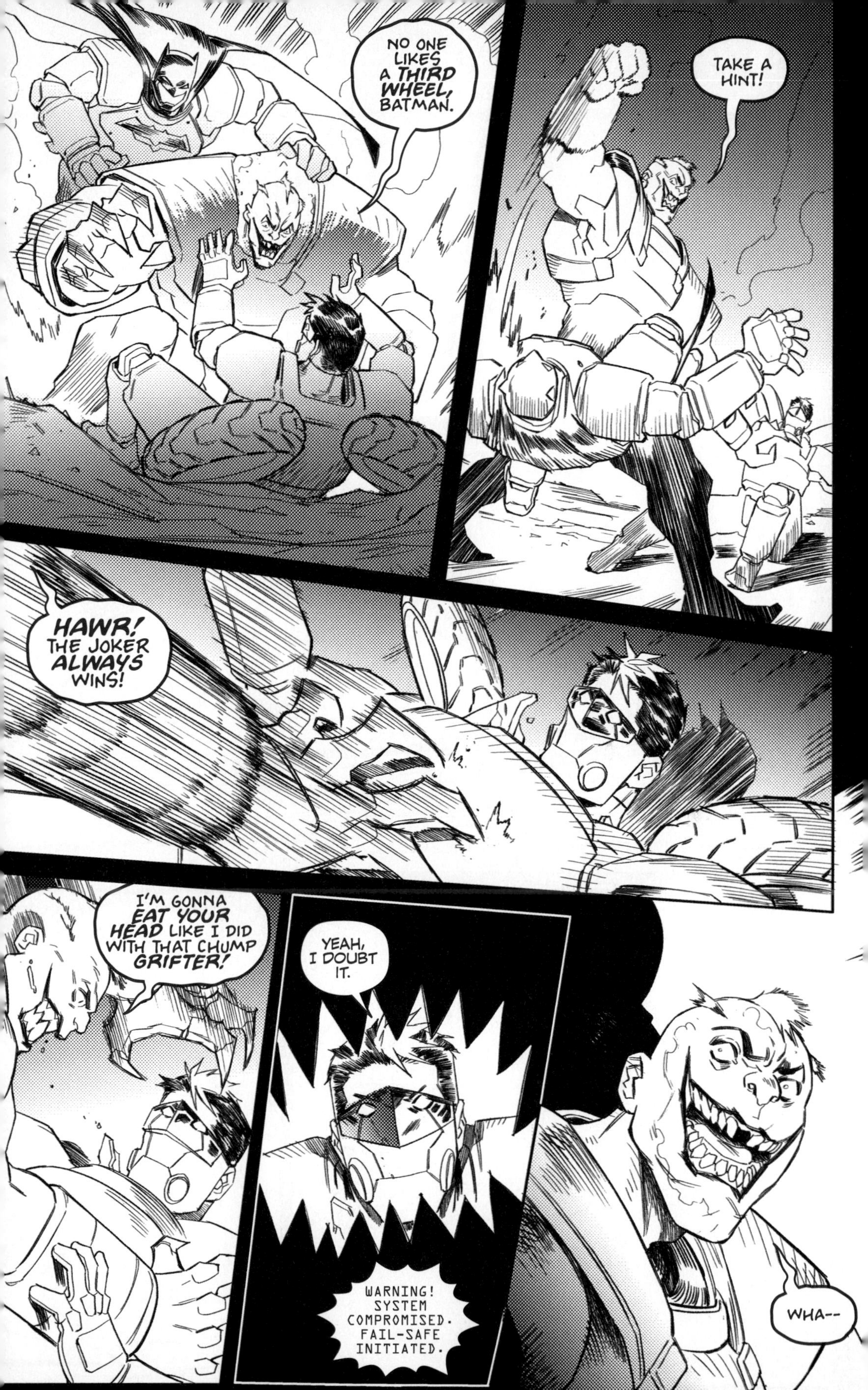
NO ONE LIKES A THIRD WHEEL, BATMAN.
TAKE A HINT!
HAWR! THE JOKER ALWAYS WINS!
I'M GONNA EAT YOUR HEAD LIKE I DID WITH THAT CHUMP GRIFTER!
YEAH, I DOUBT IT.
WARNING! SYSTEM COMPROMISED. FAIL-SAFE INITIATED.
WHA--

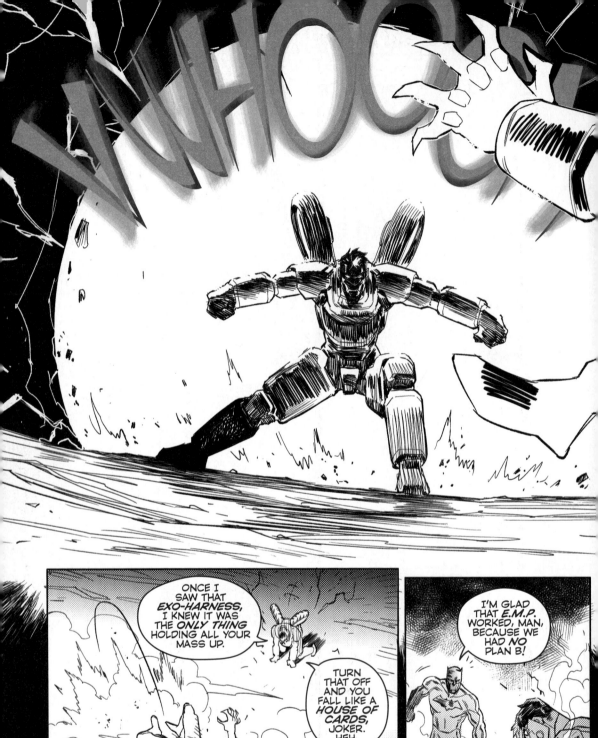

VWHOOSH!

ONCE I SAW THAT *EXO-HARNESS*, I KNEW IT WAS THE *ONLY THING* HOLDING ALL YOUR MASS UP.

TURN THAT OFF AND YOU FALL LIKE A *HOUSE OF CARDS*, JOKER. HEH.

THMP

I'M GLAD THAT *E.M.P.* WORKED, MAN, BECAUSE WE HAD *NO* PLAN B!

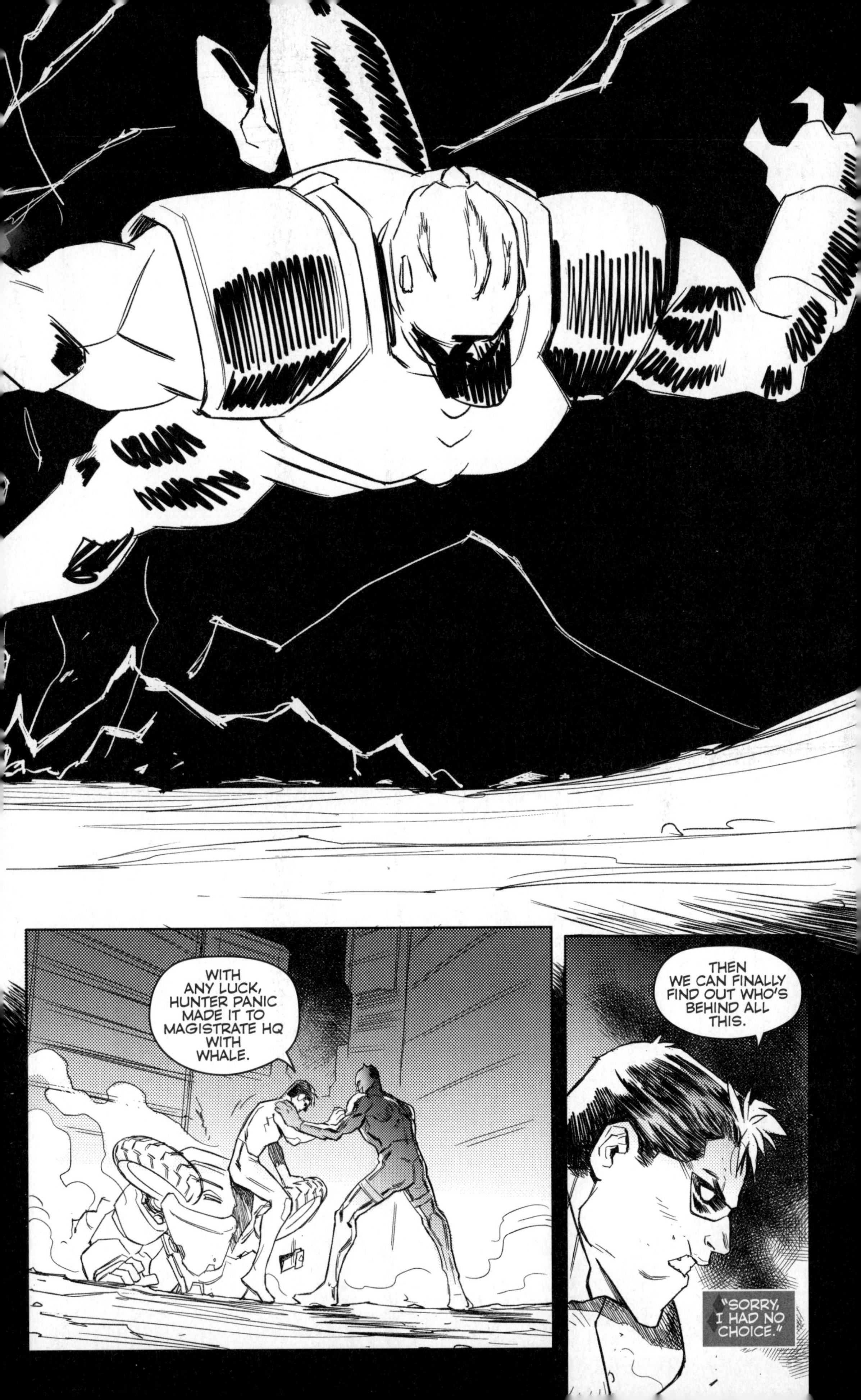
WITH ANY LUCK, HUNTER PANIC MADE IT TO MAGISTRATE HQ WITH WHALE.
THEN WE CAN FINALLY FIND OUT WHO'S BEHIND ALL THIS.
"SORRY, I HAD NO CHOICE."

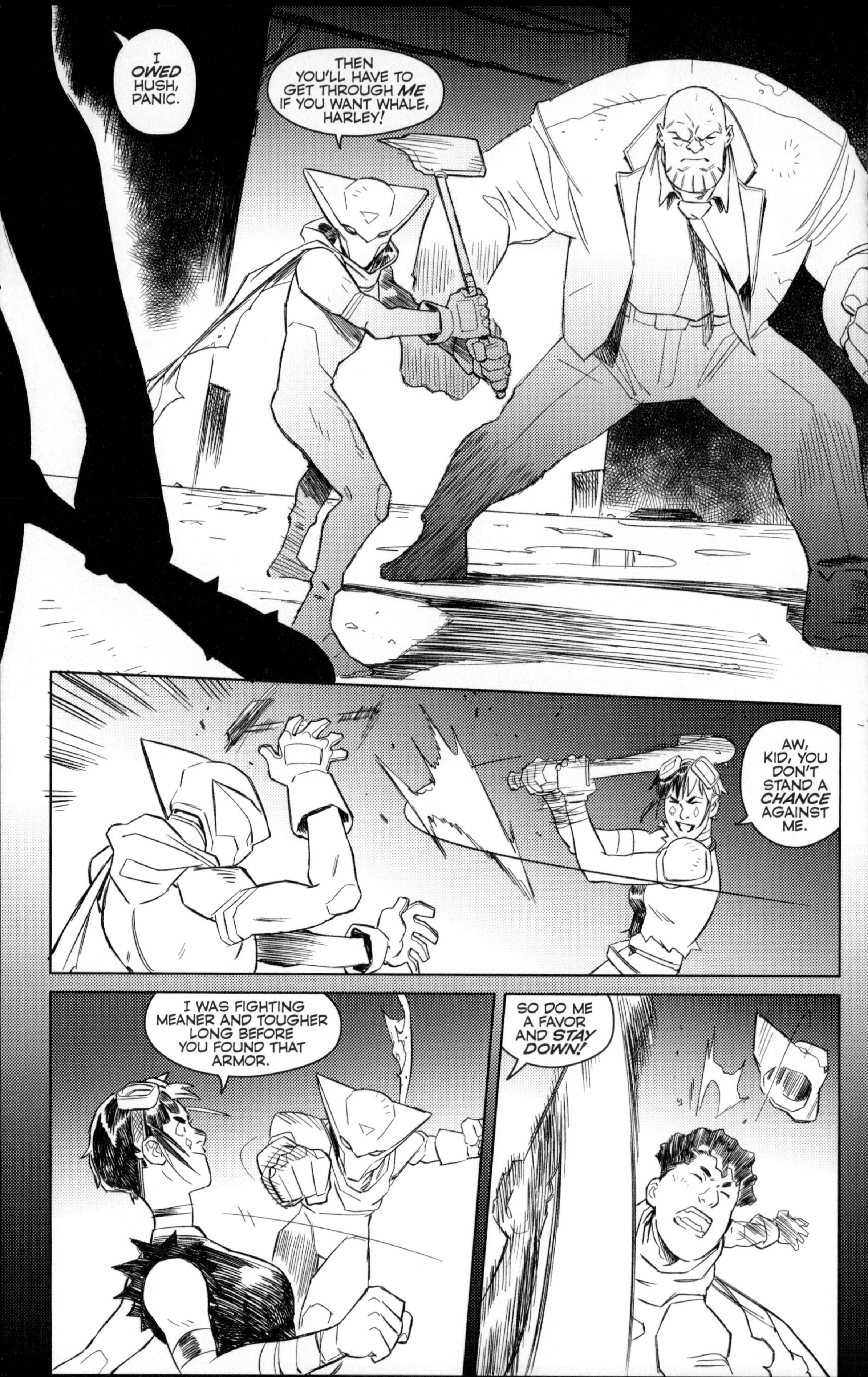
I OWED HUSH, PANIC.
THEN YOU'LL HAVE TO GET THROUGH ME IF YOU WANT WHALE, HARLEY!
AW, KID, YOU DON'T STAND A CHANCE AGAINST ME.
I WAS FIGHTING MEANER AND TOUGHER LONG BEFORE YOU FOUND THAT ARMOR.
SO DO ME A FAVOR AND STAY DOWN!

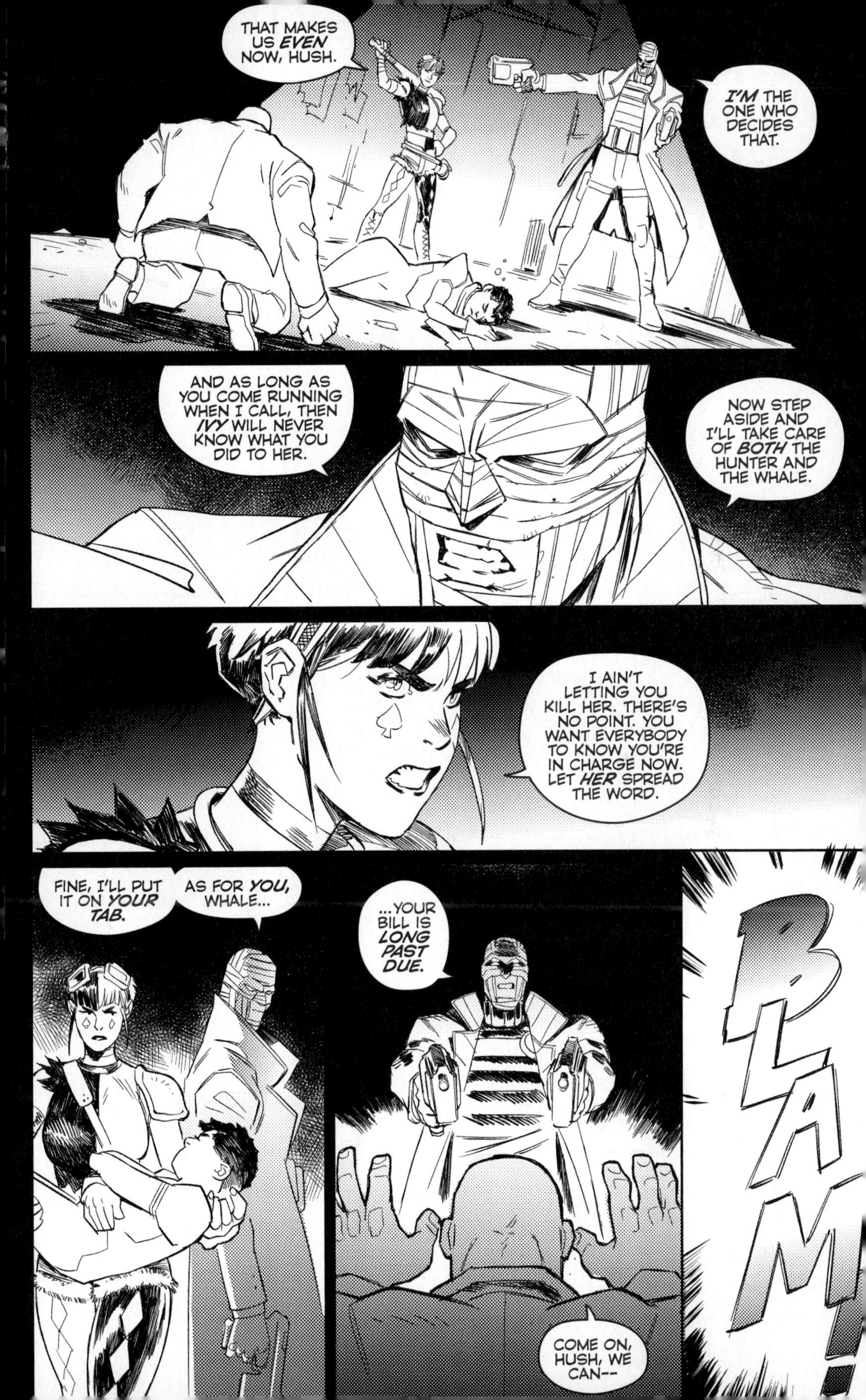
THAT MAKES US EVEN NOW, HUSH.
I'M THE ONE WHO DECIDES THAT.
AND AS LONG AS YOU COME RUNNING WHEN I CALL, THEN IVY WILL NEVER KNOW WHAT YOU DID TO HER.
NOW STEP ASIDE AND I'LL TAKE CARE OF BOTH THE HUNTER AND THE WHALE.
I AIN'T LETTING YOU KILL HER. THERE'S NO POINT. YOU WANT EVERYBODY TO KNOW YOU'RE IN CHARGE NOW. LET HER SPREAD THE WORD.
FINE, I'LL PUT IT ON YOUR TAB.
AS FOR YOU, WHALE...
...YOUR BILL IS LONG PAST DUE.
COME ON, HUSH, WE CAN--
BLAM!

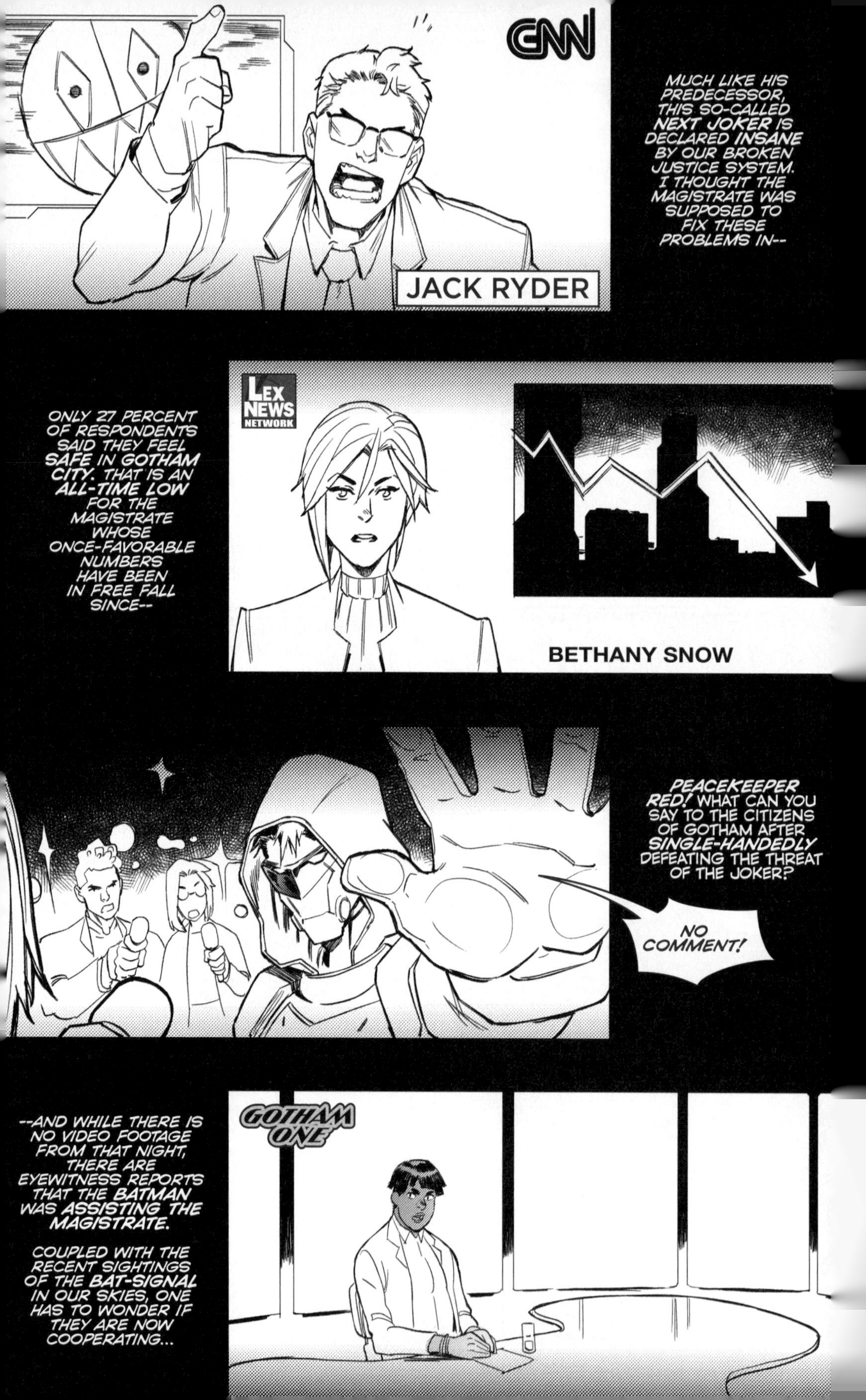
CNN
MUCH LIKE HIS PREDECESSOR, THIS SO-CALLED NEXT JOKER IS DECLARED INSANE BY OUR BROKEN JUSTICE SYSTEM. I THOUGHT THE MAGISTRATE WAS SUPPOSED TO FIX THESE PROBLEMS IN--
JACK RYDER
LEX NEWS NETWORK
ONLY 27 PERCENT OF RESPONDENTS SAID THEY FEEL SAFE IN GOTHAM CITY. THAT IS AN ALL-TIME LOW FOR THE MAGISTRATE WHOSE ONCE-FAVORABLE NUMBERS HAVE BEEN IN FREE FALL SINCE--
BETHANY SNOW
PEACEKEEPER RED! WHAT CAN YOU SAY TO THE CITIZENS OF GOTHAM AFTER SINGLE-HANDEDLY DEFEATING THE THREAT OF THE JOKER?
NO COMMENT!
GOTHAM ONE
--AND WHILE THERE IS NO VIDEO FOOTAGE FROM THAT NIGHT, THERE ARE EYEWITNESS REPORTS THAT THE BATMAN WAS ASSISTING THE MAGISTRATE.
COUPLED WITH THE RECENT SIGHTINGS OF THE BAT-SIGNAL IN OUR SKIES, ONE HAS TO WONDER IF THEY ARE NOW COOPERATING...

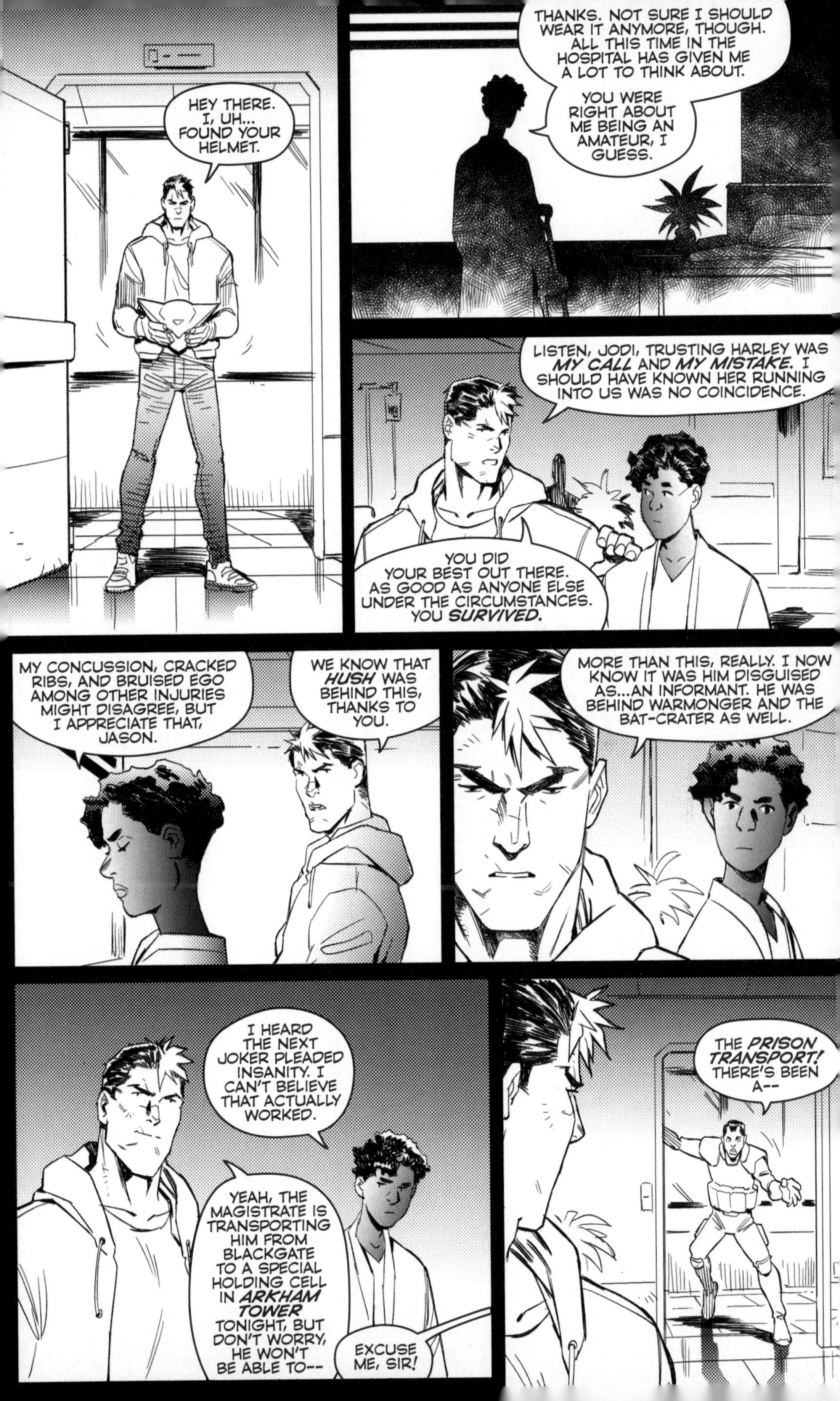
HEY THERE. I, UH... FOUND YOUR HELMET.
THANKS. NOT SURE I SHOULD WEAR IT ANYMORE, THOUGH. ALL THIS TIME IN THE HOSPITAL HAS GIVEN ME A LOT TO THINK ABOUT.
YOU WERE RIGHT ABOUT ME BEING AN AMATEUR, I GUESS.
LISTEN, JODI, TRUSTING HARLEY WAS MY CALL AND MY MISTAKE. I SHOULD HAVE KNOWN HER RUNNING INTO US WAS NO COINCIDENCE.
YOU DID YOUR BEST OUT THERE. AS GOOD AS ANYONE ELSE UNDER THE CIRCUMSTANCES. YOU SURVIVED.
MY CONCUSSION, CRACKED RIBS, AND BRUISED EGO AMONG OTHER INJURIES MIGHT DISAGREE, BUT I APPRECIATE THAT, JASON.
WE KNOW THAT HUSH WAS BEHIND THIS, THANKS TO YOU.
MORE THAN THIS, REALLY. I NOW KNOW IT WAS HIM DISGUISED AS...AN INFORMANT. HE WAS BEHIND WARMONGER AND THE BAT-CRATER AS WELL.
I HEARD THE NEXT JOKER PLEADED INSANITY. I CAN'T BELIEVE THAT ACTUALLY WORKED.
YEAH, THE MAGISTRATE IS TRANSPORTING HIM FROM BLACKGATE TO A SPECIAL HOLDING CELL IN ARKHAM TOWER TONIGHT, BUT DON'T WORRY, HE WON'T BE ABLE TO--
EXCUSE ME, SIR!
THE PRISON TRANSPORT! THERE'S BEEN A--

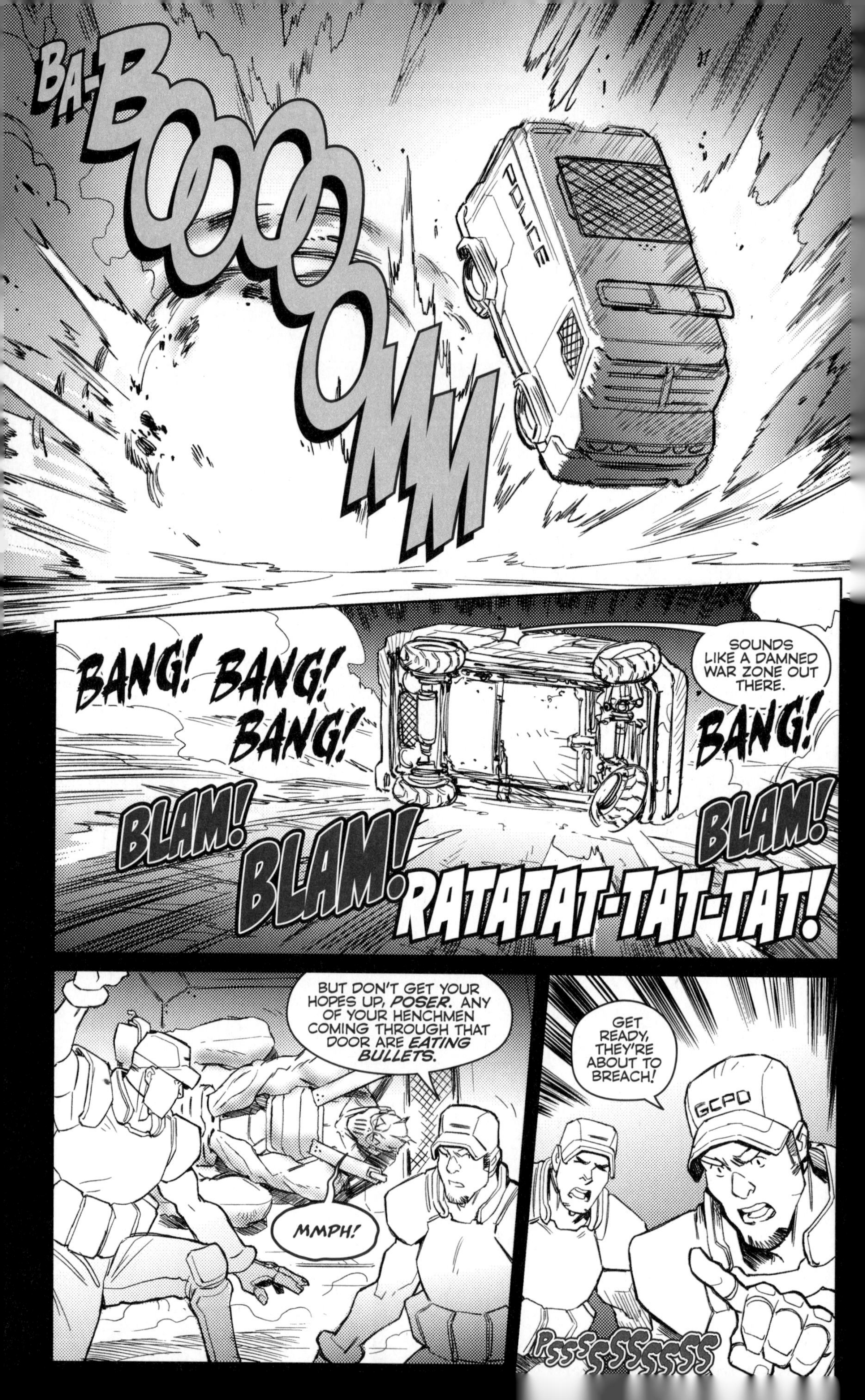
BA-BOOOOOOMM
BANG! BANG!
BANG!
SOUNDS LIKE A DAMNED WAR ZONE OUT THERE.
BANG!
BLAM!
BLAM!
BLAM!
RATATAT-TAT-TAT!
BUT DON'T GET YOUR HOPES UP, POSER. ANY OF YOUR HENCHMEN COMING THROUGH THAT DOOR ARE EATING BULLETS.
MMPH!
GET READY, THEY'RE ABOUT TO BREACH!
GCPD
PSSSSSSSSSS

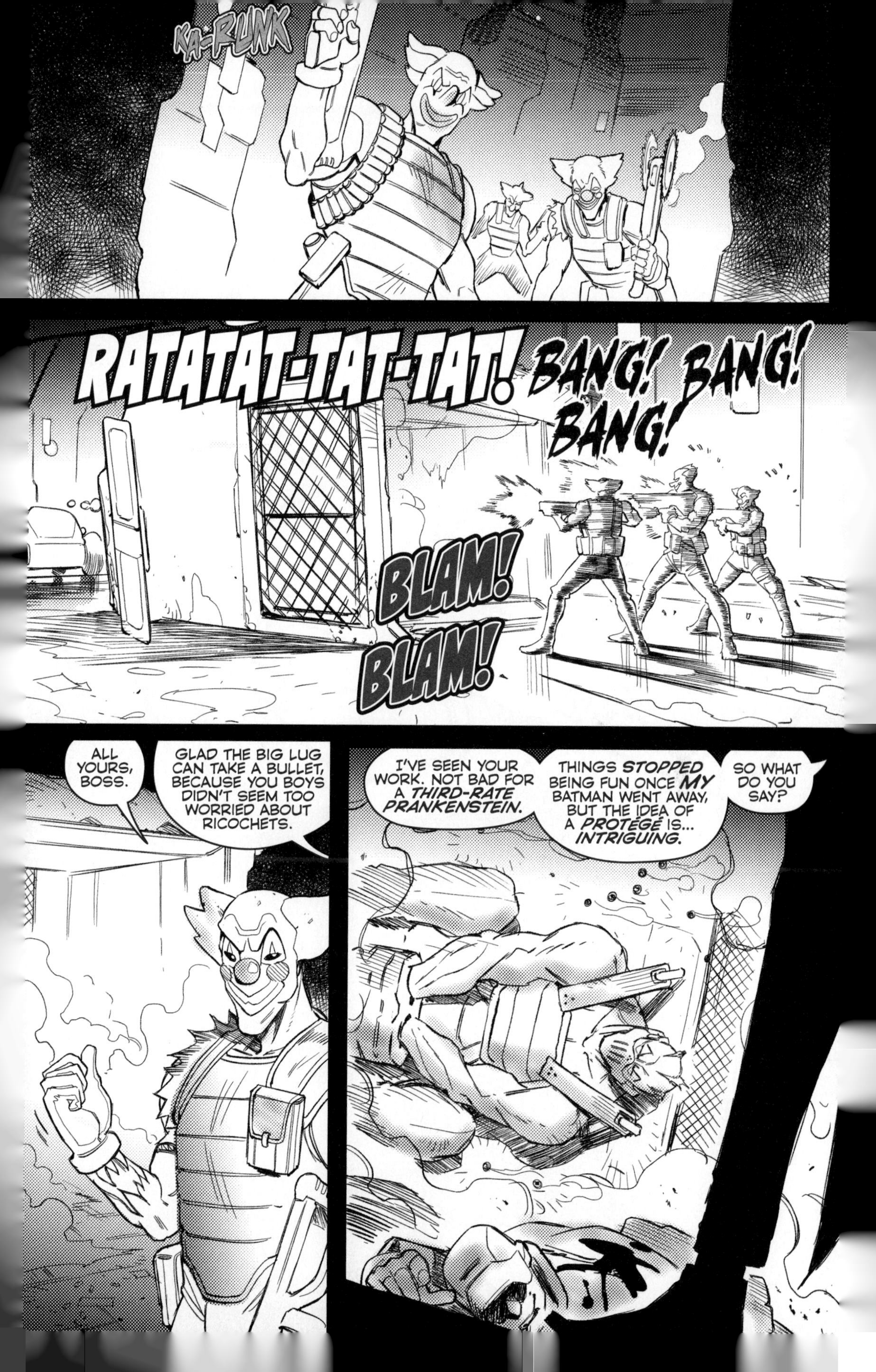
KA-RUNK
RATATAT-TAT-TAT!
BANG! BANG!
BANG!
BLAM!
BLAM!
ALL YOURS, BOSS.
GLAD THE BIG LUG CAN TAKE A BULLET, BECAUSE YOU BOYS DIDN'T SEEM TOO WORRIED ABOUT RICOCHETS.
I'VE SEEN YOUR WORK. NOT BAD FOR A THIRD-RATE PRANKENSTEIN.
THINGS STOPPED BEING FUN ONCE MY BATMAN WENT AWAY, BUT THE IDEA OF A PROTÉGÉ IS... INTRIGUING.
SO WHAT DO YOU SAY?

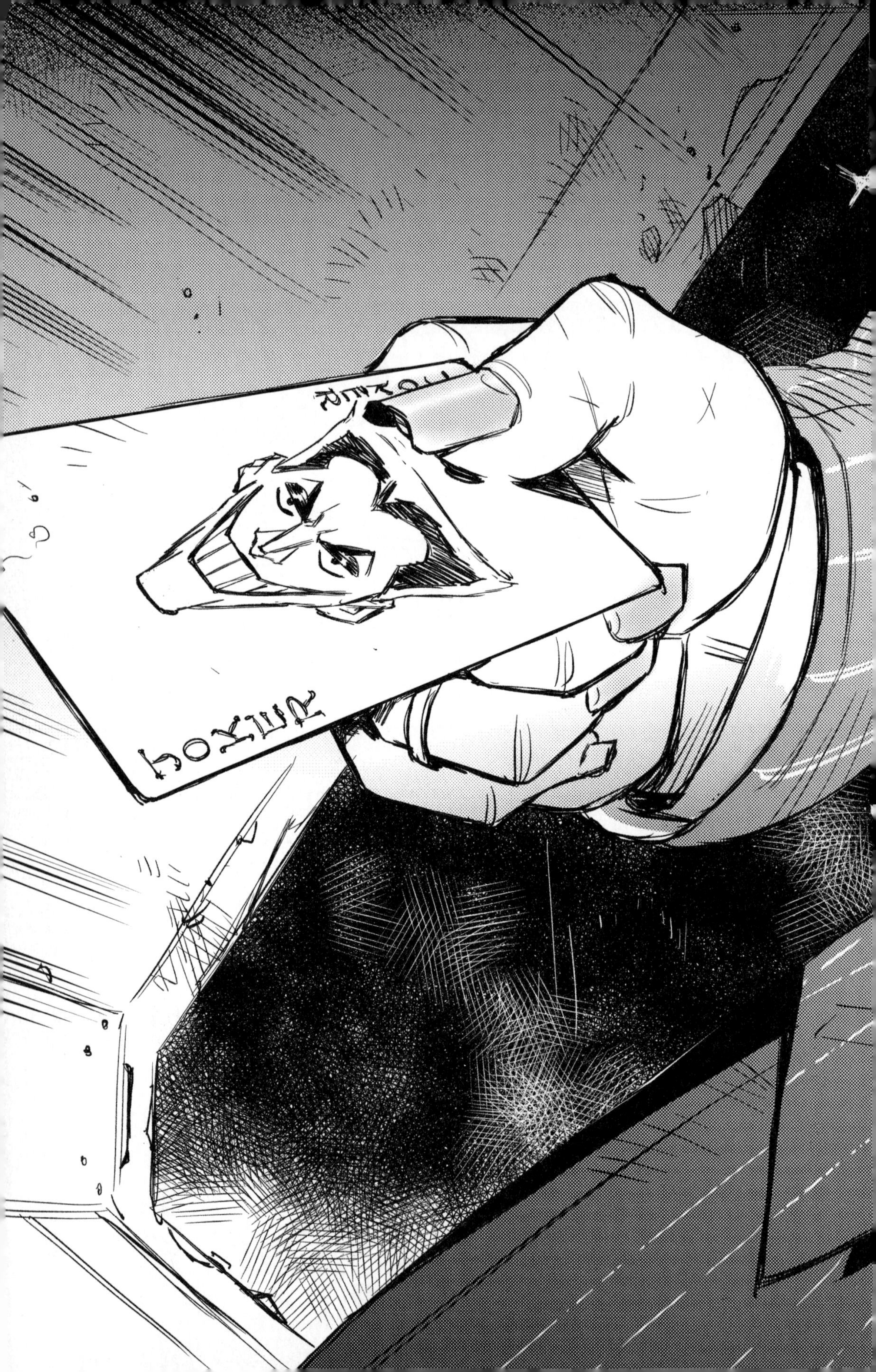
JOKER
JOKER

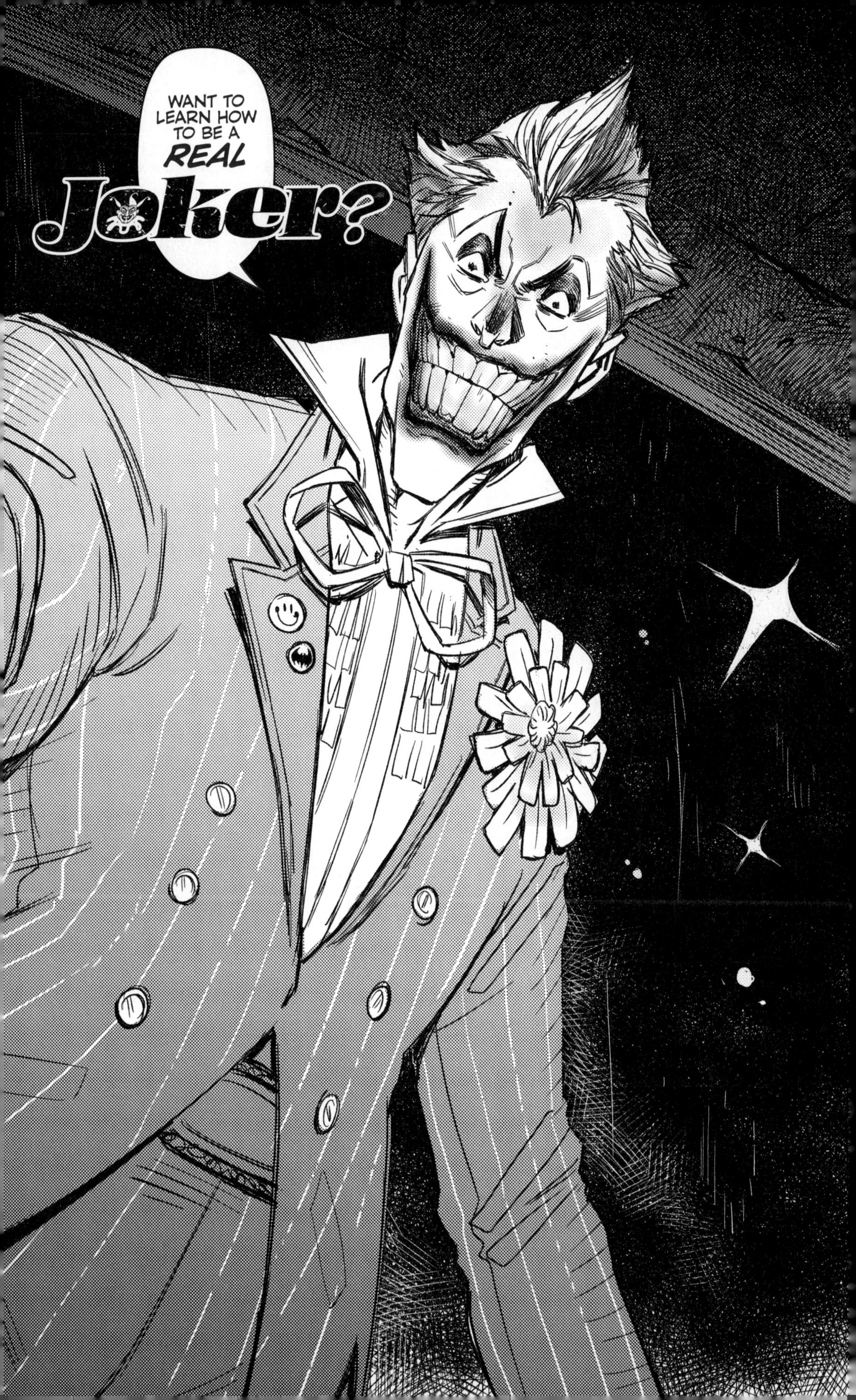
WANT TO LEARN HOW TO BE A REAL Joker?

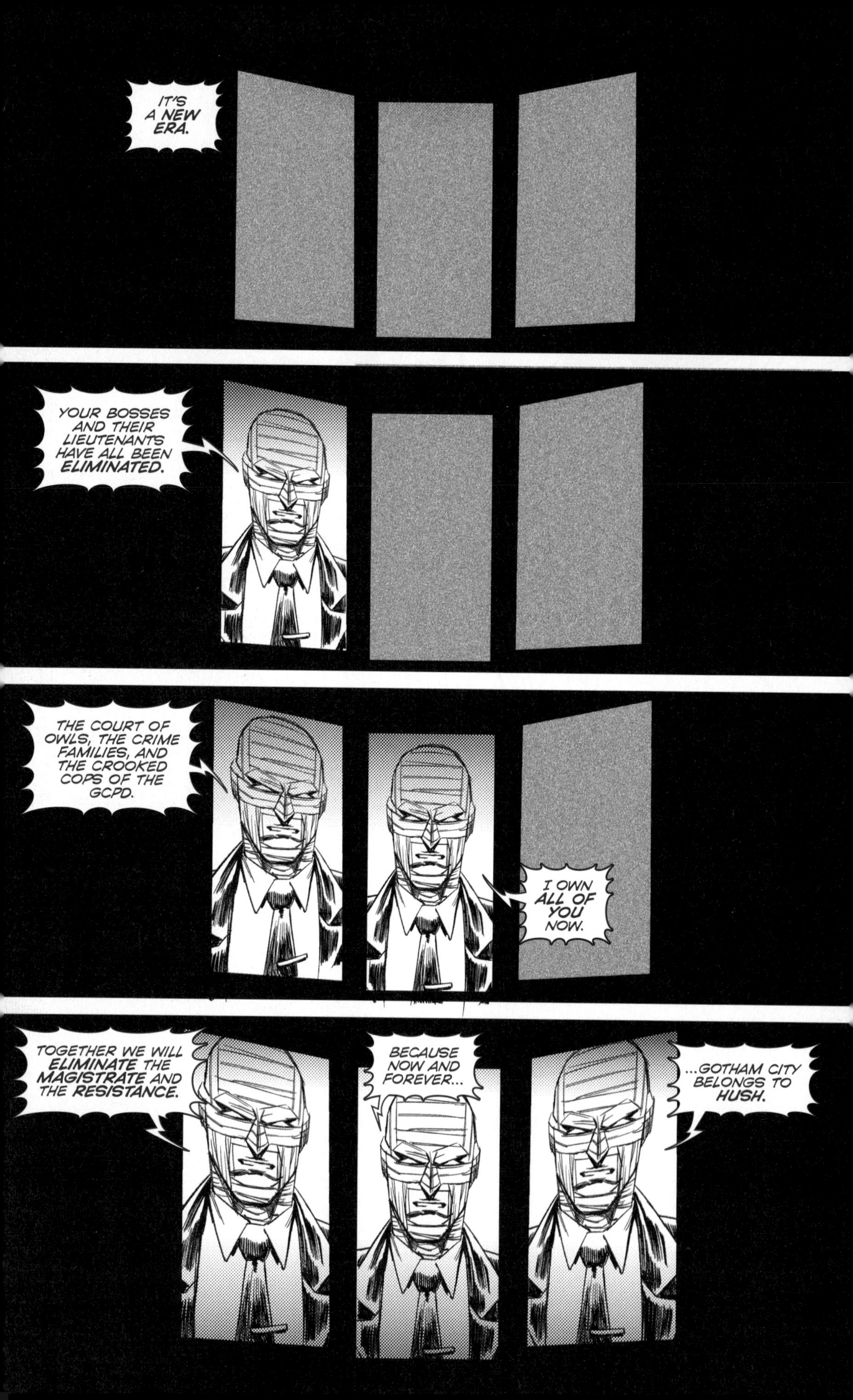
IT'S A NEW ERA.
YOUR BOSSES AND THEIR LIEUTENANTS HAVE ALL BEEN ELIMINATED.
THE COURT OF OWLS, THE CRIME FAMILIES, AND THE CROOKED COPS OF THE GCPD.
I OWN ALL OF YOU NOW.
TOGETHER WE WILL ELIMINATE THE MAGISTRATE AND THE RESISTANCE.
BECAUSE NOW AND FOREVER...
...GOTHAM CITY BELONGS TO HUSH.

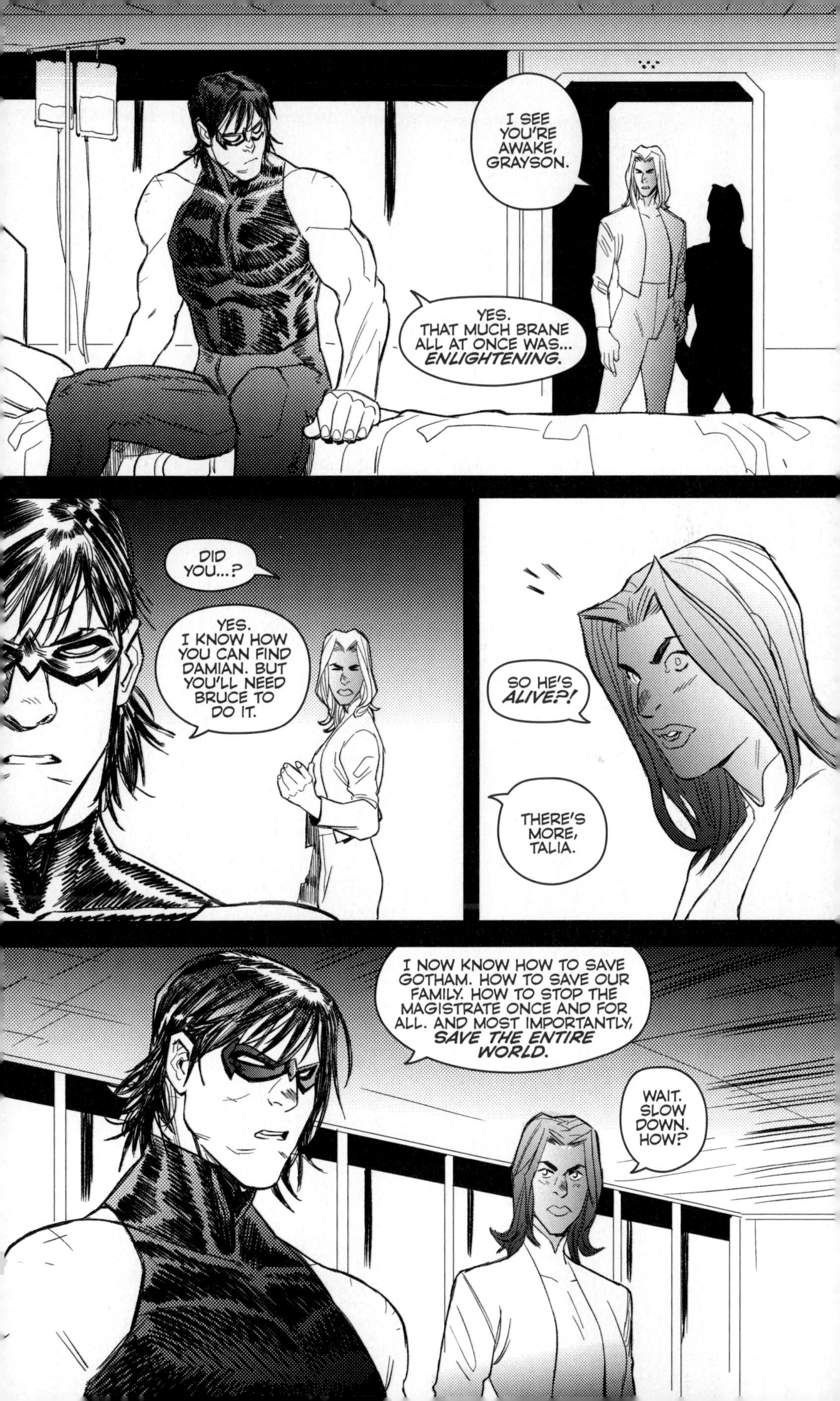
I SEE YOU'RE AWAKE, GRAYSON.
YES. THAT MUCH BRANE ALL AT ONCE WAS... *ENLIGHTENING*.
DID YOU...?
YES. I KNOW HOW YOU CAN FIND DAMIAN. BUT YOU'LL NEED BRUCE TO DO IT.
SO HE'S *ALIVE?!*
THERE'S MORE, TALIA.
I NOW KNOW HOW TO SAVE GOTHAM. HOW TO SAVE OUR FAMILY. HOW TO STOP THE MAGISTRATE ONCE AND FOR ALL. AND MOST IMPORTANTLY, *SAVE THE ENTIRE WORLD*.
WAIT. SLOW DOWN. HOW?

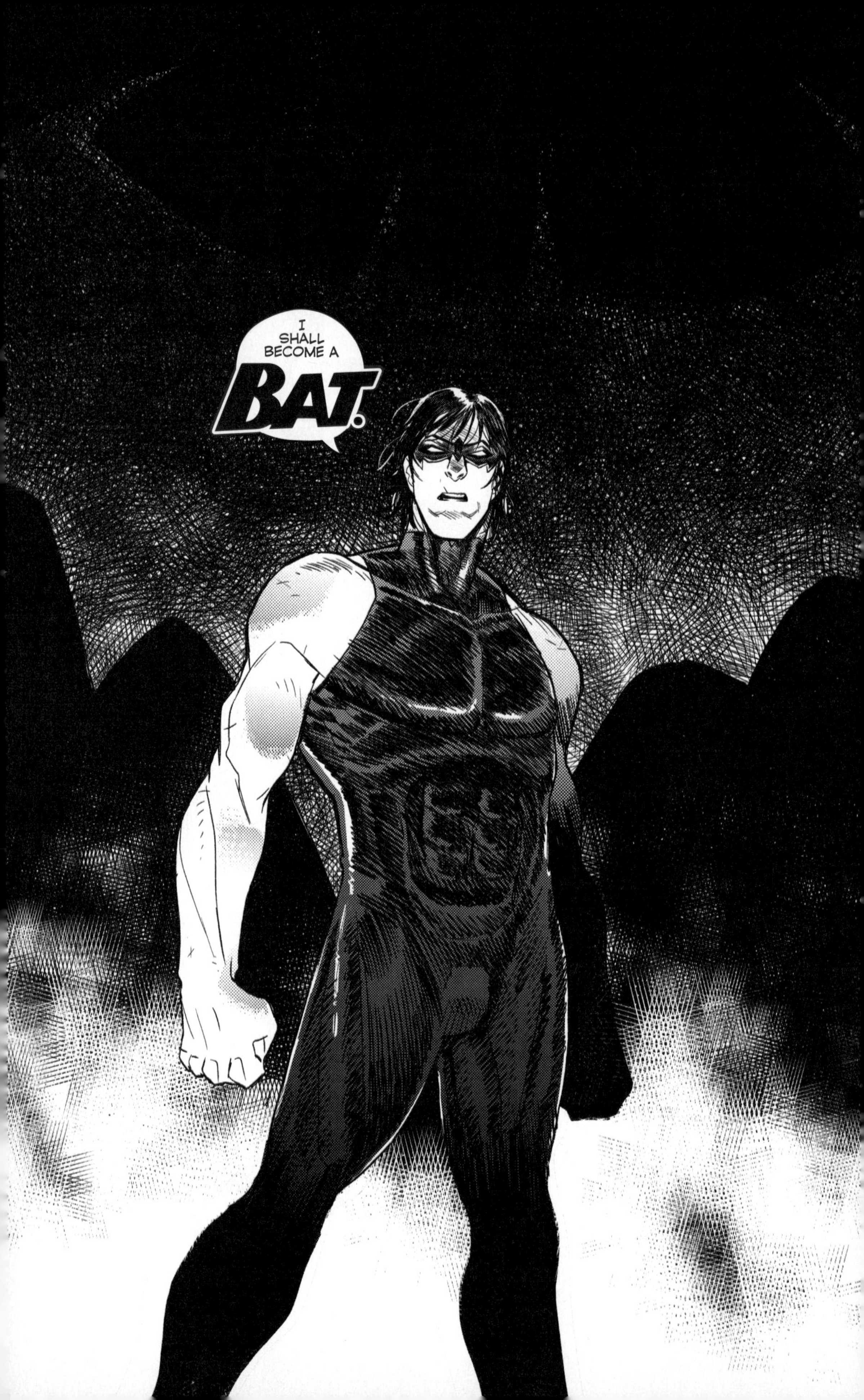
I SHALL BECOME A BAT.

Batman Urban Legends #7
cover art FRANCESCO MATTINA

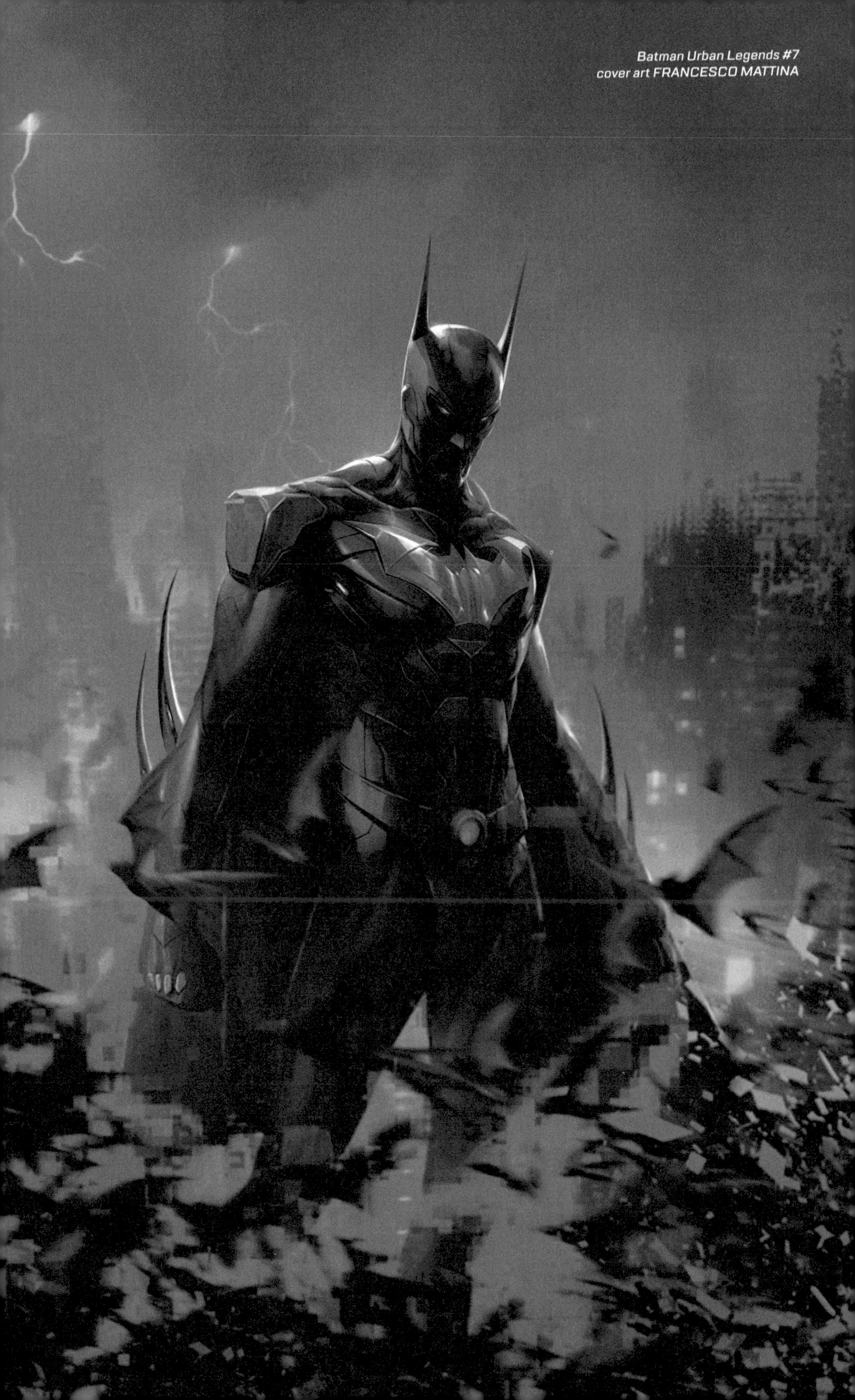

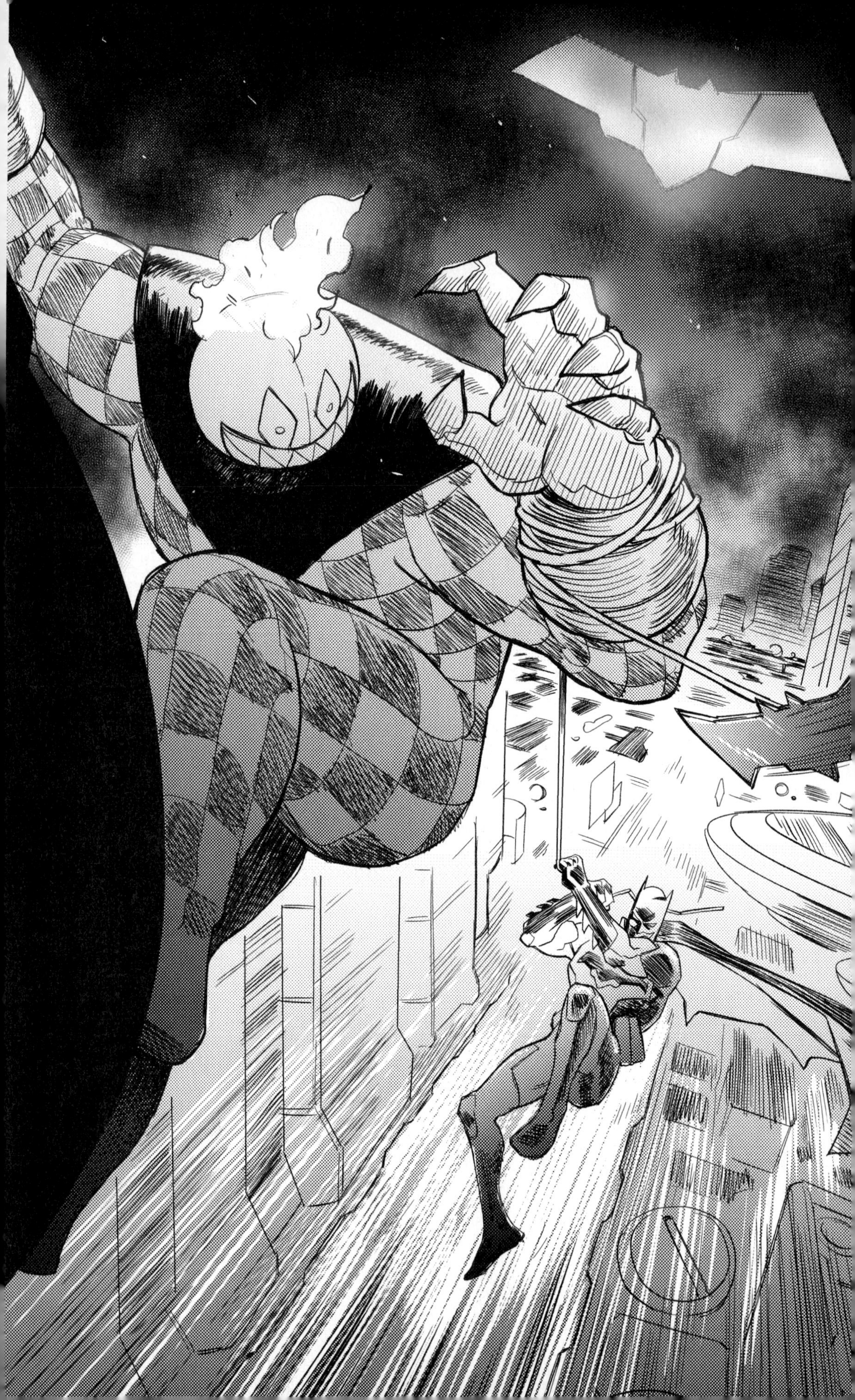

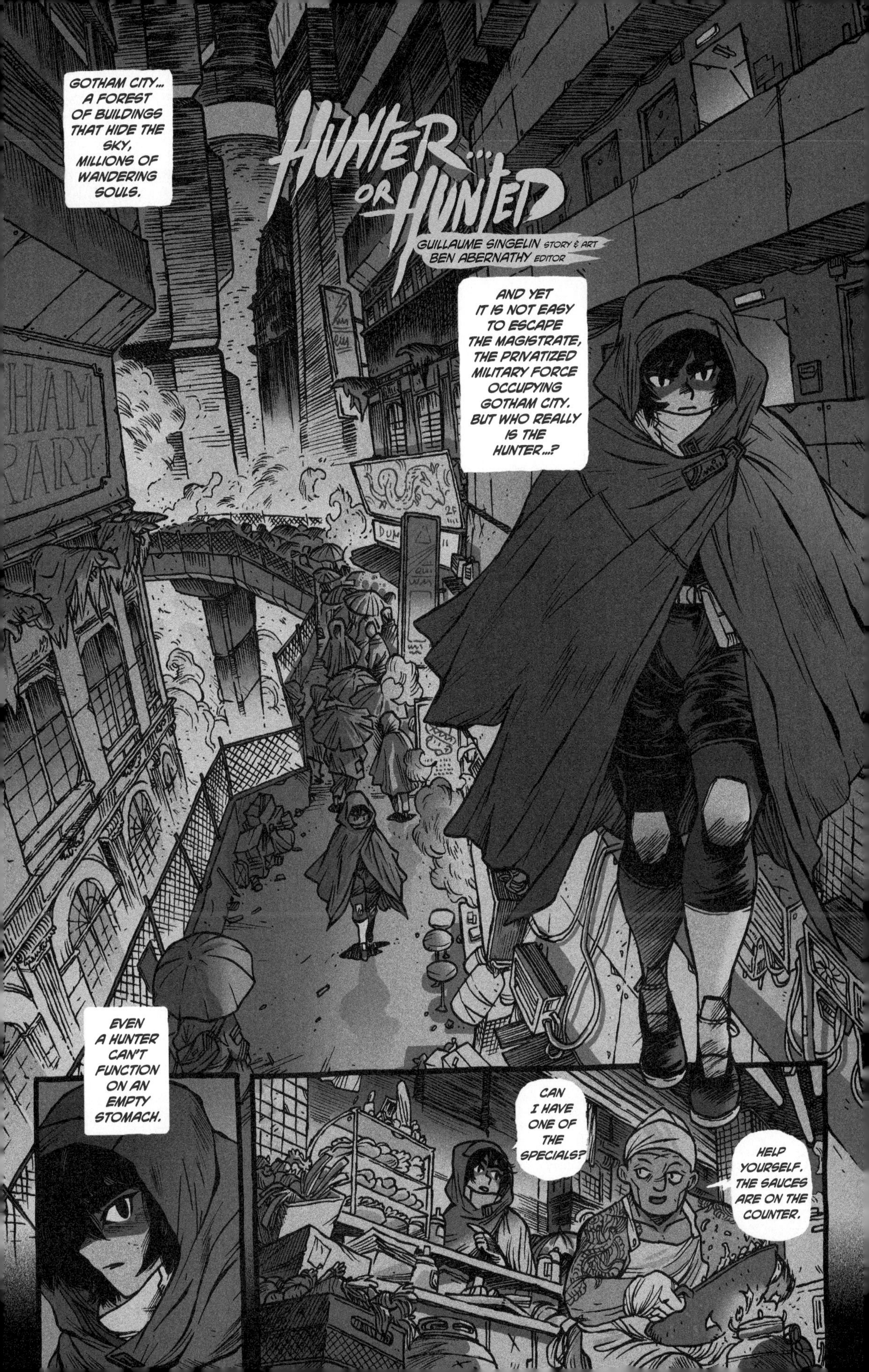
GOTHAM CITY... A FOREST OF BUILDINGS THAT HIDE THE SKY, MILLIONS OF WANDERING SOULS.
HUNTER... OR HUNTED
GUILLAUME SINGELIN STORY & ART
BEN ABERNATHY EDITOR
AND YET IT IS NOT EASY TO ESCAPE THE MAGISTRATE, THE PRIVATIZED MILITARY FORCE OCCUPYING GOTHAM CITY. BUT WHO REALLY IS THE HUNTER...?
EVEN A HUNTER CAN'T FUNCTION ON AN EMPTY STOMACH.
CAN I HAVE ONE OF THE SPECIALS?
HELP YOURSELF. THE SAUCES ARE ON THE COUNTER.

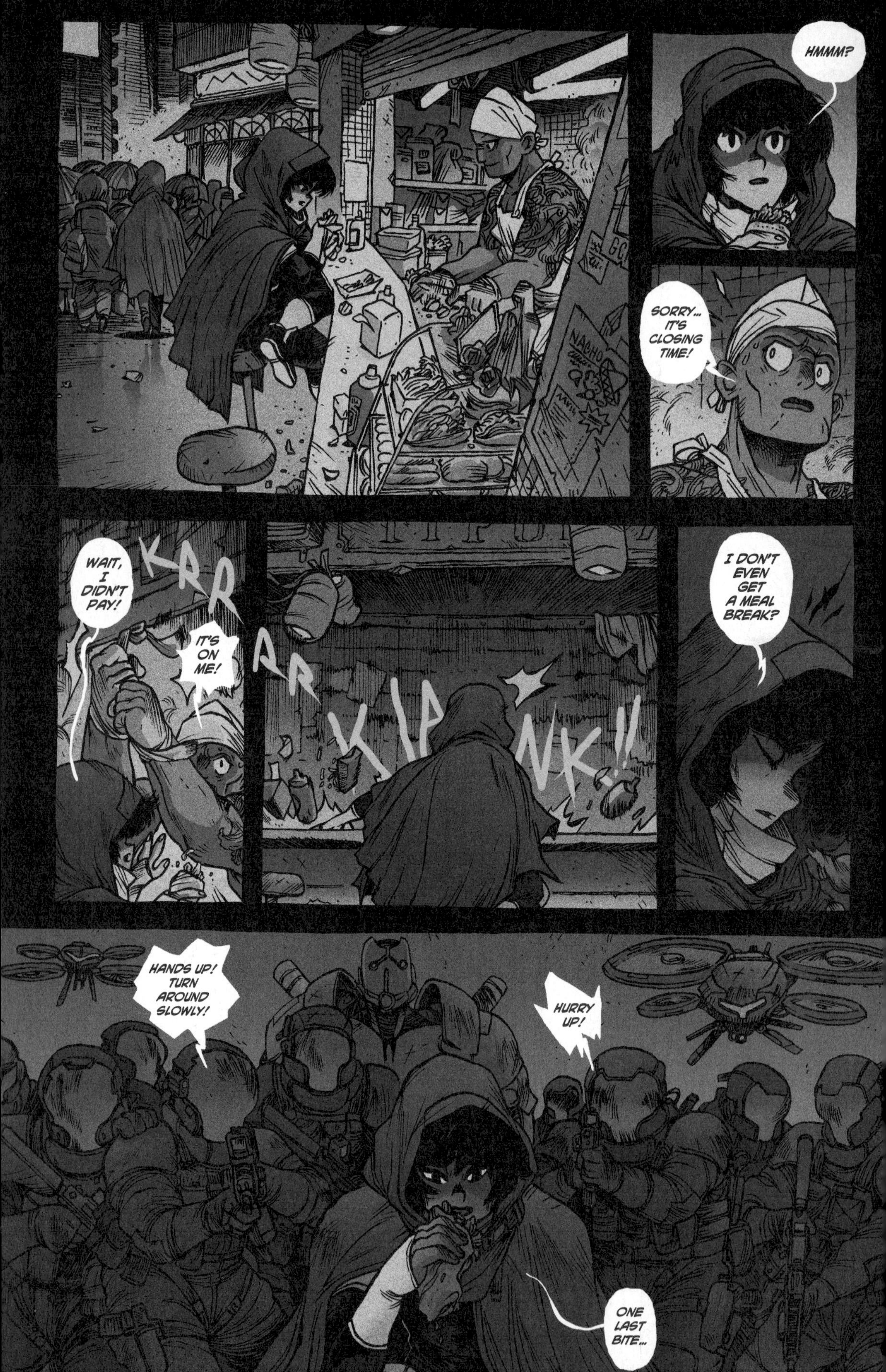
HMMM?
SORRY... IT'S CLOSING TIME!
WAIT, I DIDN'T PAY!
IT'S ON ME!
KRRRAR
KLANK!!
I DON'T EVEN GET A MEAL BREAK?
HANDS UP! TURN AROUND SLOWLY!
HURRY UP!
ONE LAST BITE...

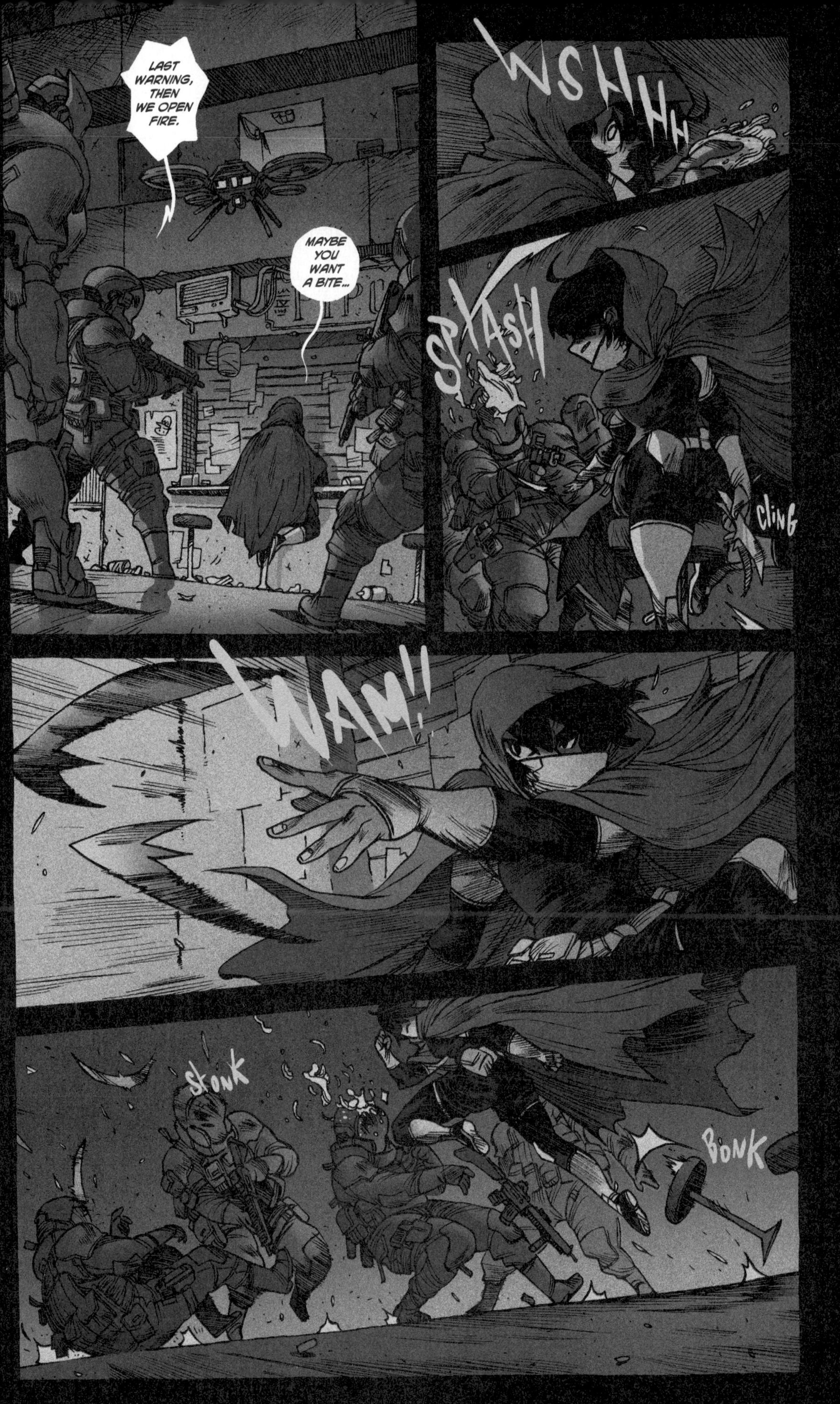
LAST WARNING, THEN WE OPEN FIRE.
MAYBE YOU WANT A BITE...
WSHHH
SPLASH
CLING
WAM!!
SKONK
BONK

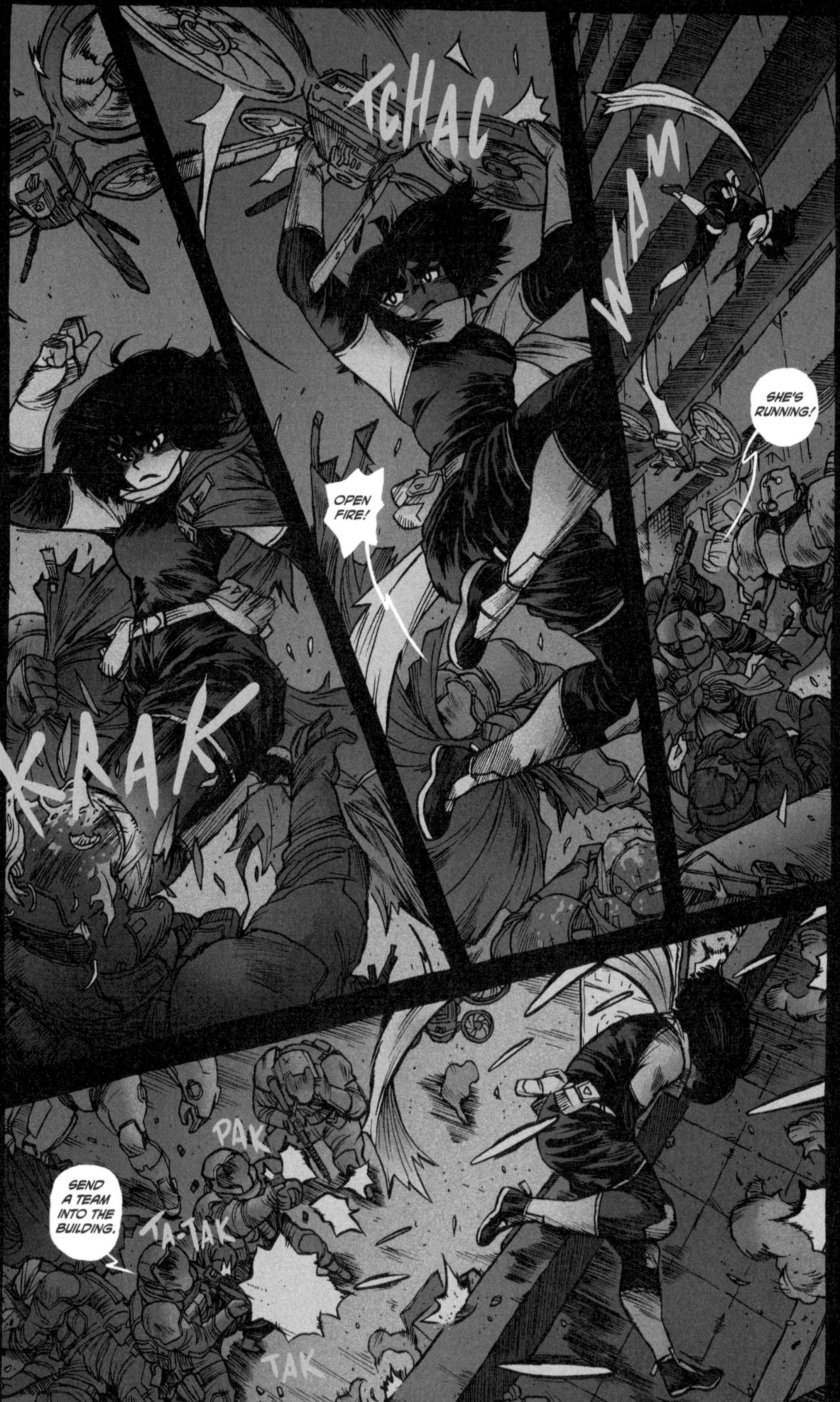
TCHAC
KRAK
OPEN FIRE!
WAM
SHE'S RUNNING!
PAK
SEND A TEAM INTO THE BUILDING.
TA-TAK
TAK

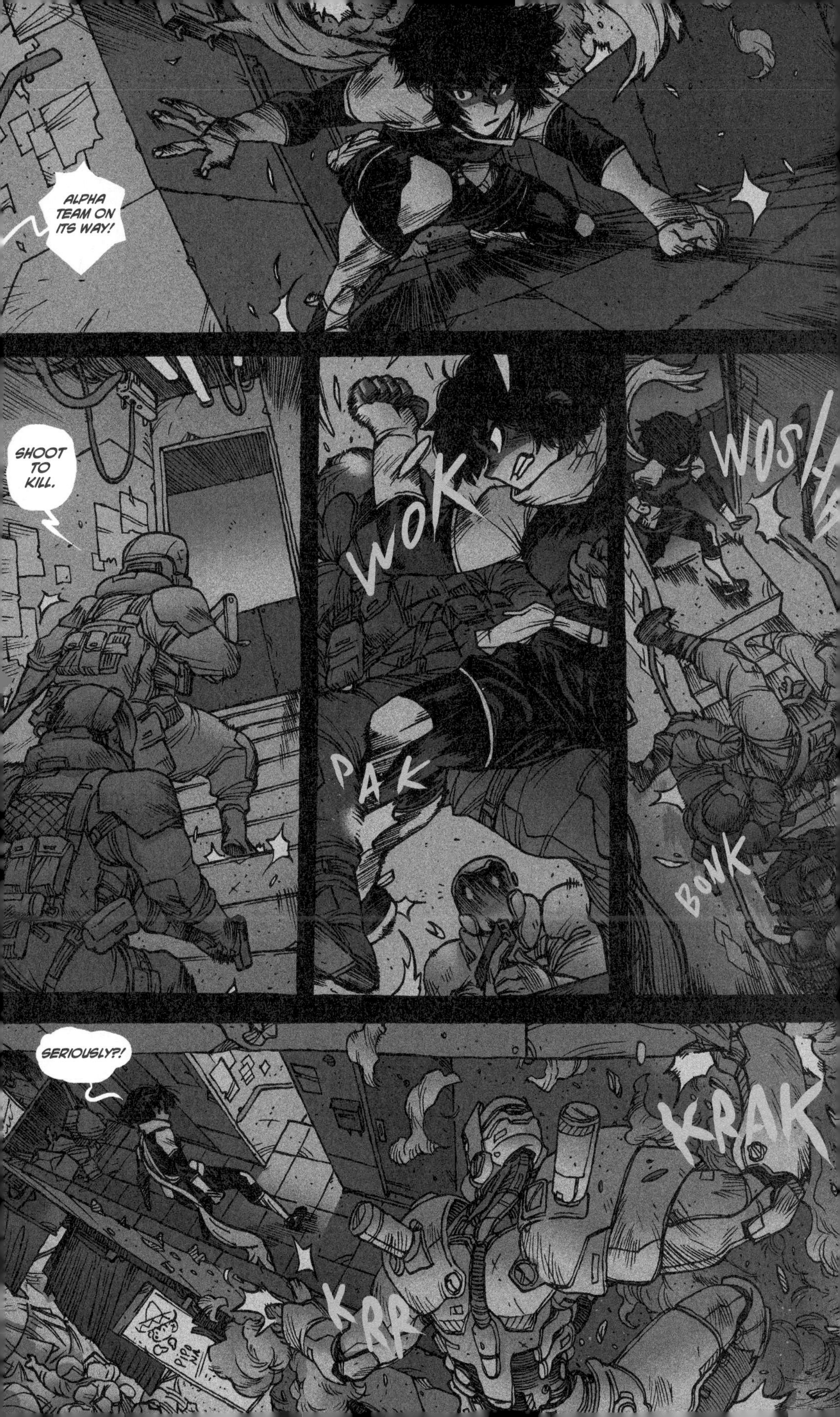
ALPHA TEAM ON ITS WAY!
SHOOT TO KILL.
WOK
PAK
WOSH
BONK
SERIOUSLY?!
KRAK
KRR

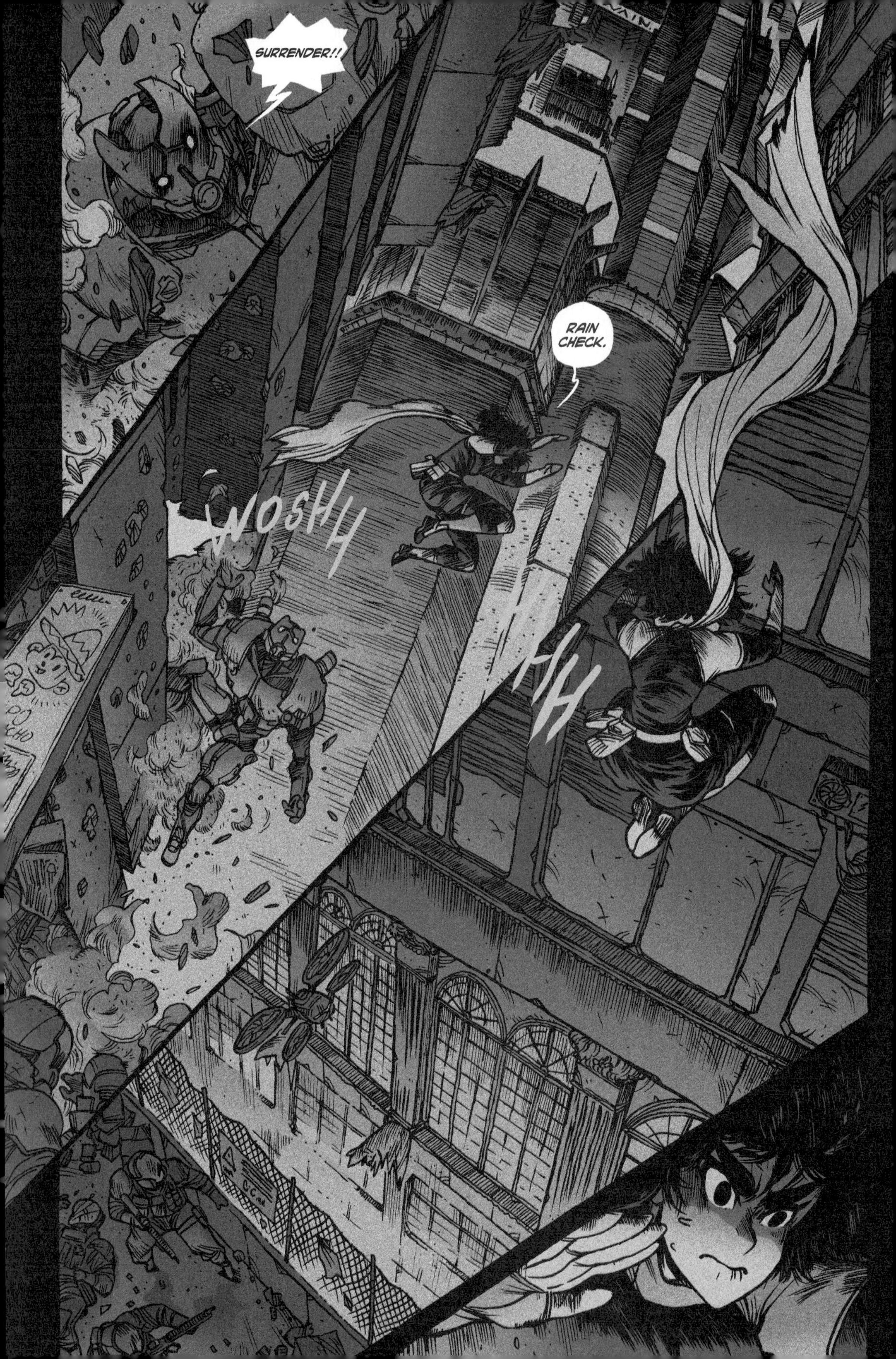
SURRENDER!!
RAIN CHECK.
WOSHHHHH

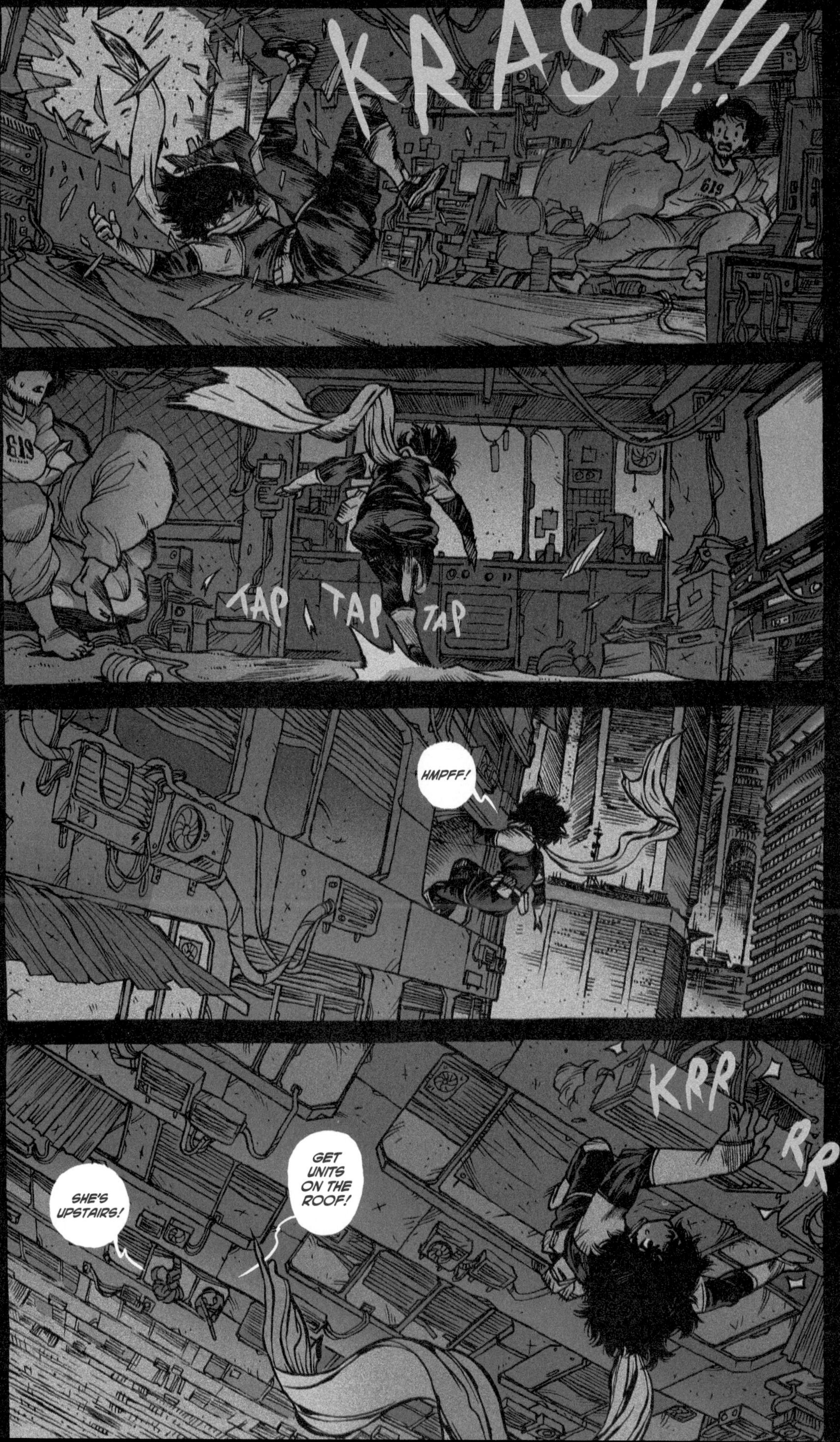
KRASH!!
TAP TAP TAP
HMPFF!
KRRRR
GET UNITS ON THE ROOF!
SHE'S UPSTAIRS!

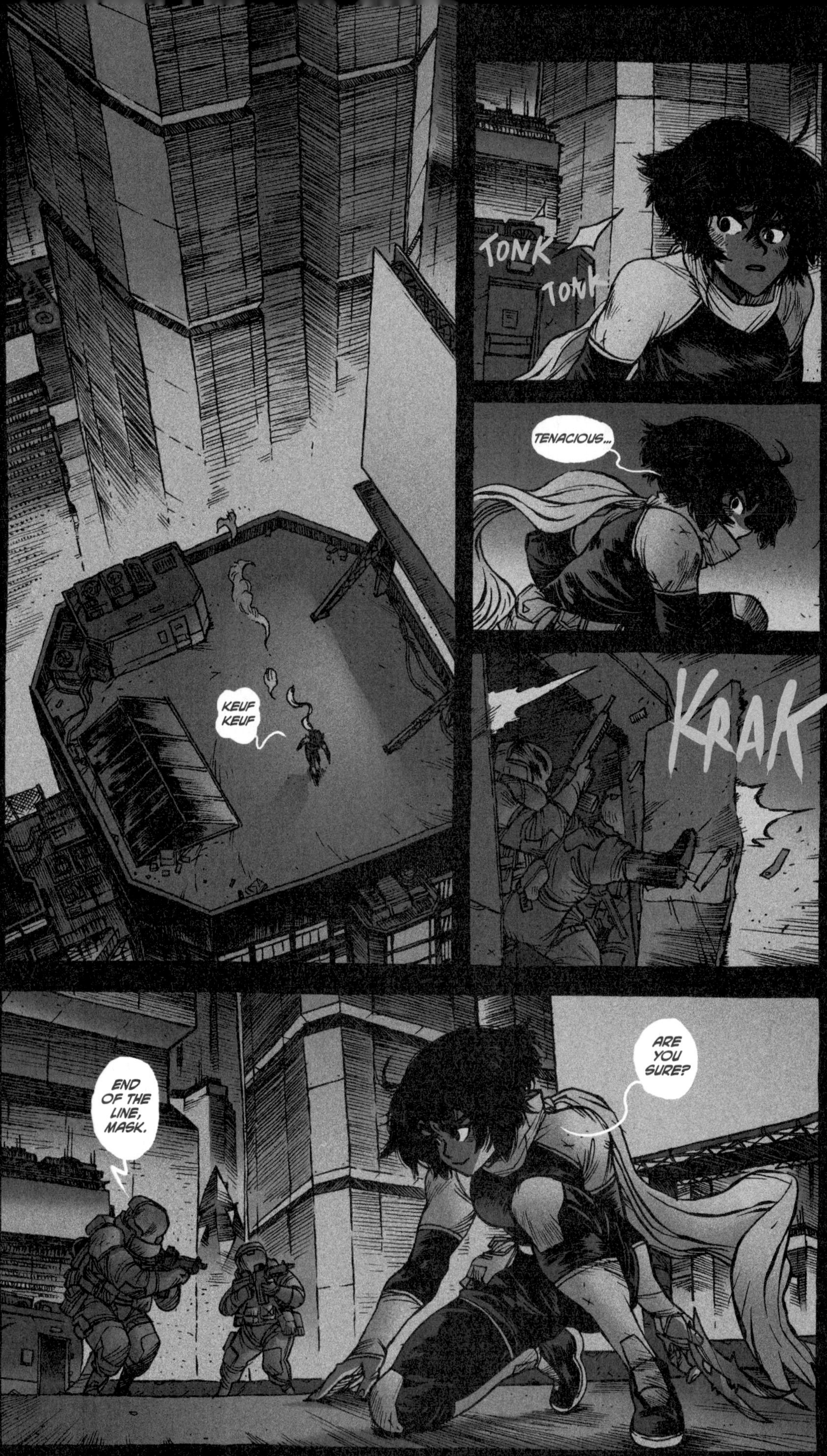
KEUF KEUF
TONK
TONK
TENACIOUS...
KRAK
END OF THE LINE, MASK.
ARE YOU SURE?

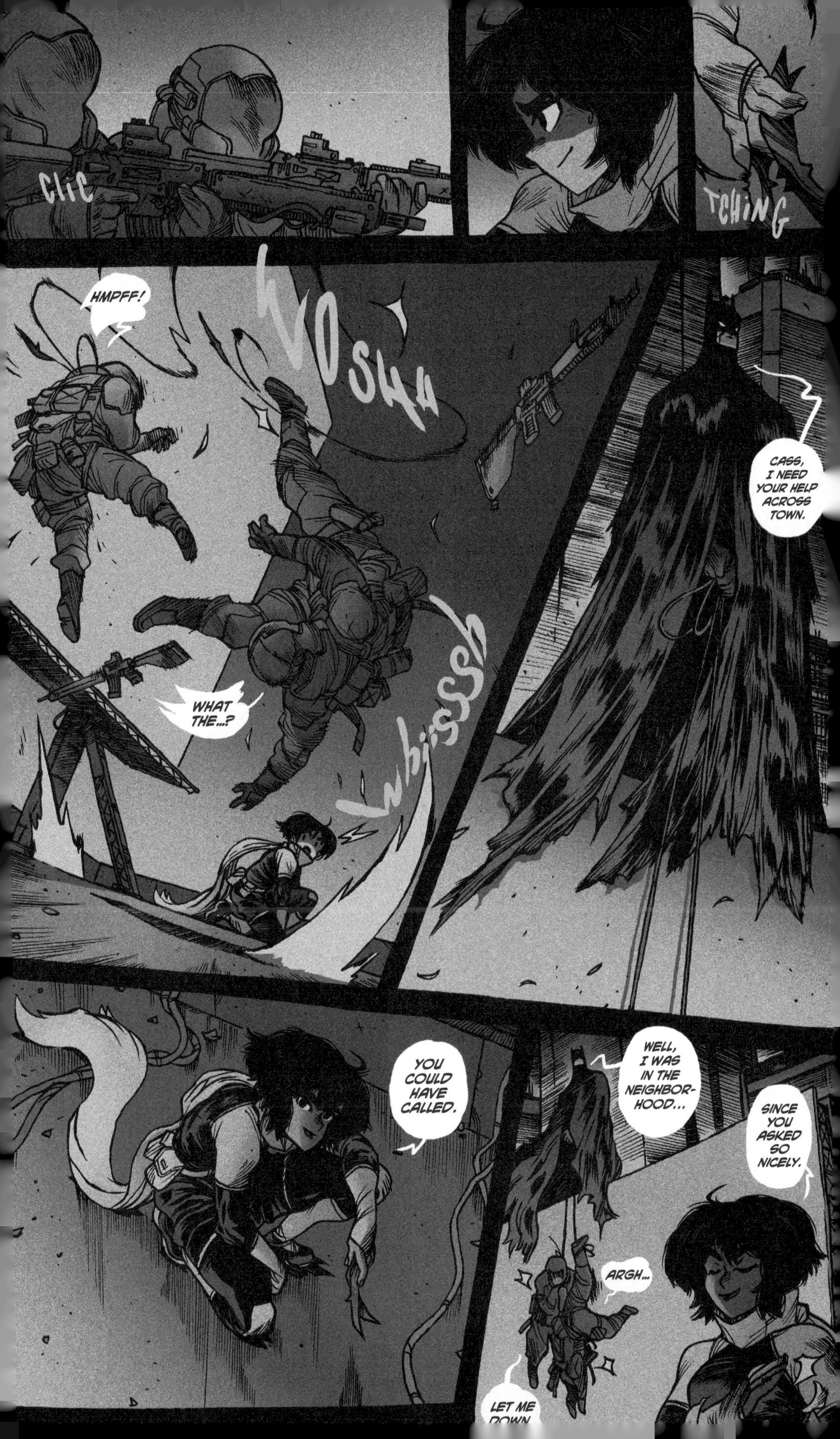
CLIC
TCHING
HMPFF!
WOSHA
CASS, I NEED YOUR HELP ACROSS TOWN.
WHAT THE...?
WHISSSH
YOU COULD HAVE CALLED.
WELL, I WAS IN THE NEIGHBOR-HOOD...
SINCE YOU ASKED SO NICELY.
ARGH...
LET ME DOWN

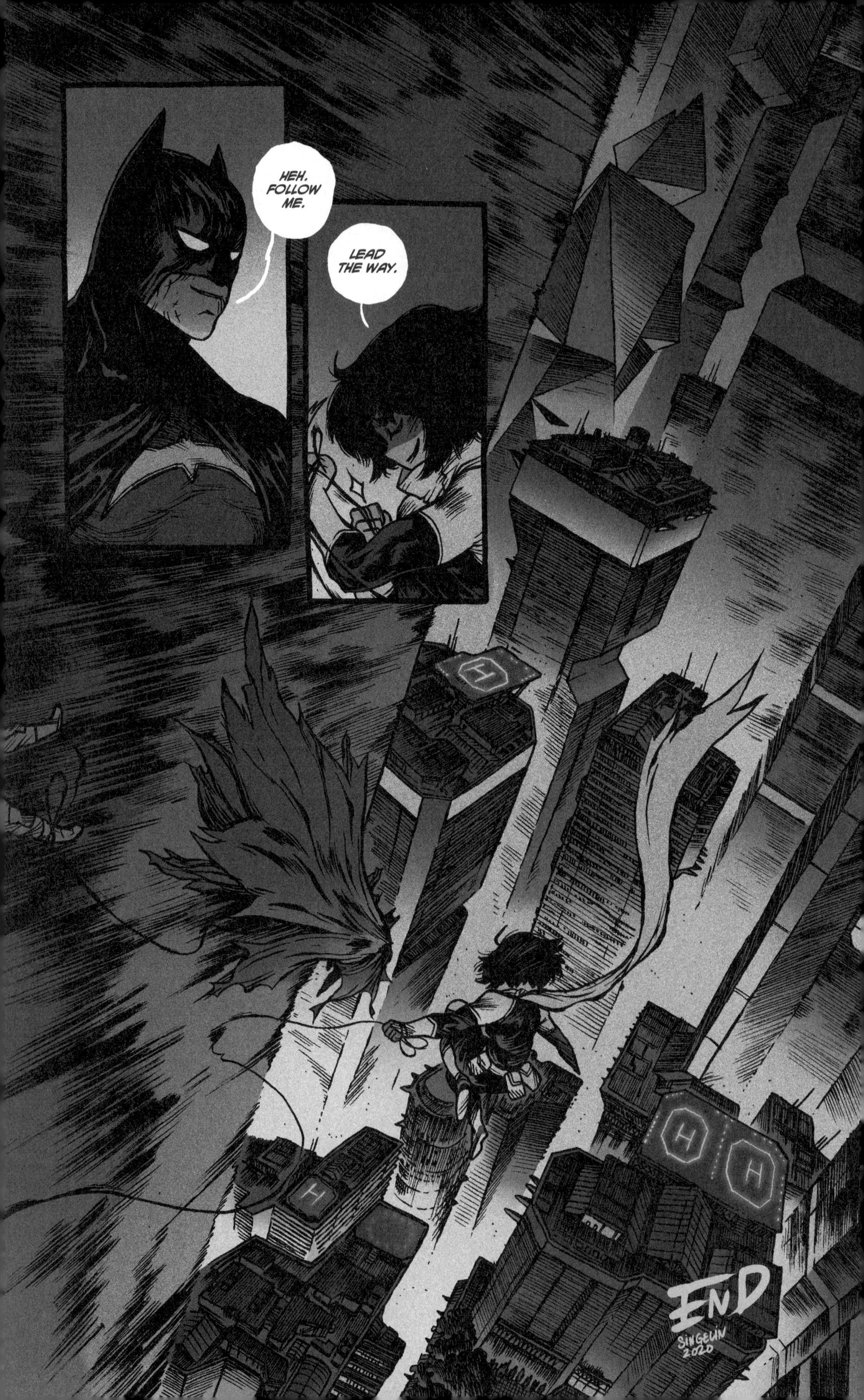
HEH. FOLLOW ME.
LEAD THE WAY.
END
SINGEUIN 2020

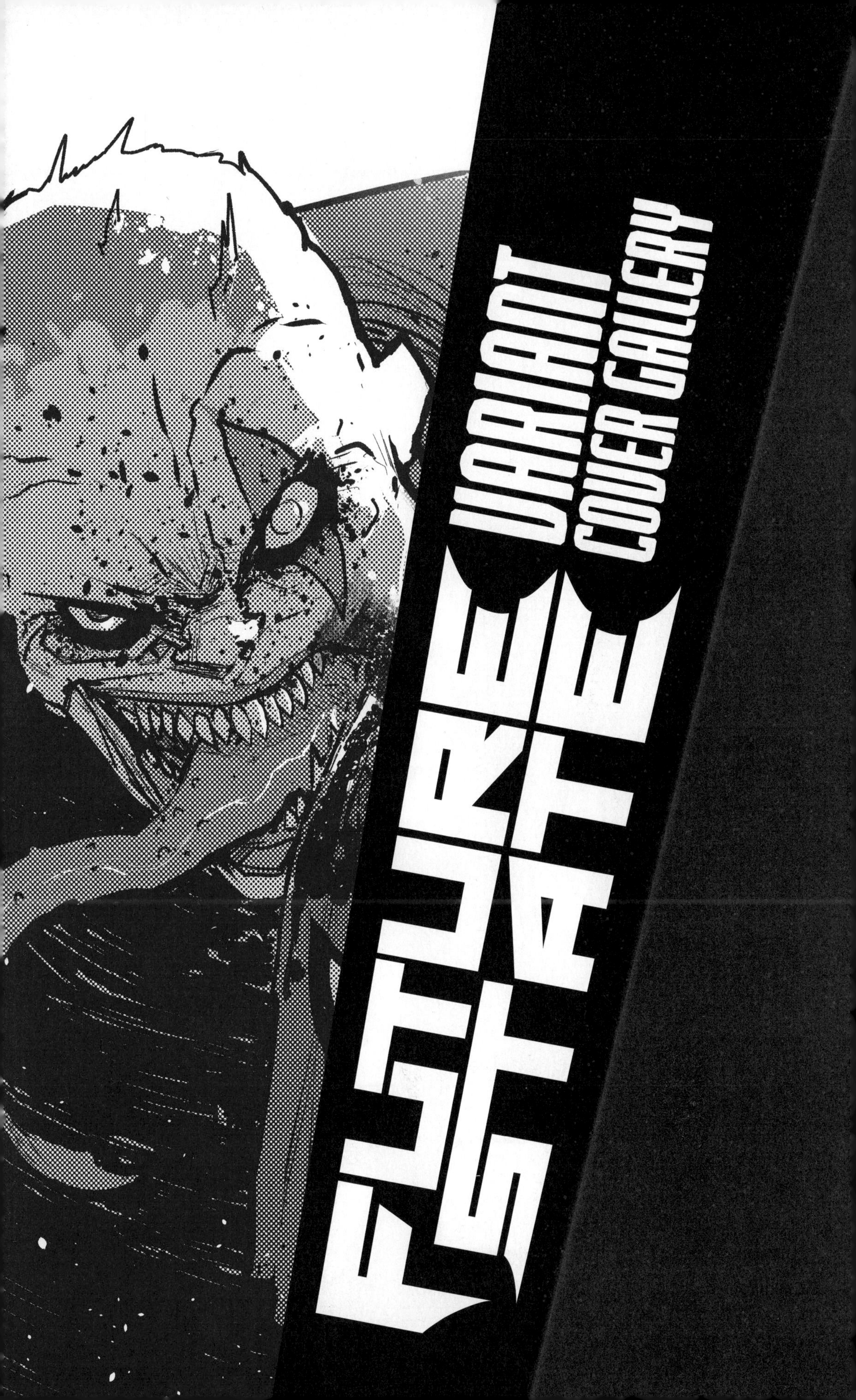

FUTURE STATE

VARIANT COVER GALLERY

Future State Gotham #8
variant cover art by KIM JACINTO

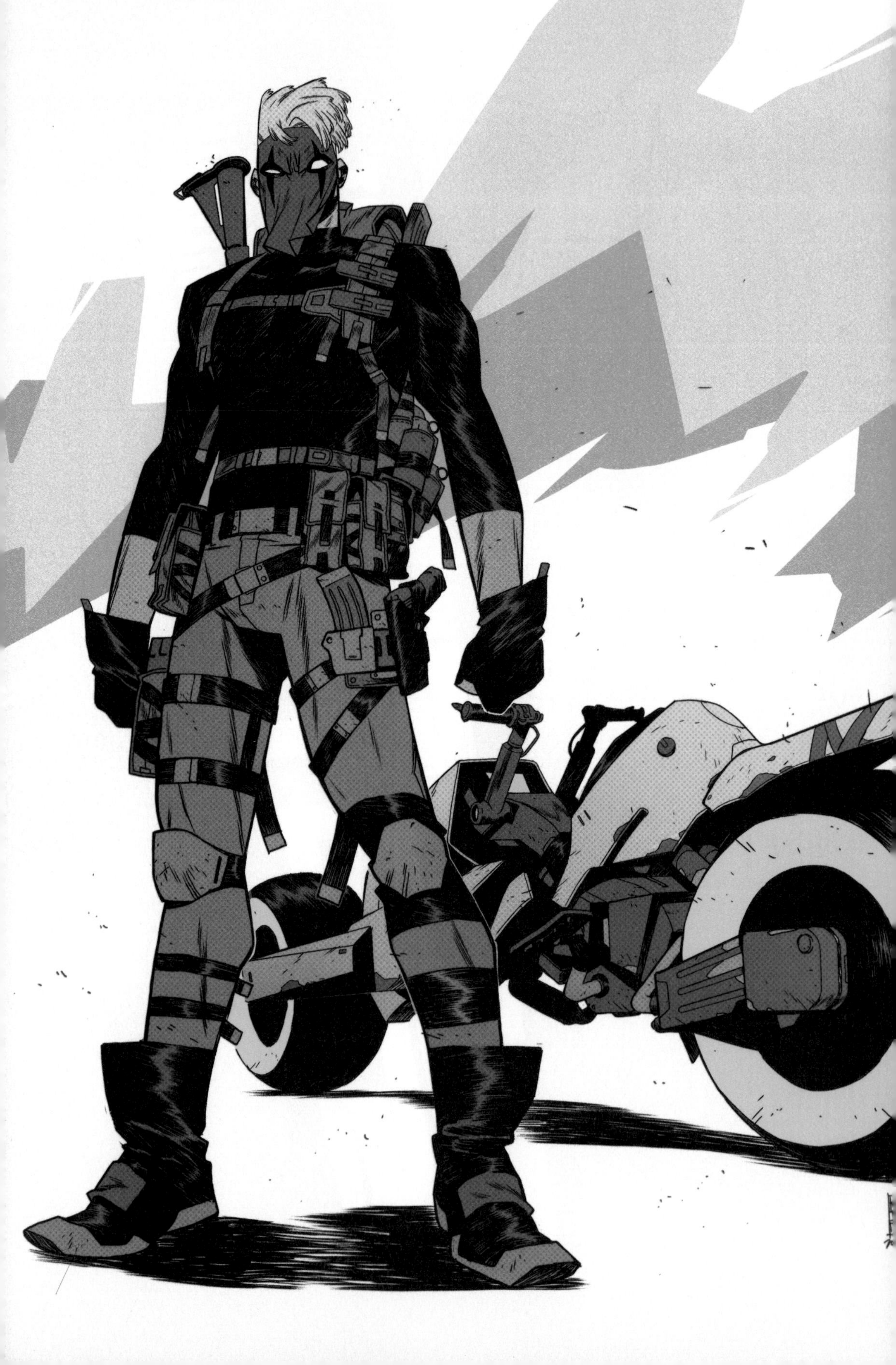

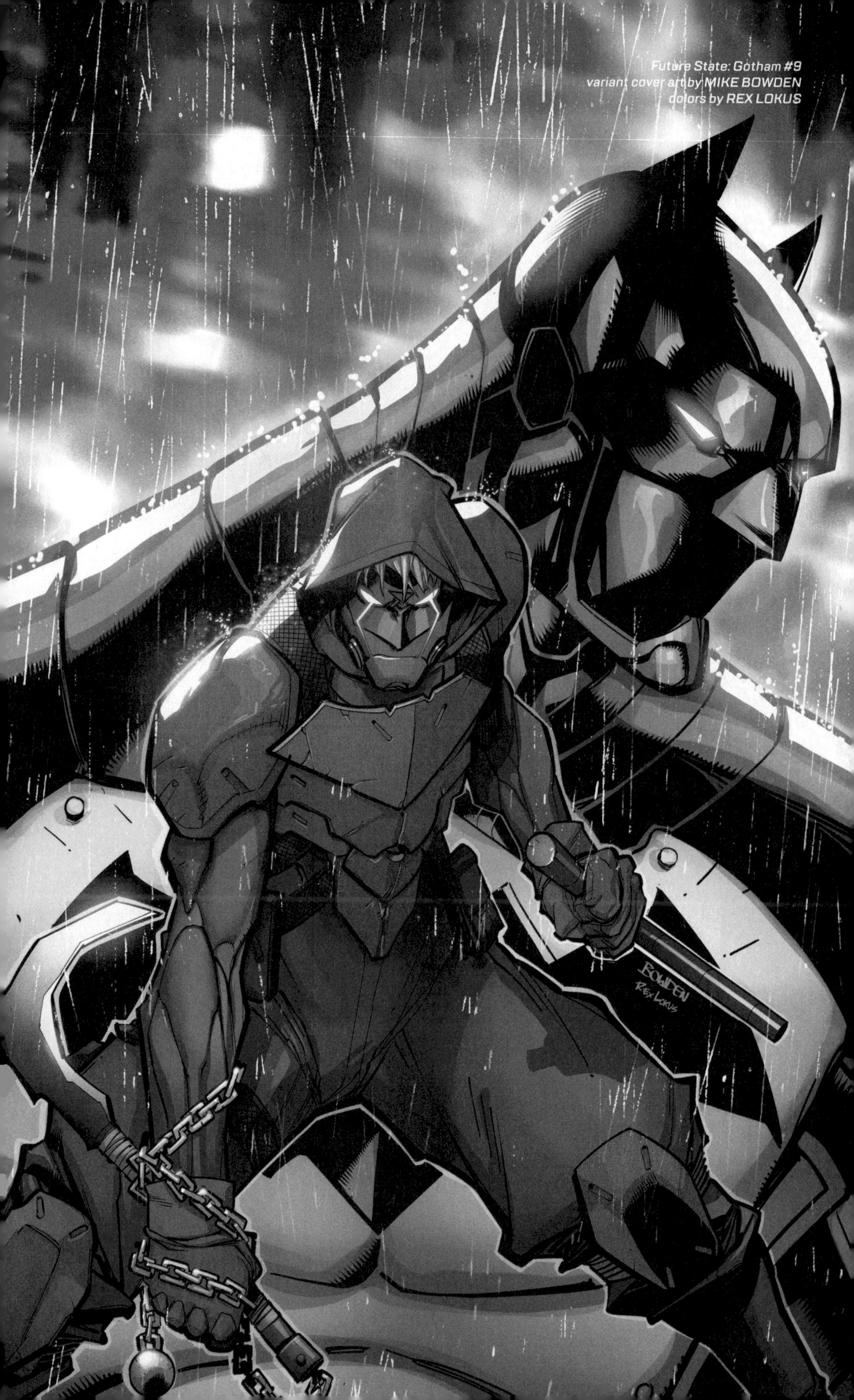
BOWDEN
REX LOKUS

Future State: Gotham #9
variant cover art by MIKE BOWDEN
colors by REX LOKUS

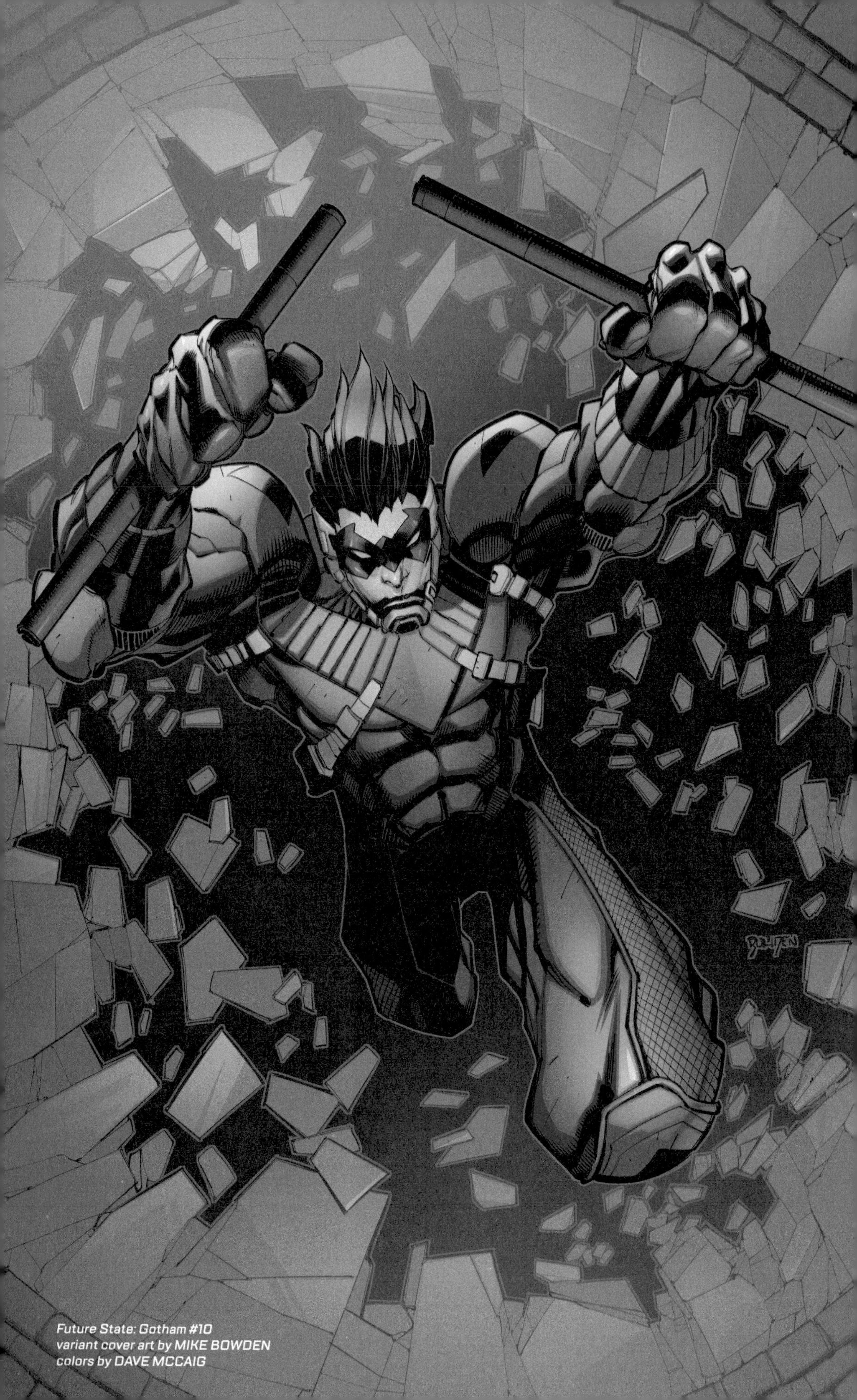

Future State: Gotham #10
variant cover art by MIKE BOWDEN
colors by DAVE MCCAIG

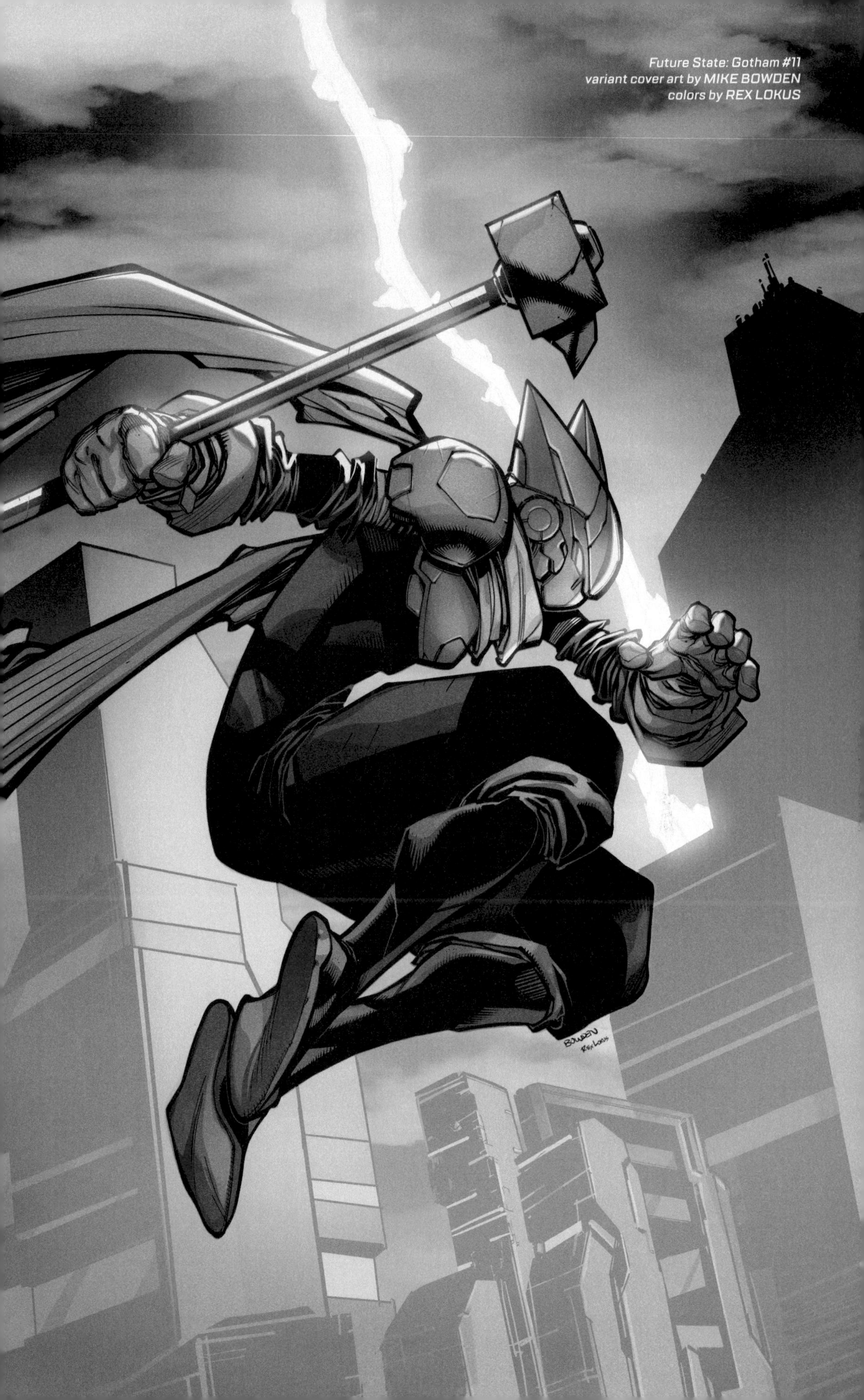

Future State: Gotham #11
variant cover art by MIKE BOWDEN
colors by REX LOKUS

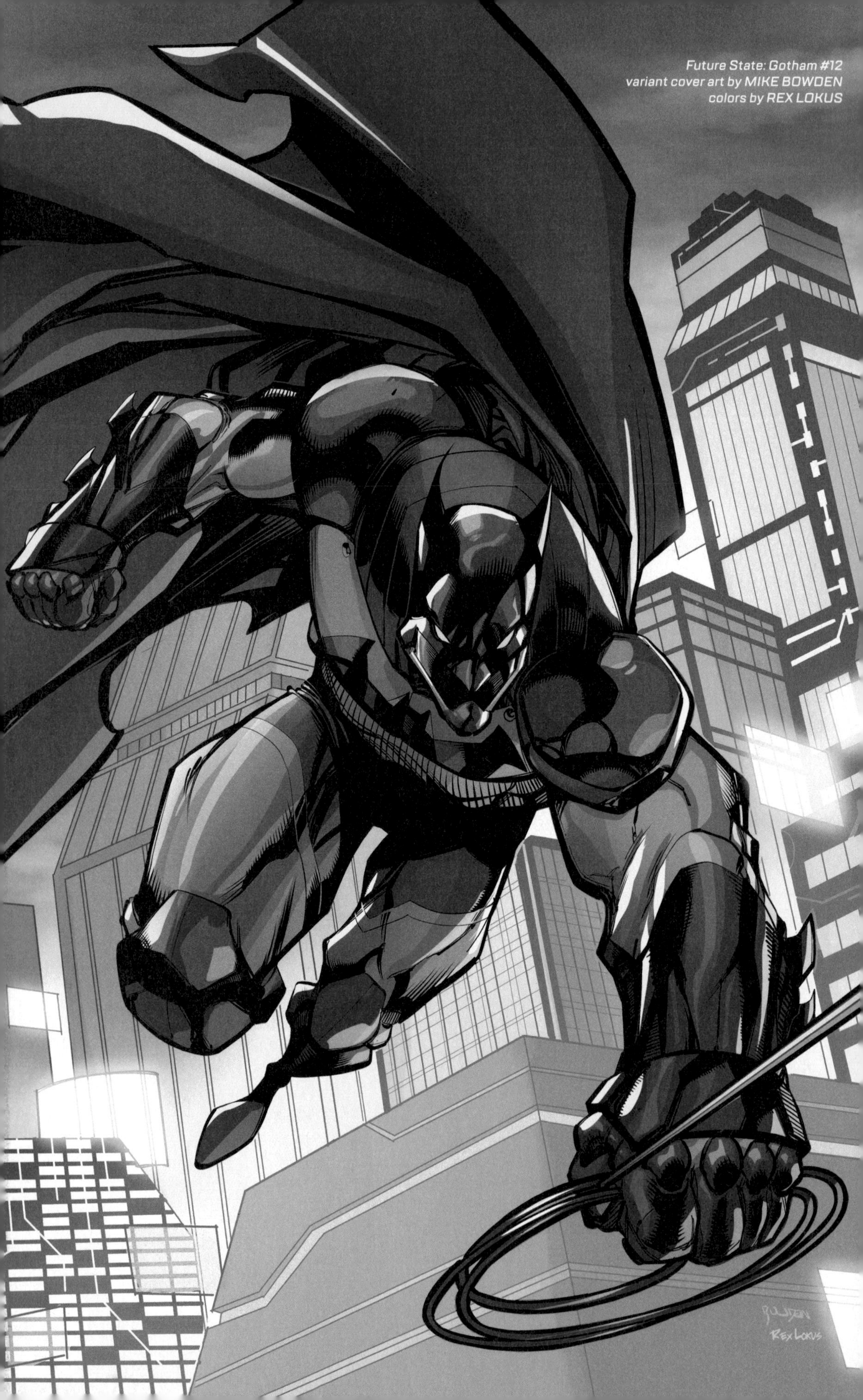

Future State: Gotham #12
variant cover art by MIKE BOWDEN
colors by REX LOKUS

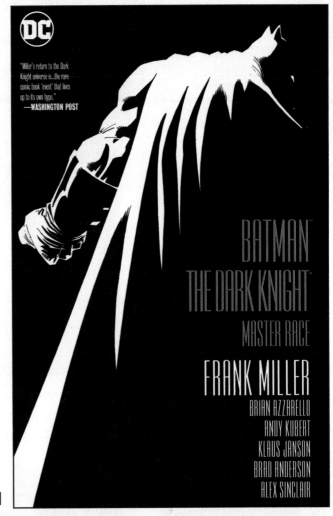

DON'T MISS THESE GRAPHIC NOVEL COLLECTIONS

DC FUTURE STATE

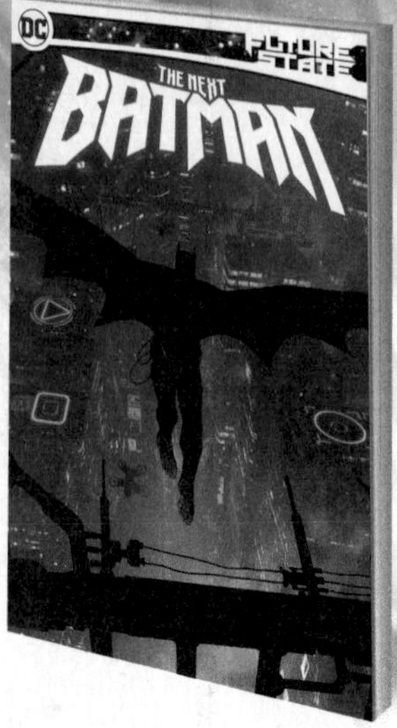
FUTURE STATE
THE NEXT BATMAN

FUTURE STATE: THE NEXT BATMAN

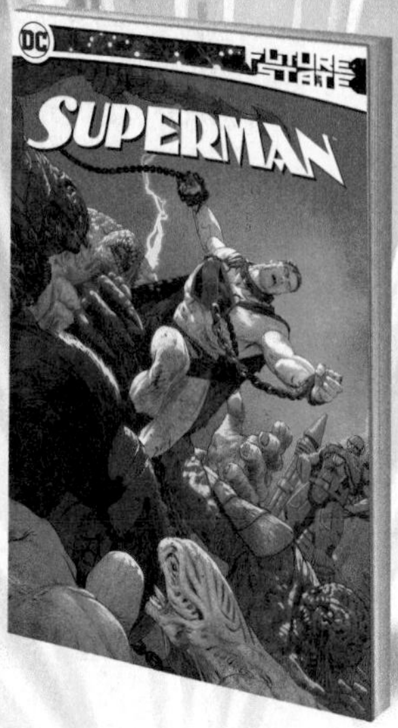
FUTURE STATE
SUPERMAN

FUTURE STATE: SUPERMAN

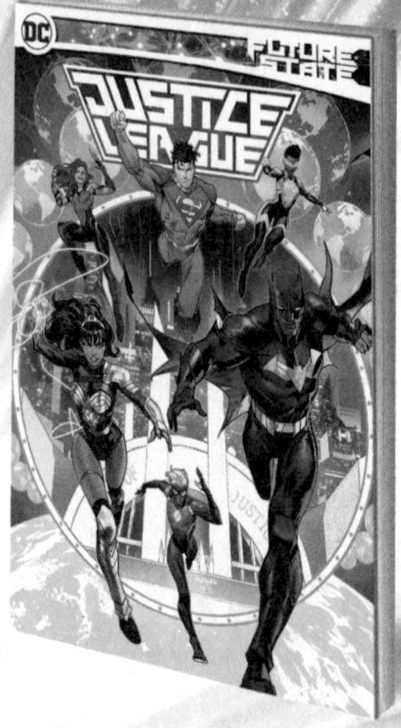
FUTURE STATE
JUSTICE LEAGUE

FUTURE STATE: JUSTICE LEAGUE

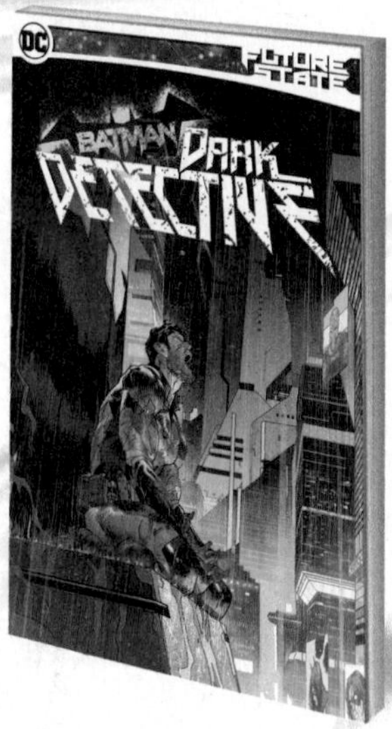
FUTURE STATE
BATMAN DARK DETECTIVE

FUTURE STATE BATMAN: DARK DETECTIVE

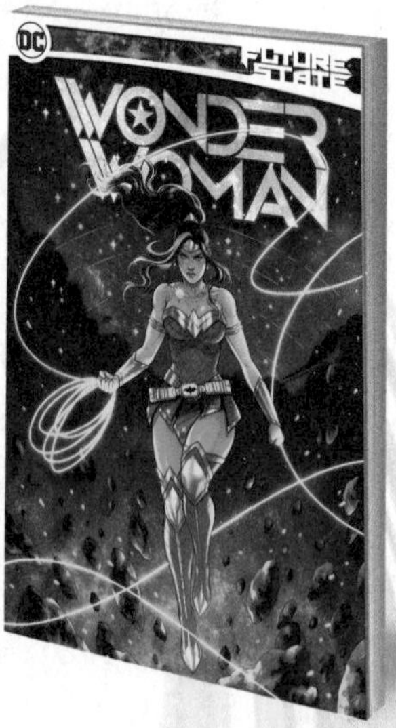
FUTURE STATE
WONDER WOMAN

FUTURE STATE: WONDER WOMAN

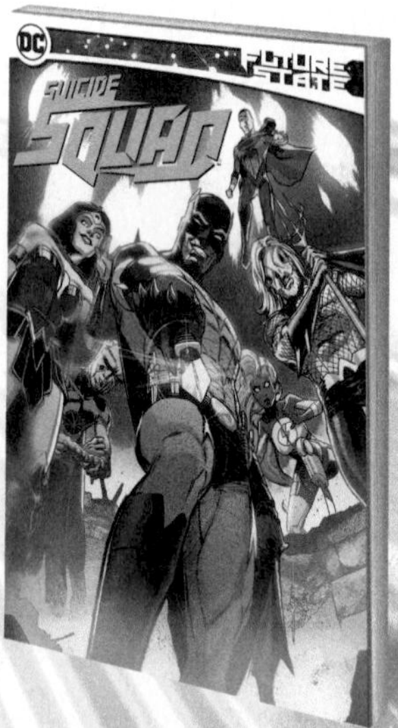
FUTURE STATE
SUICIDE SQUAD

FUTURE STATE: SUICIDE SQUAD

WRITTEN BY JOHN RIDLEY, MARIKO TAMAKI PHILLIP KENNEDY JOHNSON, AND MORE

ART BY DAN MORA, MIKEL JANÍN JOËLLE JONES, AND MORE